CONTENTS.

	PAGE
INTRODUCTION:	
§ 1. MANUSCRIPT AND EDITIONS	vii
§ 2. SOURCES	xiii
§ 3. DIALECT AND DATE	xx
§ 4. METRE	xxv
§ 5. AUTHORSHIP	xxvii
§ 6. STYLE	xxix
LE MORTE ARTHUR	1
NOTES	122
EDITIONS OF MIDDLE ENGLISH TEXTS REFERRED TO IN THE NOTES	135
GLOSSARY	137
INDEX OF NAMES	147

INTRODUCTION.

§ 1. *Manuscript and Editions*, p. vii.
§ 2. *Sources*, p. xiii.
§ 3. *Dialect and Date*, p. xx.
§ 4. *Metre*, p. xxv.
§ 5. *Authorship*, p. xxvii.
§ 6. *Style*, p. xxix.

§ 1. MANUSCRIPT AND EDITIONS.

THE metrical romance 'Le Morte Arthur,' as far as is known, exists only in the British Museum MS., Harley 2252, in which MS. it occupies leaves 86–133, back. In Ward's 'Catalogue of Romances,' I, 405, the portion of this MS. which contains our romance is assigned to the late fifteenth century, being the work of two scribes of approximately the same date. The hand-writing of the first of these scribes, who is moreover the scribe of the romance known as 'Ipomedon B.' contained in the same MS., extends only as far as the bottom of leaf 101, back. In these first sixteen leaves, there are from thirty to thirty-six lines to the page, whereas in the remaining portion the lines run from thirty-nine to forty-six to a page. As has been remarked by Ward, the MS. contains besides 'Le Morte Arthur' and 'Ipomedon B.' various miscellanies in a later hand, the most interesting of which consist of poems by Skelton and others. This later hand is probably that of John Colyns of London, who has written at the end of the copy of our romance (leaf 133, back): "Thys Boke belongythe to John Colyns me*rcer* of london dwellyng in the p*a*rysshe of *ou*r lady at wolchyrche hawe Anexid the Stocke*s* in þe pultre yn Anno domi*ni* 1517." Of this John Colyns, in connection with the affairs of his parish, there is mention in other entries in this MS., viz.: on leaf 163 and leaf 165. Still further, the inscription "Sum Roberti Farrer," dating from the sixteenth century, is found on leaf 1, back, and it appears from another entry (leaf 162, back) that the book was in the possession of this "Robert Farrers" in 1570.

The earliest notice of 'Le Morte Arthur,' as far as I have been able to discover, is that which is found in the 'Catalogue of the Harleian Manuscripts,' II, 584. It runs as follows: "I know not who this Poet was, but guess that he lived about the time of K. Henry VII., and that he might have been a Northern man. He

viii § 1. *Early views regarding the Date and Source of the Poem.*

useth many Saxon or obsolete Words, and very often delighted himself (as did the Author of 'Piers Plowman') in the Chime of words beginning with the same letter, as (that I may give one example) 'For welle the wiste withouten wene,' fol. 117 ᵇ. I suppose he enlarged upon the story (which was too large before) in that he mentioneth the Tower of London, Syr Lucan de Botellere," etc.

That the date which Wanley, the compiler of the above catalogue, here assigns to 'Le Morte Arthur' is too late was objected already by Bishop Percy in his 'Reliques of Ancient English Poetry'[1] published in 1765. He bases his objection, however, on the absurd ground, that the formula with which our romance opens, " Lordingis that are leff And dere," seems to be quoted in 'Syr Bevis.' Warton in his 'History of English Poetry' (1774–1781) approached the subject with a knowledge of the Middle English romances, which neither Wanley nor Percy possessed, but in classing[2] the poem with the work of the " nameless minstrels who probably flourished before or about the reign of Edward II.," he makes the mistake of dating it too early.

It is curious that Ritson should have reverted to Wanley's erroneous view with regard to the date. In the brief passage dealing with our romance in the preface of his 'Ancient English Metrical Romances,'[3] after speaking in uncomplimentary fashion of Percy's views on this subject, he says that it " is in fact nothing more than part of the 'Morte Darthur' of Caxton turned into easy alternate verse, a very unusual circumstance, no doubt, in the time of Henry the Seventh, to which Wanley properly allots it. The antiquated words used by this versifier are manifestly affected. Caxton's book is the only one known by the name of 'La Morte D'Arthur,' which he took as he found it."

The fame of the 'Morte Darthur' evidently blinded Ritson to the possibility that Malory instead of the old romancer may have been the real borrower—a view which has found favour in recent years— or the still further possibility, which we believe to deserve most consideration, that they borrowed from a common original. It is not at all likely, however, that Ritson made any detailed comparison of the two works with each other, to say nothing of the Old French 'Mort Artus.'

Just three years later, in 1805, Ellis in his 'Specimens of Early

[1] See the edition of this work by A. Schröer, II, 551. Berlin, 1893.
[2] See the revised edition, II, 190. London, 1871.
[3] See the revised edition by Edmund Goldsmid, p. 56. Edinburgh, 1884.

§ 1. *The Roxburghe Club Edition, and Dr. Furnivall's.*

English Metrical Romances,' I, 308, in commenting on the above passage in Ritson's Preface remarks that our romance "differs most essentially from Malory's work, which was a mere compilation; whilst it follows, with tolerable exactness, the French Romance of 'Lancelot,'[1] and its phraseology which perfectly resembles that of Chester and other authors of the fifteenth century, betrays no marks of affectation."[2] We shall see later on how these statements of Ellis also need correction. It was he, however, that first made the story of the Harleian 'Morte Arthur' accessible to readers generally, for on pp. 328–387 of his first volume he gives a full outline of our romance with occasional specimens of the original text.

At last in 1819 the romance was printed for the Roxburghe Club at the cost of Thomas Ponton. In this edition the type is black letter, and there is no pagination. As a matter of fact, however, the text covers one hundred and twenty-nine pages, and the glossary which is added covers four. There is, moreover, a facsimile prefixed of the two different hands which appear in our copy of the poem, and on the title-page a design "which represents the intrusion of Sir Agravaine and his companions on the slumbers of the guilty pair and the punishment inflicted by Sir Launcelot on their temerity."

A list of the mistakes in the Roxburghe edition noted by R. F. Weymouth appeared in the 'Transactions of the Philological Society for 1860–61,' pp. 279–281, but the romance was not republished until 1864, when Dr. Furnivall through the firm of Macmillan and Co. brought out the very attractive edition which has since generally superseded that of the Roxburghe Club. It is almost needless to say that there are very few errors in Dr. Furnivall's text, and that his glossary marks a great advance over that which is contained in the edition of 1819. Moreover, the discussion of the dialect and metre of the poems in the preface to his edition is still of interest. Time has dealt more hardly, however, with the prefatory essay on the Arthurian legend by Mr. Herbert Coleridge which follows immediately on that discussion.

In the present edition I have endeavoured to lay before the reader all the facts of importance which relate to the dialect, date and metre of the poem. I have, moreover, investigated with a great deal

---

[1] That this statement is not correct was pointed out already by Sir F. Madden in the Introduction to his 'Syr Gawayne' (published for the Bannatyne Club. London, 1839). See p. xxii, note.

[2] See also pp. 327 f. of the same volume.

x § 1. *Differences between the present and Dr. Furnivall's Edition.*

of care the question of the source of the romance and its relation to Sir Thomas Malory's famous work, and I hope that I have been able to put these matters at last in their true light. I have still further endeavoured to bring the glossary up to the level of present knowledge, and I have also laboured by repeated collations to correct whatever errors had crept into Dr. Furnivall's text. The most frequent differences between the text of his edition and my own are in letters at the beginning of lines and in *e*'s at the end of words. It is not always easy in our MS. to say whether the initial letter is intended as a capital or not, and, on the other hand, a good many of the *e*'s used in Dr. Furnivall's edition for indicating the cross of preceding double *l* or the curl of preceding *d* and *r* were left unitalicised by mistake. The list, however, of even these unimportant differences is not long. The following are the only instances in which mistakes of reading in Dr. Furnivall's edition affect the sense (I place his reading first and the corrected reading after): 497, *Sute–Sitte*; 1324, *hyr–hym*; 1455, *not–non*; 1617, *Auauncement–Auauntement*; 2663, *ouer–euer*; 2912, *gryfely–grysely*; 3205, *the–tho*; 3326, *prices–princes*; 3419, *Refte–Reste*;[1] 3468, *be–me*; 3759, *the–tho*; 3826, *the–tho*. It should perhaps be noted also that the name of King Banndemagew is wrongly given in Dr. Furnivall's edition as Baundemorgew (l. 2564).

In regard to the numbering of the lines, I have decided notwithstanding the new arrangement in eight-line stanzas to retain the numbering of Dr. Furnivall's edition. Any change in this matter would have rendered comparison between that and the present edition (including the discussions of language and metre in the prefaces) very difficult, nor could Dr. Seyferth's dissertation, which contains a complete classification of the grammatical forms of our poem and is based on Dr. Furnivall's edition, have been used without very great inconvenience, if such a change had been made.[2] The numbering I have retained has at least the justification of representing the actual number of lines in the only extant MS. of our poem plus an allowance for those which the missing leaf between leaf 102 and leaf 103 contained.

In the numbering he has adopted Dr. Furnivall makes such an allowance for the loss of "one or more leaves," so that in his edition, although the last line before the gap is numbered 1181, the first one

[1] The sense requires, however, *Refte*, so that I have adopted it in my text.
[2] Prof. W. W. Skeat says rightly, I think: "An old numbering, even if faulty, should be adhered to, where possible, for the sake of convenience of reference." ('Wars of Alexander,' Preface, p. xiii, E. E. T. S., 1886.)

§ 1. *Dr. Sommer's views concerning the Gap in the MS.*

after the gap is numbered 1318. As already stated, I have adhered to his numbering for the sake of convenience, but I think that he has assumed here a greater loss than actually occurred. Each side of a leaf in this part of the MS. contains, as has already been said, from thirty-nine to forty-six lines. Now, if one compares the Middle-English romance with the Old French Vulgate-Lancelot, it will be seen that very little is missing from the former at this place. Judging by this comparison, the missing passage would have included a description of the funeral of the Maid of Ascalot, and possibly[1] some of the details of Lancelot's sojourn in the forest. I do not believe, however, that any one who has made the comparison will regard it as probable that more than one leaf from the Harleian MS. is lost, and that would mean the loss of either ten or eleven stanzas (of eight lines each) plus the two lines which are missing in the MS. from the last stanza before the gap and the same number which are missing from the first stanza after the gap—so a total of either eighty-four or ninety-two lines.

In a letter to the 'Academy' of November 15, 1890, the substance of which he has repeated in a note to his 'Studies on the Sources of the Morte Darthur' (pp. 11 f.), Dr. H. O. Sommer has argued that the gap in the Harleian MS. is after all only apparent, that as a matter of fact the leaves have simply been misplaced. To quote from the 'Studies' Dr. Sommer says:—

"The gap which is caused by the deficiency of the leaf can be filled up as nearly as possible by ll. 832–951, which are, as above stated, misplaced. By transposing these lines into the gap after fol. 102, the episode of 'Guenevere and Mador de la Porte' becomes a complete whole, if we omit ll. 912-927 because they are to a certain extent repeated by ll. 1318–1331 (comp. *e. g.* ll. 916, 917, and 919 to ll. 1318, 1320 and 1321), and also ll. 928–951 as being an apparent contradiction to ll. 1467–1503.

"How did this confusion arise? I venture to think that I can satisfactorily answer this question. The poet while transcribing the French prose into English verse, finding that he had so far abandoned his source that it was impossible for him to connect his narrative

---

[1] One has to remember that the Old French Vulgate-Lancelot is not the source of the Harleian romance, although their narratives are similar. The latter shows many transpositions of episodes, as I have pointed out in 'Anglia,' xxiii, 87 ff., so that one cannot speak positively about this matter, and hence I have not tried to supply the missing portion of the story by extracts from the French romance.

xii   § 1. *Reasons for rejecting Dr. Sommer's proposed Changes.*

with the ensuing events, re-wrote a part of his work, and very likely marked the portions which he wished to be omitted. The scribes afterwards neglected or did not understand his indications, and so the Harl. MS. contains a certain portion twice which varied only in the end. Thus the folio missing after 102 evidently contained ll. 832–911 + two lines rhyming with ll. 1318 and 1319, and completing ll. 1318–1323 to a stanza of eight lines—or eighty-two lines, the exact number of lines contained by several folios of the Harl. MS.

"If these proposed emendations are accepted, the episode of 'Guinever and Mador de la Porte' would consist of (1) ll. 832–910; (2) two lines + 1318–1671, and thus arranged would be in accordance with the account given of this episode by the various MSS. of the 'Lancelot' in the British Museum, and with that of Malory's 'Le Morte Darthur,' book XVIII, chaps. iii to viii."

With reference to all these arbitrary and complicated changes which Dr. Sommer proposes,[1] I need only say that they are wholly uncalled for. The occasion for his proposing the transposition of ll. 832 ff., as he says elsewhere in the note from which I have just been quoting, is that they interrupt "the episode of Lancelot and the Fair Maiden of Ascolot." But notwithstanding the erroneous statement in the last paragraph we find the same arrangement exactly in the Old French Vulgate-Lancelot, both in the printed texts and the British Museum MSS.[2]—only in the Vulgate-Lancelot the narrative is broken by the insertion of still other material. One simply has to collate our poem with the Old French romance to convince oneself of the truth of this assertion, and it is difficult to see how Dr. Sommer could ever have proposed his rearrangement of the former, if he had really made this collation.[3]

Apart from the arrangement in stanzas the most notable difference in appearance between the present edition and Dr. Furnivall's is due to the use of italicised *e*, which is made in the latter wherever the preceding double *l* has the cross-line drawn through it (ƚƚ) or the preceding *d* or *r* ends with a flourish. In accordance with the practice

---

[1] Seyferth in his 'Sprache und Metrik des mittelenglischen strophischen Gedichtes, ' Le Morte Arthur' und sein Verhältniss zu 'The Lyfe of Ipomydon' (Berlin, 1895), p. 74, accepts them without further examination.
[2] The MSS. break the episode of 'Mador de la Porte' even more than the printed text, inasmuch as they interrupt it also with the story of Lancelot's accidental wounding, and Bors' search for him. Cp. Additional MS. 10294, leaf 64, col. 3—leaf 65, col. 2.
[3] What the order of incidents is in the Vulgate-Lancelot as compared with the Harleian romance, I have set forth in my article in 'Anglia,' xxiii, pp. 83 f.

§ 2. *Dr. Sommer's views concerning the Sources of the Poem.* xiii

of the Early English Text Society, a special type has been, of course, employed in the present edition to reproduce these peculiar forms, and also *m* and *n* with the flourish.

I have moreover expanded the MS. contraction 'w^t' into *with*, instead of *wyth*, which Dr. Furnivall adopts in his edition.[1] The matter is of no great importance, but where the uncontracted form is used in the MS., *with* and *withe* greatly preponderate over *wyth* and *wythe*. I find indeed *wyth* only once, l. 99, and *wythe* only three times, ll. 1963, 2447, 2625, whereas *with* occurs five times, ll. 45, 51, 842, 1606, 2127, and *withe* eighteen times, ll. 955, 1638, 1642, 1723, 1778, 1820, 2031, 2101, 2155, 2159, 2181, 2307, 2442, 2464, 2535, 2552, 2577, 2602. Nearly all these uncontracted forms occur at the beginning of lines.[2]

§ 2. SOURCES.

It will have been observed from the above section that both Ritson and Ellis hazarded suggestions regarding the source of our romance, and the same is true of still other scholars of later date. This question, however, was first discussed in detail by Dr. H. Oskar Sommer in the third volume of his edition of Malory's[3] 'Morte Darthur' (London, 1889–91), especially pp. 249 ff. Nevertheless in his discussion Dr. Sommer in the main simply develops suggestions of earlier scholars, for the most part ill-founded, with reference to the source of our romance and its relation to the other Death of Arthur romances. For instance, his notion that the portion of our romance which follows the gap in the Harleian MS. is the original of the latter part of Malory is derived from Branscheid ('Anzeiger' to 'Anglia,' viii (1885), 220), and the further notion that the Old French Vulgate-Lancelot constitutes the source of the Harleian 'Morte Arthur' down to the gap seems a partial and ill-considered

---

[1] The late Prof. Koelbing expands also by *with*, in his edition of 'The Lyfe of Ipomydon,' which is contained in the same MS. as our poem, having been copied by the same scribe that copied ll. 1–1091 of 'Le Morte Arthur.'

[2] It should perhaps be added that at the beginning of certain divisions of the story (*e. g.* 424, 832, etc.) the scribes left space for the illumination of the initial letters, although they were never actually illuminated. The initial letters in such cases are small letters, but with reference to the scribes' intention I have represented them in this edition, as they were in Dr. Furnivall's, by large, heavily leaded capitals.

[3] I have confined myself in the following to a discussion of the immediate sources of our romance. The ultimate sources I expect to discuss in an edition of the Old French 'Mort Artus' (the last branch of the prose 'Lancelot du Lac') which I am now engaged in preparing.

xiv § 2. *Sources. A Discussion of Dr. Sommer's views.*

adoption of Ellis' erroneous view, cited above, with regard to the relation of our poem and the old French romance.[1]

In an article which appeared in 'Anglia,' xxiii (1900), pp. 67 ff.,[2] I submitted Dr. Sommer's discussion to a detailed examination, and succeeded, I hope, in fixing the true relations to each other of the Harleian 'Morte Arthur,' Malory's work, and the Old French Vulgate-Lancelot. The conclusions of this article I will summarise as follows, referring the reader for the full argument to the article itself:

I. Dr. Sommer wavers between two opinions, (1) that the portion of the Harleian romance after the gap in the MS. is the original of the corresponding portion of Malory's 'Morte D'Arthur'; (2) that this part of the Harleian romance and the corresponding portion of Malory are derived from a common source. The second of these views, however, is evidently the correct one,[3] only it should be recognised that the poet of the Harleian romance does not begin to draw from the same source as Malory just after the gap in the MS. (l. 1318), but somewhat later (l. 1672), or to state the matter conversely, it is only the twentieth and twenty-first books of Malory which are drawn from the same source as the latter part of the metrical romance, not any portion of the eighteenth.

The following passages in Malory, which have nothing corresponding in the English metrical romance, show that he was not dependent on the latter. The citations are from Sommer's edition (vol. i.), London, 1889–91.

1. The long conversation between Lancelot and Guinevere when the former has been espied in the Queen's chamber (pp. 801–802).

2. The latter part of Lancelot's speech to Agravain and his knights whilst Lancelot is still in the Queen's chamber, together with the reply of Agravain and Mordred (pp. 802–803).

3. Lancelot's parting with Guinevere after he has slain Agravain and his knights (p. 803).

---

[1] Dr. Furnivall devotes very little space to the discussion of sources, and with regard to the relation of our romance to Malory, he seems to have remained in doubt as to whether the latter was dependent on the former or whether both were derived from a common original. He noticed, however, correctly that the Harleian romance could not have been based on what is known as the Vulgate-Lancelot. See Preface to his edition, pp. xvi f.

[2] The full title is: 'The Middle English metrical romance, "Le Morte Arthur" (Harleian MS. 2252): its sources and its relation to Thomas Malory's "Morte Darthur."'

[3] E. Wechssler has adopted it from Sommer in his 'Ueber die verschiedenen Radaktionen des Robert von Borron zugeschriebenen Graal-Lancelot-Cyklus' (Halle, 1895), p. 36.

§ 2. *Sources. The relation of the Poem to Malory's last two Books.* xv

4. Lancelot's interview with the knights who assemble to join him after the affair with Agravain (pp. 804–807).

5. The latter part of Arthur's speech on his being told that Guinevere has been carried off, and that his knights have been slain (pp. 811–812).

6. Lancelot's long speech in excuse of himself when he brings Guinevere back (p. 824).

7. Lancelot's consultation with his knights before leaving Arthur's kingdom (pp. 828–829).

8. Lancelot's consultation with his knights before going out to meet Gawain at the siege of Benwyk (p. 834).

9. Gawain's death-bed conversation with Arthur and his letter to Lancelot (pp. 841–843).

10. Lancelot's speech on hearing of the revolt of Mordred (p. 852).

11. The visit of Lancelot to Gawain's tomb (p. 853).

12. The warning which Lancelot receives in a vision to go to Guinevere, together with her death and burial (pp. 856–858).

13. Hector's lament over Lancelot (p. 860).

There is, furthermore, nothing in the Old French Vulgate-Lancelot to correspond to the above passages, except in the case of those numbered 6 and 9, and even in these cases there is no direct dependence. Nevertheless, these passages 6 and 9 and many others of less extent show that there is a connection of some sort between Malory and the Old French romance, and all the difficulties of the situation are best explained, if we assume that the author of the Middle English romance and Malory drew from a common source, which in its turn was a modification of the Old French Vulgate-Lancelot. The similarities and occasional coincidences of phraseology which one observes in comparing Malory and the Middle English metrical romance are only such as must occur where two writers are following closely the same original.[1]

[1] In his selections from 'Morte Darthur' (Boston, 1897), pp. 305 ff., Dr. W. E. Mead has discussed this question from the point of view of phraseology alone, without making the investigation as to source. His conclusions agree with mine. W. W. Newell, who in his 'King Arthur and the Table Round' (London, 1897), ii, pp. 201–239, and pp. 262 f., has given an abstract of our romance, remarks, p. 262 : 'The exquisitely beautiful work of the beginning of the fifteenth century (?) depends on the French prose romance, but with variations ; the writer perhaps obtained his material from oral recitation, and the poem may not have been written, but only recited, and recorded by another hand at a date considerably after the time of its composition." After the discussion in the text, I do not believe that it is necessary to consider this statement more particularly.

§ 2. *The Source of Lines* 1318–1671.

II. *a.* As already stated, it is not at l. 1318 that the poet of the Harleian romance began to use the same source as Malory, but at l. 1672. The lines that lie between (1318–1671) deal with the episode of Mador de la Porte. Now, apart from the very important difference that in Malory this episode occurs at a different point in the order of the narrative, the chief variations between the account of these incidents in our metrical romance as compared with Malory are as follows :—

1. We have in MH. (the romance of the Harleian MS.) two separate appeals of Guinevere to Bors before he consents to defend her, viz. ll. 1340 ff. and 1422 ff., whereas in Malory there is only one (pp. 731 f).

2. In MH. (1357 ff.) the Queen also appeals to Gawain, to which there is nothing to correspond in Malory.

3. The circumstances of Lancelot's meeting with Bors in the forest are different in the two works. In MH. Bors and Lionel have gone forth to offer up their orisons at a chapel in the forest before the battle (1459 ff.) and meet Lancelot riding there by chance. In Malory (p. 732) Bors, who is alone, goes forth on purpose to seek Lancelot.

4. The scene and speech of the Queen in her chamber alone when she laments the absence of Lancelot, ll. 1404 ff. Not in Malory, pp. 730 ff.

5. In MH. they sit at the "borde" before the battle (1504 ff.), of which there is nothing in Malory (pp. 732 f.).

6. In MH. both Mador and Lancelot are unhorsed in their encounter (1584); in Malory only Mador, whilst Lancelot of his own accord after the first encounter descends from his steed (p. 735).

7. In MH. Mador asks Lancelot to reveal to him his name (1604 ff.); there is nothing similar to this scene in Malory (pp. 736 f.).

8. In MH. the squires are put to the torture, and in this way the true author of the death of Mador's brother is forced to confess his crime (1648 ff.). In Malory it is the "damoysel of the lake," Nymue, who reveals the criminal (p. 737).

Now in regard to all the points just enumerated, in which MH. differs from Malory, with the exception of the last, which is found only in MH., a comparison shows that it stands in close relation to the Vulgate-Lancelot, so that there can be no doubt that these features of the metrical romance are derived ultimately from that

§ 2. *Errors of Dr. Sommer regarding these Lines.* xvii

work (or its source), although several of them have undergone transposition or alteration in the process. In fact, whilst differing markedly from Malory, as the above enumeration sufficiently shows, the relation to the Vulgate-Lancelot is just the same as that of the whole preceding portion of the romance down to l. 1318—a relation not of direct dependence, but of ultimate derivation from it through an intermediate version of the part of the Lancelot-story based on that romance (or its source) of the same general nature as the common source of MH., ll. 1672–3969, and the last two books of the 'Morte Darthur.'[1]

b. Dr. Sommer's view, then, that the lines which came just after the gap in the Harleian MS. are derived from a different source from the portion of the romance that precedes that gap is erroneous. But this erroneous view has led him (p. 250) to look for contradictions between these portions of our poem where none really exist. The only point of this kind he has cited which is really worth considering is that of the two accounts which Lancelot receives concerning Queen Guinevere's troubles over the poisoning of the Scottish knight—the one occurring before the gap, ll. 928 ff., and the other after, in ll. 1467 ff. In the first case he hears the story by general report whilst he is lying ill in the forest under the care of a hermit, and in the second he hears it from Bors after he has recovered and is riding about. There is, however, really no inconsistency here, for in the Vulgate-Lancelot also, at exactly corresponding places in the narrative, Lancelot is told twice of these events. The apparent inconsistency is simply due to the fact that the author of the English romance has neglected to make Lancelot remark in the second instance that he had heard of the incident before.[2] The author of the French romance had properly made him say this. The awkwardness, however, of the English poet in this passage is nothing as compared with that which he has been guilty of in leaving the cause of Lancelot's illness unaccounted for in ll. 933 ff. The last time we had heard of Lancelot before, viz. in ll. 780 ff., he was in perfect health. As a matter of fact, the poet in this instance went so far in the condensation of the story of his source that he has

---

[1] The fact that we have after the gap *Bors,* and *Estor* (prevailingly), as the forms for the proper names which appear as *Boerte* and *Ector* in the earlier part of our text is due no doubt to a preference of the second scribe who began writing at l. 1092. As it happens, the names do not occur between l. 1092 and the gap.

[2] As far as Lancelot's inquiry on meeting Bors, l. 1482, is concerned: "how now farys my lady bryght," this is purely conventional. Such conventional inquiries are especially common in ballad literature.

§ 2. *The Source of Lines* 1–1671.

become unintelligible without reference to that source. If we refer to the corresponding place in the Vulgate-Lancelot (which, though not the actual source of MH., undoubtedly gives us the main outline of the story of that source), we learn that the cause of Lancelot's illness is an accidental wound, which he has received from one of the king's huntsmen.[1]

III. The source of the Harleian romance from l. 1672 to the end is unquestionably the same as that of Malory's twentieth and twenty-first books. Now, what is the source of the portion which goes before l. 1672? As I have already had occasion to say in another connection, the source of the earlier portion—from the beginning of the poem down to l. 1672—was a modification of the Vulgate-Lancelot different from the common source of MH., ll. 1672–3969, and Malory's last two books, although of the same general nature. For this earlier portion we have no parallel version as we have for the later portion in Malory's last two books, but a comparison with Malory and the Vulgate-Lancelot shows that the author of the Harleian romance in this later portion followed very closely the source used by himself and Malory, and there is no reason to suppose that his method of dealing with his source in the earlier portion was different. Making the comparison for the later portion, viz. that which extends from l. 1672 to the end, we find that wherever the poem of the Harleian MS. has any incident not in Malory, something parallel to it may still be found in the Vulgate-Lancelot, showing that in such instances the poem represents their common original more accurately than Malory.[2]

The fact that the Harleian romance and Malory take up the incidents in this later portion of the narrative in exactly the same order shows still further that the Middle English poet followed his source closely. There is only one transposition, indeed, of any importance which he has allowed himself, as a comparison with Malory shows, and the reason in that case is obvious. I refer to the end of the story, where the author, being in a hurry to conclude his poem, suppresses the story of how Lancelot and his fellows went to Almesbury and fetched the dead Queen's body to Glastonbury (Malory, Book XXI, Ch. xi), but further on (ll. 3954–3961), after describing Lancelot's death, relates in the briefest way that his companions did this.

[1] Cp. Additional MS. 10294, leaf 64, col. 3—leaf 64, back, col. 3.
[2] I have discussed this at great length in 'Anglia,' xxiii, pp. 96 ff.

§ 2. *Relation of Ll.* 1–1181 *to Malory & the Vulgate-Lancelot.* xix

I repeat then that since our author can be shown to have followed his original closely in the only part of his work where the means of control exist, there can be no reasonable doubt that he did the same thing in the earlier part too, where such means are wanting.

I have already pointed out differences between Malory and the poem for the lines after the gap in the MS. down to l. 1671, which show that the two are independent of each other in that part of the narrative,[1] and I will now do the same thing for the portion before the gap, ll. 1–1181. In all of the points of difference I am about to cite there is an agreement between the Harleian romance and the Vulgate-Lancelot as against Malory. I follow Dr. Sommer's enumeration (pp. 249 f.)—only I leave out the first point he makes as being incorrect.

1. In the Harleian poem (= MH., ll. 63 ff.) when Arthur has left for Winchester, Lancelot comes to Guinevere with the intention of taking leave and going to the tournament, whereas in Malory Guinevere suggests that he should go.

2. The armour of Lancelot is red in MH. (l. 176), and the colour of the sleeve is not mentioned, whereas in Malory the sleeve is red and the colour of the armour is not specified (except in the case of the shield, which is white).

3. Lancelot in MH. (ll. 245 ff. and 321 ff.) stays both before and after the tournament at the house of his host's sister, whereas in Malory he stays before the tournament at the house of a rich "burgeis," and after it, at a hermitage.

4. When Lancelot hears of the new tournament to which he cannot go, in MH. (ll. 382 ff.) his wound breaks open from the violence of his emotion; in Malory he overstrains himself by attempting to ride.

5. The maiden's letter which in MH. (ll. 1078 ff.) reproaches Lancelot with cruelty, does not do so in Malory.

6. Whilst in MH. (ll. 952 ff.) Lancelot is absent from court when the maiden's body arrives, he is present in Malory.

On the other hand, Dr. Sommer's assertion (p. 249) that the sequence of incidents in MH. and the Vulgate-Lancelot is the same is erroneous. "A minute examination of the first part of MH.," he says (p. 250), "discloses several points which do not agree with P.L. (= the 1513 print of the Vulgate-Lancelot), but they are of very secondary importance and can be explained without

---
[1] See p. xvi, above.

§ 3. *Various opinions as to the Dialect of the Poem.*

exception as the poet's modifications of the source in order to adapt his material to the exigencies of his metre; thus in his tendency to avoid proper names, he gives no names for the localities where the events he relates take place." These words, however, give an utterly false idea of the real relation of MH. and P.L. As a matter of fact, when we compare the former with the latter, we discover that the English poem exhibits numberless transpositions of material, and indeed in the part covered by ll. 504–831, the two works are so unlike that it is difficult to keep up any comparison at all. I have set forth the whole matter, however, in great detail in 'Anglia,' xxiii, pp. 87 ff., and must refer the reader to that place for the proof of my assertion. It is only in the part of the narrative, covered by ll. 832–1181, that the English and French romances run closely together. To conclude, as I have already said more than once, the source of ll. 1–1671 is not the Vulgate-Lancelot, but some modification of the Vulgate-Lancelot (or, possibly, its source) no longer in existence.

§ 3. DIALECT AND DATE.

The dialect of our poem has been generally recognized as Midland by all recent students[1] who have expressed themselves on the subject. The only question has been whether the language was that of the East or West Midland. In his edition of our poem[2] Dr. Furnivall adopts the view of the late Dr. Richard Morris to the effect that it is East Midland, but the value of Dr. Morris' conclusions is impaired by his failure to distinguish between the language of the poet and that of the scribes. On the other hand, Professor Alois Brandl in the Introduction to his edition of 'Thomas of Erceldoune'[3] (p. 55) speaks of our poem as West Midland, and Dr. Seyferth in his dissertation[4] (p. 57) has since assigned it more definitely to the Northern border of the West Midland region. I believe that Dr. Seyferth's view of the origin of our poem is the correct one. But let us see what is the evidence of the forms (*i. e.* those fixed by rime) in regard to the language of the poet as distinguished from that of the scribes.[5] As Dr. Seyferth has remarked, we have in our poem as characteristic of

---

[1] Wanley's opinion, which I have quoted above (p. vii) in another connection, has of course no value.
[2] See Preface, pp. xiv f.   [3] Published at Berlin in 1880.
[4] For the title of this study, which is an enlargement of a dissertation presented previously for the doctorate, see above, p. xii, note 1.
[5] Dr. Seyferth, pp. 54 ff., has already discussed the question of dialect very fully. What I have to say here is in the main based on the materials he has collected in his dissertation.

§ 3. *Phonological Peculiarities of the Text.* xxi

a Midland document a mixture of Northern and Southern peculiarities of speech. To take some of the common dialect tests, O.E. *á* yields *ó* as a rule in our text. Cp. the rimes, 761 ff. *stone : torne : mone : none*, 976 ff. *tho : go : so : therto*, 1073 ff. *woo : goo : ther-to : fo*, 1112 ff. *thoo : do : therto : so*, 2803 ff. *bone* (= request) *: done : none : one*, 2938 ff. *two : go : thro : to*, 2898 ff. *none* (= noon) *: vppon : A-none : one* (cp. also 1792 ff.), 3678 ff. *doo : mo*. On the other hand, where the *á* was followed by *r*, we have resulting sometimes *á* and sometimes *ó*, but the former much more frequently. For *ó* cp. 1169 ff. *sore : more : bore* (= born), 3715 ff. *more : ore : therfore : sore*. On the other hand, for *á* cp. the rime of *mare* with *fare*, 434, 2040, 2052, 2111, 2238, 2601, 3769, 3837, with *care*, 557, 685, 687, 771, 1091, 1125, 1426, 3605, 3737, 3760; again of *sare* with *fare*, 511, 802, 2046, 2117, 2216, 2244, 2442, 2458, 2501, 2597, 2801, 3835, with *care*, 559, 681, 3599, 3756, with *bare*, 3069. Notice besides that *á* is kept in *bare*, 951, riming with *fare*, and with *care*, 951, 2101, 2214, and 2606.

O.E. *þǽr*, *wǽron* show as their vowel in our text sometimes *á*, sometimes *ê*, and *wǽron* shows in two instances also *ó*, viz. in 1172 and 2099. In both of these instances the scribe has written *were*, but the rime with *bore* (= born), 1174, 2101, shows that the original form was *wore*. For examples of *there* as fixed by rime see 552 ff. (*fere : there : were : here*), 641 ff. (*lere : were : here : there*), 720 ff. (*there : nere : brere : chere*), 825 ff. (*there : chere : nere : here*), 1721 ff. (*here : there : *swere : yere*), etc.; for *thare* cp. 507, 2042, 2452, 2577 (*: fare*), 775, 804, 979, 1422 (*: care*), etc. On the other hand, for *were* cp. 3 (*: dere*), 159 (*: sopere : bachelere : dere*), 413 (*: fere*), 435 (*: dere : nere*), 480 (*: chere*), 556 (*: here : fere*), 643 (*here : lere*), 2224 (*nere : fere*), 2766 (*: clere*), and 3238 (*: Boteler : here : fere*); and for *ware* cp. 220 (*: fare*), 345, 351 (*: fare*), 769 (*: care*), 949 (*fare : care*), 1095 (*care : bare*, adj.), 2115 (*: fare*), 2797 (*: fare*), etc. In addition to these words notice that *whar* in 3603 stands in rime with *care*. The mixture of the *a*, *e*, and *o* forms in these words is characteristic of the Northern and North Midland districts.[1]

W.S. *ea* before *l* + consonant yields sometimes *ē* and sometimes *ō*. For the former cp. 920, 1928, 2917 (*welde : shelde*), 3405 (*feld : weld*), and for the latter 712 (*folde : golde : wolde*), 803, 3917

[1] See on this subject F. J. Curtis, 'Anglia,' xvi, 449 f. It is often impossible to say which of these variant forms our poet used in a particular case, so, on the whole, I have thought it better to follow Dr. Furnivall in leaving the MS. forms unchanged.

xxii   § 3. *Inflexional Forms.*

(*wolde* : *bolde*), 1705, 2302, 2548, 3589 (*holde* : *wolde*), 3302, 3686 (*holde* : *molde*).

As regards the representatives of O.E. y̆ (the result of mutation), we have both *i* (appearing often as *y*) and *e* in our text, but the evidence under this heading is not very important, especially since in the case of sounds that, comparatively speaking, differ so little it is impossible to say how far the forms even in rime are due to the scribes.

Looking now at the evidence of the inflexional forms, we observe as characteristic of the North and North Midland the present participle in *-and*, which occurs three times in rime, viz. 2365 ff., *lande* : *garlande* : *hande* : *synghand*; 2661 ff., *honde* : *stonde* : *londe* : *lyvande*, and 2834, *stonde* : *londe* : *hond* : *levande*. Indeed, the only present participle in *-ynge* fixed by rime is *lastynge*, 3676, which rimes with *kynge*, *thynge*, and *sokerynge* (verbal noun).

The 2 sing. of the present indicative ends in *-ys* in the only instance where it is fixed by rime, namely, in 1572, *gredys* riming with *dedys* : *nedys* : *wedys. One is tempted to cite three more such forms in our poem which do not occur in rime, especially as two of them occur in the portion of the text which was written by a scribe evidently more Southern than the poet, I mean, viz. *semys* 165, *presons* 1853, *lystenes* 2402, but this is hardly safe. Similarly there is but one instance in our poem of the 2 sing. pret. indic. standing in rime, and that like the 2 pres. indic. points to the North, viz. 3430 *Radde* (N.B. without the inflexional *-est*) riming with *sprad* (3 sg. pret. ind.) and *by-stadde*.[1] The evidence here is, of course, rather scanty, but as far as it goes it points to North or North Midland.

In the only instances where the 3 sing. pres. indic. occurs in rime it ends in *s*, viz. *tase*, 956, *has*, 958 (*was* : *case*). These forms like the others cited point to the North or North Midland.

The forms of the 3 pl. pres. indic. which are fixed by rime end in *-e* (doubtless mute), *see* 1685, *here* 1733, *ryde* 2569—that is to say, are Midland in character. (The forms *dwelle* 232, and *byde* 243, probably also belong here, though they may be subjunctives.) We have besides occurring not in rime, but probably due to the poet

---

[1] Dr. Seyferth has pointed out, moreover, that wherever 2 sing. pret. indic. forms in *-iste*, *-yst(e)* occur in our poem, even though not in rime, except in l. 1155, —viz. in 1148, 1152, 1160, 2832, 3942, 3945, "verlangt der vers die dem norden eigene abwerfung der endung." This is certainly true from the point of view of strict regularity, yet I can't say that the change would improve the rhythm.

§ 3. *Inflexional Forms and Vocabulary.*   xxiii

rather than to his more Southern scribe, the following instances of the 3 pl. pres. indic. ending in -*s*, viz. *buskes* 2525, 2715; *graythes* 2530, and *has* 2599. These forms are Northern or North Midland.

To judge by the rimes the preterite form *was* was pronounced *wes*, as in many Northern texts (Barbour's 'Bruce,' 'Sir Tristrem,' 'Octavian B'). Only twice does it rime with *a*, namely, in 952, 1135. In all other places the pronunciation *wes* is required, viz. 274, 421, 994, 998, 1514, 1717, 1863, 2349, 2518, 2730, 2955, 3559.

It is to be noted that there are several instances of the inflected infinitive fixed by rime in our text: *sayne*, 861, 1028, 1106, 1130, 1587, etc.; *slayne*, 2410; *sene*, 1971, 2435, 2671, 3342; *bene*, 1503, 1925, 2022, 2268, 2284; *done*, 1122, 2068, 2805. On the other hand, the infinitive without ending is the rule, being so frequent as to need no illustration. The [infinitive ending *i* (*y*) from O.E. -*ian* (second class of weak verbs), which is common in the South, is not found in our text.

The past participle, *drayne* = (drawn), 859, 1997, 2164, 3014, 3325, is also characteristic of the North (cp. 'Sir Tristrem,' 'Sir Degrevant,' 'Octavian B'). For the rest, the ending -(*e*)*n* is found in the following forms fixed by rime: *borne*, 3115, 3335, 3553, 3741; *lorne*, 3117, 3331, 3551, 3739; *forlorne*, 3209; *sene*, 522, 550, 691, etc.; *bene*, 524, 1588, 1734, etc.; *done*, 370; *goone*, 3113. On the other hand, we have as past part. *be*, 3641; *agoo*, 149; *take*, 582.—
The prefix -*i* of the past participle is found only in the following cases: *imanased*, 479; *iwounded*, 934; *ibente*, 1035; *ibrowghte*, 1093; *idighte*, 610, 970, 972; *irade*, 2651. In each of these cases the prefix, being required by the metre, is evidently due to the poet.

The following words also indicate Northern or North Midland origin: *fone* (= few), 2378, and *sitte* (*sytte*), 497, 870, from O.N. *sȳti* (= sorrow). Somewhat less significant are *dede* (= death), 911, and *till* (= to), 191, 837, 1786, etc. Of more force, perhaps, is *to* in conjunctive use (= until), 374, 3437, although from its nature it does not occur in rime. The words, *sprente* (= sprang), 1846, 1949, 3357, etc.; *glente*, 3493; *þro*, 589, 1526, 2389, etc.; *layne*, 989, 1108, 2650, etc., belong also to the more Northern dialects.[1] To these the words *busk* and *graythe* and *bayne*, all three of Scandinavian origin, should probably be added.

As regards final *e*, of course, not all such -*e*'s which we find in

[1] Cp. G. Sarrazin's edition of 'Octavian' (Heilbronn, 1885), Introduction, pp. xxxvii f.

§ 3. *Reasons for assuming a Midland origin for the Poem.*

our text are due to the poet. Nevertheless, the rhythm constantly requires the pronunciation of the final *-e*. On the other hand, the following rimes seem to show that it was not always pronounced: 1792 ff. *sone : vppon : fone : mone*; 2062 ff. *come : sone : vppon : done*; 2445 ff. *wone : on : mone : sone*; 146 ff. *newe : show* (for *shewe*) : *hewe : knew*; 593 ff. *shewe : knew : newe : drewe* (in this instance, however, *knew* may stand for *knewe*, the subj.) ; 2396 ff. *he : me : the : bye*; 2126 ff. *ascrye : by : why : cowardly*; 809 ff. *day : away : lay : playe* (similarly 728 ff.) ; 2954 ff., *Mordreid : rede*; 2653 ff., *sped* (p.p.) : *wede : nede : lede*. Especially frequent are the rimes of the pret. ind. *mighte* with *knight*, 161, 583, 616, 872, *bright*, 841, *light*, 583, 708, *sight*, 616. There is always the possibility of a slovenly rime in such cases, but on the whole it can hardly be doubted that our poet often did not sound his final *-e*'s.

It is a peculiarity of our text[1] that the rimes seem often to require as a plural form, *knight* (also once *right*, 2720) as in 677, 919, 925, 1048, 1480, etc. Such a plural form for this word, however, as far as I am aware, is not found in any dialect, and one is at a loss to explain whether we have here simply an arbitrary change of the grammatical form for the sake of rime or whether the poet's own form was the usual *knightis*, so that in such cases we have simply bad rimes as in 812, *nakyd : make*; 529, *lyff : swithe*, etc. The latter is, of course, more likely.

From the above it will be seen that the language of the poet as distinguished from that of the scribes abounds in peculiarities of the Northern dialect. The representation of O.E. *á* by *ó* (except where *r* follows) everywhere in the forms fixed by rime, and still more the prevailing plural indic. endings in *-e* show, however, that the dialect is Midland.[2] In the absence of marked distinctions between the East and West Midland dialects[3] it is difficult to say to which group the language of our poet belonged, but in view of the form *tase* (= takes), to say nothing of the forms of the 2 sing. pres. indic. not in rime, the predominance of *ande* (not *ende*) as the pres. part. ending, and lastly in view of the fact that the 2 sing. pret. ind. seems to have ended like the first person, though only one of these forms is fixed by rime, the West Midland seems more likely. We should accord-

---

[1] See the Preface to Dr. Furnivall's edition, p. xxiv, note.
[2] Moreover the infinitives in *-n* do not belong to strictly Northern dialects, nor do the past participles with prefix *i*.
[3] See on this subject Morsbach, 'Mittelenglische Grammatik,' Halle, 1896, p. 15.

§ 3. *Conclusions as to Dialect and Date of the Poem.* xxv

ingly assign our poem to the Northern boundary of the North-west Midland region.

As regards the time that 'Le Morte Arthur' was composed, Dr. Seyferth has cited (p. 58), the occurrence in our text of the words *fele*, 6, 228, 2019, 2032, 2157, etc.; *lede*, 653, 2569; *blee*, 739, 3504, 3779, 3896; and *wynne* (= come), 1830, as proof that our poem was written before the end of the fourteenth century. Dr. Sarrazin has observed[1] that these words had disappeared even in the Northern dialects by the beginning of the fifteenth century. This would accord with the general condition of inflexions in our poem, so that one will hardly go wrong in placing our romance about the end of the fourteenth century.[2]

The language of the scribes like that of the author of our poem was Midland, of course, as our text shows. It is worthy of remark, however, that the second scribe shows more Southern peculiarities than could be attributed, as is evident from the above analysis, to the poet himself, or, we may add, than are found in the work of the first scribe. Thus in the portion of our text written by the first scribe we find all forms of the plural pres. indic. ending in -*e*, whereas we have in that written by the second scribe besides these prevailing forms in -*e* ten instances of plural pres. indic. in -*en* and two in -*eth*. Again, the portion written by the first scribe shows forty-six forms in -*s* for the 3 sing. pres. ind. and twenty-four in *th*, whilst that written by the second scribe shows fifty-five instances of each. It accords with this that the first scribe uses for the pronoun of the third person plural exclusively the forms *theym*, *them*, *their*, *there*, whereas the second scribe has sixty instances of *hem* to thirty-one of *theym* and *them*, and seventeen of *her* and *hyr* to twenty-eight of *their* and *there*.[3]

§ 4. METRE.

'Le Morte Arthur' is composed in stanzas of eight lines with four accents to the line. The prevailing rhythm is iambic and the usual rime-order is ab ab ab ab. This form of stanza is found in lyrical poetry, as for instance in ' Specimens of Lyrical Poetry,' ed. T. Wright,

---

[1] 'Englische Studien,' vii, 137.
[2] Brandl in his article on Middle English Literature, Paul's 'Grundriss II, Abtheilung I,' p. 708, discusses our romance under the heading of fifteenth century literature, but says nothing specifically about the date.
[3] Cp. Seyferth, pp. 58 f.—also pp. 43, 51 f. I don't think that the evidence is sufficient for us to assign these scribes so exactly as Seyferth does to the East and South-east Midland respectively.

xxvi § 4. *Metre. Defective Stanzas and inexact Rimes.*

London, 1842, p. 99; 'Alya Cantica,' 'Political, Religious and Love Poems,' ed. F. J. Furnivall, E. E. T. S. 1886, p. 109), and the first of 'Laurence Minot's Poems' (ed. J. Hall, Oxford, 1897). It occurs, moreover, sporadically in the 'Chester Plays' (cp. The Fall of Lucifer), and is the prevailing stanza form in the 'Legend of St. Gregory' contained in the Auchinleck MS. (ed. Fritz Schulz, Königsberg, 1876). The stanza was perhaps too exacting for the writers of romances[1]—at least I know of no other romance which is written in it. The Prologue to 'Thomas of Erceldoune' (see Brandl's edition, Berlin, 1880) furnishes the nearest approach to it, but only one of the three stanzas there conforms to the normal rime-order of the stanza in 'Le Morte Arthur.' Even in our romance we have variations from this normal rime-order in the following stanzas: In st. 365, 398, 421, 445, 478 we have the rime-order ab ab ac ac; in st. 147, 372, ab ab ba ba; in st. 1 ab ab cb cb.[2]

It is to be noted, moreover, that st. 46, 177, 186 contain only seven lines, st. 187, 241, 291, 341, 393, 429, only six, and st. 462 only four. In all these apparently defective stanzas the sense is complete in the text as it stands; nevertheless, it is probable that in each instance except the last the lines necessary to make up the full stanza were lost in copying. At the same time, it would not be remarkable if a medieval poet of the minstrel class in composing a poem which was intended practically only for recitation should occasionally omit a line or lines either through inadvertence or through a momentary difficulty in supplying the full complement of lines. In the case of st. 462 especially, which contains only four lines, it seems to me in the highest degree unlikely that anything stood between l. 3681 and l. 3682. And if the poet has allowed himself here a stanza of four lines, why should he not allow himself occasionally a stanza of six lines at any rate?

The rimes in our poem are frequently inexact. Examples of some of the more pronounced instances which cannot be set down to the account of the scribes are as follows: 712 ff. *lade : ledde : sade : glade*; 761 ff. *stone : torne : mone : none*; 808 ff. *sake : lake : nakyd : make*; 2818 ff. *hede : leuyd : wavyd : levyd* (though *hede* here may be for *heved*); 2979 ff. *come : crowne : towne : bowne*; 3224 ff. *dyde :*

---

[1] Cp. on the subject of this stanza J. Schipper's 'Altenglische Metrik' (Bonn, 1881), pp. 346 f. There are variations as to rime-order in the 'Coventry Mysteries' and the other poems which he cites.

[2] Seyferth (p. 59) proposes to get rid of some of these irregularities by changes in the text, but I don't think that this is warranted.

§ 5. *Authorship. Relation of our poem to 'Ipomedon B.'*

stad; 3288 ff. *lese : chese : pease : dayes*, 3320 ff. *caste : truste : fuste : praste*; 3392 ff. *breste : loste : caste : creste*. Many other instances of inexact correspondence of vowels in the rime might be cited, such as 2810 ff. *socoure : indure : stoure : coloure*. There are also many instances where the consonants do not correspond; e.g. 1380 ff. *take : lake : make : shape* (similar 1468 ff.); 368 ff. *sone : done : mone : come* (similar 2062 ff.); 2508 ff. *bydene : bytwene : ʒeme : bydene* (similar 2669 ff.); 2660 ff. *heste : pees : resse : lese* (also 2684 ff.); 3858 ff. *land : found : wode : strond* (where the first two words should no doubt be emended to *lond : fond*); 3272 ff. *spede : bede : lende : stede*. Of especially frequent occurrence in our poem is the riming of *f(f)*, *th* and *gh* (labial, dental and guttural spirants) with one another—so of *ff* with *th* in 529 ff. *lyff : swithe : kithe : blithe*, and similarly, 632 ff., 865 ff., 1561 ff., 1609 ff., 2015 ff., 3566 ff., 3598 ff., 3699 ff.—of *f* with *gh* in 840 ff. *thought : wrought : brought : lofte* (similar 1966 ff.)—of *th* and *gh* in 2677 ff. *inoughe : treuthe : boughe : inoghe*.

I have already referred to the numerous instances where the plural of *knight*[1] also disturbs the rime.

Finally it will be observed that our poet like most of the romance writers makes a large use of alliteration in addition to rime. According to Dr. Seyferth's counting (p. 61) about forty-two per cent. of the lines of our poem show alliteration—in all but a few instances consonantal.

§ 5. AUTHORSHIP.

In a note to his discussion of the sources of Malory (p. 250, note 2) Dr. Sommer has thrown out the suggestion that 'Le Morte Arthur' is by the same author as 'The Lyfe of Ipomydon,' also contained in MS. Harley 2252. The only reasons he offers, however, for this supposition are (1) that the 'Lyfe of Ipomydon,' or 'Ipomedon B,' as it is generally called, is in the same handwriting as the first part of 'Le Morte Arthur' (ll. 1–1091); (2) that the relation of 'Le Morte Arthur,' to the Prose-Lancelot (the source of 'Le Morte Arthur,' ll. 1–1181, as Dr. Sommer holds) is the same as that of 'Ipomedon B' to its source. With reference to the first of these points, the fact that the same scribe copied the two romances is, of course, no argument whatever for identity of authorship; and with reference to the second, since I have shown, as I believe I have, that

[1] See note above, p. xxiv.

§ 5. *Differences of Vocabulary & Forms between the 2 Poems.*

the Prose-Lancelot in its existing form is not the source of any part of 'Le Morte Arthur,' there is no basis of analogy in this case.

One may add, moreover, on this subject that apart from the difference in metrical form ('Ipomedon B' is in short rimed couplets) there are marked differences of style between the two works. In the case of 'Ipomedon B' the narrative is much more condensed than in 'Le Morte Arthur.' Then, the latter poem abounds in the usual formulas of the romances to a far greater degree than 'Ipomedon B.' *Is not to hyde*, etc., are pressed into service by the author of 'Le Morte Arthur' to an extent that is hardly exceeded in the case of any of the other Middle English romances, whereas such expressions are not particularly frequent in 'Ipomedon B.'

Dr. Paul Seyferth in his dissertation on our poem [1] has still further called attention to the pretty frequent use which the author of 'Le Morte Arthur' makes of the words *layne* (= deny) and *thro* (= bold, fierce) in his rimes (*layne* thirteen times, *thro* twelve times), whilst these words do not occur at all in 'Ipomedon B.' [2] He points out, moreover, that the form *yode* occurs in rime fourteen times in 'Le Morte Arthur' (*yede* occurs twelve times), but in 'Ipomedon B' does not occur at all (*yede* occurs eight times). Still further, the infinitive *bene* which occurs seven times in rhyme in 'Le Morte Arthur' does not occur at all in 'Ipomedon B,' and *sene* (infinitive) which occurs four times in rhyme in the former is not found at all in the latter (although it has *se* sixteen times). On the other hand, we find *gone* (infinitive) eleven times in the rhymes of 'Ipomedon B' (*go* ten times), but only *go* (twelve times) in 'Le Morte Arthur.' [3]

In conclusion, we may safely assume that a poem which is so completely in the usual romance style was the work of a professional minstrel. The fact which Dr. Seyferth points [4] out that there is no mention of minstrels in the poem cannot be allowed any weight as against the evidence of style.

---

[1] Sprache und Metrik des mittelenglischen strophischen Gedichtes 'Le Morte Arthur' und sein Verhältnis zu 'The Lyfe of Ipomydon,' Berlin, 1895, see pp. 76 ff.

[2] Dr. Seyferth's statistics regarding the relative occurrence of words of romance and Scandinavian origin in the two poems do not seem to me to have much force.

[3] Dr. Seyferth presents other statistics besides these, but the above points are the telling ones, as it seems to me. It is safer, perhaps, not to use the great number of examples of *wes* for *was* which he cites, since they are based on changes in the MS. readings which at best must remain uncertain, especially in view of our poet's tolerance for inexact rhymes.

[4] Page 77.

§ 6. STYLE.

Readers generally will hardly go so far as Mr. W. W. Newell in pronouncing our poem an "exquisitely beautiful work,"[1] yet I should say for my own part that it is only the adverb which we have a right to demur to here. Our poet lays himself open to criticism most of all in the matter of rimes. As far as inexactness goes, he has, of course, suffered much at the hands of his scribes, yet there remain too large a number of instances which cannot thus be explained away. Worse than this, however, is his constant use of the same rime-words, in which respect, owing to the exigencies of his eight-lined stanza, no doubt, he seems to me to sin beyond what we find elsewhere even in the Middle English romances. The ordinary formulas of the romances, moreover, seem to me to be more frequently repeated in this work than in any other. Such are the special limitations of our poem, to say nothing of those which it has in common with all Middle English romances. We have here, however, a famous and often lovely story told in a style of charming *naïveté* which stands in striking contrast to the ornate and courtly prose of the Old French romances to which his originals belonged. In the English poem indeed we breathe almost the atmosphere of the ballad. Yet it is doubtful whether there is anything in the Vulgate-Lancelot that brings home to our hearts more directly the pathos of the tragedy of Guinevere and Lancelot than that exclamation of the knights:

"Allas, they sayd, Launcelot du lake
That euyr shuldistow se the quene!" (ll. 796 f.)[2]

The reputation of our poem has been eclipsed in a large measure by that of the 'Morte Arthure' of the Lincoln MS. The many problems connected with the origin of that poem which have given rise to such prolonged controversy, and the fact that in parts it represents elements of Arthurian tradition which but for it would have been lost, have drawn the attention of the learned world to it in an unusual degree. It illustrates, moreover, that curious revival of alliterative verse which is one of the most interesting phenomena of fourteenth century literature in England. The Harleian 'Morte

---

[1] See passage quoted in note above, p. xv. Mr. Newell says even more enthusiastically ('King Arthur and the Table Round,' II, p. 264): "The noble conclusion, scarce rivalled in its way in English literature, makes a grand and fitting close to Arthurian Story."

[2] There are passages in the Vulgate-Lancelot corresponding to this, but they do not produce the same effect.

§ 6. *The Merits of the Harleian Romance.*

Arthur' has none of these adventitious sources of interest, nor can one claim for it the rush and vigour of the better-known romance. On the other hand, it is free from the uncouthness which, as I think even professional students will usually find, renders the reading at one time of any considerable portion of the poem of the Lincoln MS. a labour that is by no means light. The main story and the episodes our poem embraces, moreover, far surpass in human interest those of the alliterative poem, as indeed is shown perhaps by the fact that it is the material of the former and not of the latter which has entered into the life-blood of English literature in later centuries. This then, along with its quiet, simple beauty, constitutes the chief claim of our old romance to consideration by the modern world—namely, that it is the earliest work in English verse of all that have survived to present the sorrows of the 'Lily Maid of Astolat' and the story moreover of the end of the Table Round in just that form which seems surest of immortality.

Le Morte Arthur.

[Harleian MS. 2252.]

(1)

Lordingis that ar leff And dere,
    lystenyth and I shall you tell
By old[e] dayes what aunturs were
    Amonge oure eldris þat by-felle :   4
In Arthur dayes, that noble kinge,
    By-felle Aunturs ferly fele,
And I shall telle of there endinge
    That mykell wiste of wo and wele.   8

[leaf 86] The poet is going to tell of adventures in Arthur's days.

(2)

The knightis of the table Round,
    The sangrayle whan they had sought,
Aunturs that they by-fore them found
    Fynisshid and to end[e] brought ;   12
Their enemyes they bette & bound,
    For gold on lyff they lefte them noght.
Foure yere they lyved sound,
    Whan they had these werkis wroght,   16

After the quest of the Holy Grail was ended, the knights of the Round Table lived four years in quiet.

(3)

Tille on a tyme þat it by-felle
    The kinge in bed lay by the quene,
Off Aunturs they by-ganne to telle,
    Many that in þat land had bene :   20
"Sir, yif that it were youre wille,
    Of a wondir thinge I wold you mene,
How your courte by-gynnyth to spill
    Off duoghty knightis all by-dene ;   24

Queen Guinevere begins to fear a decline in the renown of Arthur's Court,

(4)

Syr, your honour by-gynnys to falle,
    That wount was wide in world to sprede,

     Off launcelott and of other all
      That euyr so doughty were in dede."   28
     "Dame, there-to thy counsell I calle:
and advises   What were best for suche a nede?"
[leaf 86, back] "yiff ye your honoure holde shalle,
him to pro-
claim a   A turnement were best to bede,   32
tournament.

         (5)
     For-why that Auntre shall by-gynne
      And by spoke of on euery syde,
     That knightis shall there worship wynne
      To dede of Armys for to Ryde.   36
     Sir, lettis thus youre courte no blynne
      But lyve in honour and in pride."
     "Certys, dame," the kinge said thenne,
      "Thys ne shall no lenger abyde."   40

         (6)
Arthur has A turnement the king lett bede,
a tournament
at Win-   At Wynchester shuld it be,
chester pro-
claimed in Yonge Galehod was good in nede,
which
Galehod is to The Chefteyne of the Crye was he,   44
be leader.
     With knightis þat were stiff on stede,
      That ladyes and maydens might se
     Who that beste were of dede
      Thrughe doughtynesse to have the gre.   48

         (7)
The knights Knightis Arme them by-dene
go to the
tournament, To the turnemente to Ride,
but Lancelot
stays behind With sheldis brode and helmys shene
to see the
queen.   To wynne grete honoure and pride.   52
     launcelot lefte withe the quene
      And seke he lay that ylke tyde;
     for loue þat was theym by-twene
      he made inchessoun for to abyde.   56

         (8)
     The kynge satte vppon his stede
      And forthe is went vppon his way;
Agraveyne Sir Agraveyne for suche a nede
also stays
at home   At home by-lefte, for soth to say,   60

For men tolde in many a thede
  That launcelot by the quene lay;
For to take them with the dede
  he Awaytes both nyght and day. 64

to watch Lancelot and the queen.

[leaf 87]

(9)

launcelott forth wendys he,
  Unto the chambyr to the quene,
And sette hym downe vpon his kne
  And salues there that lady shene. 68
"launcelott, what dostow here with me?
  The kinge is went and þe courte by-dene;
I drede we shall discouerid be,
  Off the loue is vs by-twene; 72

When Lancelot goes to the queen's chamber,

she is alarmed lest they should be discovered.

(10)

Sir agravayne at home is he,
  nyght & day he waytes vs two."
"Nay," he sayd, "my lady fre,
  I ne thinke not it shall be so; 76
I come to take my leve of the,
  Oute of courte or that I go."
"ya swithe þat thou Armyd be,
  For thy dwellynge me is full woo." 80

Lancelot says that he has come to take leave of her.

(11)

launcelott to his chambyr yede,
  There Riche atyre lay hym by-fore,
Armyd hym in noble wede,
  Off that Armure gentylly was shore; 84
Swerd and sheld were good at nede
  In many batayles þat he had bore,
And horsyd hym on a grey stede
  kyng Arthur had hym yeve by-fore; 88

He goes to his own chamber, arms himself,

(12)

haldys he none highe way,
  The knight þat was hardy and fre,
Bot hastis bothe night and day
  Faste toward that Riche Cite,— 92

and avoiding the high ways hastens toward Winchester.

Wynchester it hight, for sothe to say,—
  There the turnament shuld be;
kinge Arthur in a castell lay,
  Full myche there was of gam) and gle. 96

(13)

For-why men wold launcelott by-hold,
  And he ne wold not hym-self shewe,
Wyth his shuldres gonne he fold
  And downe he hangid his hede full low, 100
As he ne might hys lymmys weld;
  Kepit he no bugle blowe;
Wele he semyd As he were old,
  For-thy ne couth hym no man knowe. 104

(14)

The kinge stode on a toure on highte,
  Sir Evway[n]e clepis he þat tyde;
"Syr' evwayne, knowistow any wight
  This knight þat Rides here by-syde?" 108
Sir Evwayne spekis wordis Right
  That Ay is hend, is not to hyde:
"Sir, it is som old knighte
  Is come to se þe yonge knightis Ride." 112

(15)

They by-held hym bothe Anone
  A stounde for the stedis sake;
his hors stomelyd at a stone
  That alle his body there-with gan shake; 116
The knight þan braundisshid yche a bone,
  As he the bridelle vp gan take;
There-by wiste they bothe Anone
  That it was launcelott du lake. 120

(16)

kynge Arthur than spekis he
  To sir evwayne there wordis Right:
"Welle may launcelot holden be
  Off alle þe world the beste knight 124

Sidenotes:
As he passes the castle where Arthur is,
he tries to disguise himself. [leaf 87, back]
The king asks Evwayne who the strange knight is, and Evwayne replies it is probably an old knight come to witness the tournament.
Lancelot's horse stumbles and the king and Evwayne recognize him.

Off biaute and of bounte,
  And sithe is none so moche of myght,
At every dede beste is he,
  And sithe he nold it wist no wight,[1] 128

(17)

Sir Evwayn, wiƚƚ we done hym byde;
  he wenys þat we know hym noght."
"Sir, it is better lette hym Ride
  And lette hym do as he hath thoght; 132
he wolle be here nere by-syde,
  Sithe he þus ferre hedyr hath sought;
We shalle hym know by his dede
  And by the hors þat he hath brought." 136

Arthur wishes to detain him but is dis- [leaf 88] *suaded.*

(18)

An Erle woundyd there be-syde,
  The lord of Ascolot was hight;
launcelot gonne thedyr Ride
  And sayd he wolle there dweƚƚ aƚƚ night; 140
They resseyvid hym with grete pryde.
  A Riche soper there was dight;
his name ganne he hele and hyde
  And sayd he was a strange knight. 144

Lancelot rides to the dwelling of the lord of Ascalot and is well re- ceived.

(19)

Thanne had the erle sonnys two
  That were knightis makid newe;
In þat tyme was the maner so,
  Whan yonge knightis shuld sheldis show, 148
Tille þe friste yere were agoo,
  To bere Armys of one hewe,
Rede or white, yelew or bloo;
  There-by men yonge knightis knew. 152

This lord had two sons, recently knighted, and, as with other young knights in the first year of knighthood, their arms were of one colour.

(20)

As they satte at there sopere,
  launcelot to the erle spake thare:
"Sir, ys here Any Bachelere
  That to the turnament wolle fare?" 156

Lancelot inquires whether there is any young bachelor

[1] MS. might.

there who is
going to the
tournament.
The lord of
Ascalot
wishes one of
his sons to go,
and Lancelot
agrees.

"I haue two sonnys that me is dere,
    And now that oon*n*e is seke full sare;
So in companye þ*at* he were
    myne other sonne I wold were thare."   160

(21)

"Sir, and thy sonne wille thedir Right,
    The lenger I wolle hym abyde,
And helpe hym there w*ith* all my myght
[leaf 88, back]   That hym none harme shall be-tyde."   164
"Sir, the semys a noble kn[i]ght,
    Courteyse and hend, is not to hyde;
At morow shall ye dyne and dight,
    Togedir I rede welle þat ye Ride."   168

(22)

For the sake
of disguise)
Lancelot
wishes to
borrow a suit
of armour.

"Syr, of one thinge I wolle you mynne
    And be-seche you for to spede,
yif here were Any Armure Inne,
    That I might borow it to this dede."   172

The lord of
Ascalot gives
him the
armour of
his son who
is ill.

"Sir, my sonne lieth seke here-in;
    Take his Armure and his stede;
For my sonnys men shall you kenne,
    Off Rede shall be your bothis wede."   176

(23)

The daughter
of the lord of
Ascalot falls
in love with
Lancelot.

Therle had a doughter þat was hym dere,
    Mykell launcelott she beheld;
hyr Rode was rede as blossom on brere
    Or floure þat springith in the feld;   180
Glad she was to sitte hym nere,
    The noble knight vndir sheld;
Wepinge was hyr moste chere,
    So mykell on hym hyr herte gan held.   184

(24)

Vp̄ than Rose þat mayden stille
    And to hyr chamber wente she tho;
Downe vppon hir bedde she felle,
    That nighe hyr herte brast in two.   188

launcelot wiste what was hyr wyll,   *Lancelot recognizes*
   Welle he knew by other mo,   *the cause of her sorrow,*
hyr brother klepitte he hym tylle
   And to hyr chamber gonne they go;   192

(25)

he satte hym downe for the maydens sake
   vpon hyr bedde there she lay,
Courtessely to hyr he spake,   *and tries to comfort her.*
   For to comforte þat fayre may;   196
In hyr Armys she gan hym take
   And these wordis ganne she say: *[leaf 89]*
"Sir, bot yif that ye it make,   *When she confesses*
   Saff my lyff no leche may."   200   *her love,*

(26)

"lady," he sayd, "thou moste lette,   *he says that his heart is*
   For me ne giff the no-thynge Ille;   *already given away, but*
In Another stede myne hert is sette,   *that he will be her*
   It is not at myne owne wille;   204   *knight.*
In erthe is no thinge that shall me lette
   To be thy knight lowde and stille;
A-nother tyme we may be mette
   Whan thou may better speke thy fille."   208

(27)

"Sithe I of the ne may haue more,
   As thou arte hardy knight and fre,
In the turnement þat thou wold bere
   Sum signe of myne þat men might se."   212
"lady, thy sleve thou shalte of-shere,   *He agrees to wear her*
   I wolle it take for the love of the;   *sleeve as a sign in the*
So did I neuyr no ladyes ere   *tournament.*
   Bot one that most hathe lovid me."   216

(28)

On the morow whan it was day   *The next day Lancelot*
   They dyned and made them yare,   *rides forth with the*
And þan they went forthe on there way   *brother of the Maid of*
   To-gedyr as they bretherne were.   220   *Ascalot to*

They mette a squyer by the way
 That frome the turnament gan fare,
And askyd yif he couthe them say
 Whiche party was the bygger thare. 224

take part in the tournament.

(29)

"Sir Galehod hathe folke þe more,
 For sothe, lordingis, as I you telle,
But Arthur is the bigger there;
 he hath knightis stiff and felle; 228
They Ar bold and breme as bare,
 Evwayne and boert and lyonelle."
Therlys sonne to hym spake thare :
 "Sir, with them I rede we dwelle." 232

They learn that Arthur's party in the tournament [leaf 89, back] includes the best knights,

(30)

launcelotte spake, as I you rede :
 "Sithe they ar men of grete valour,
how might we amonge them spede
 There alle are stiffe & stronge in stowre? 236
helpe we them þat hath most nede ;
 Ageyne the beste we shall welle dore ;
And we might there do Any dede,
 It wold vs torne to more honour." 240

so, to win greater glory, they decide to aid the other side.

(31)

launcelot spekis in that tyde
 As knight þat was hardy and fre :
"To-night with-oute I rede we byde ;
 The presse is grete in the Cite." 244
"Sir, I haue An Aunte here beside,
 A lady of swith grete biaute ;
Were it your wille thedir to Ride,
 Glad of vs than wold she be." 248

They decide to spend that night outside the city at the house of an aunt of the young knight of Ascalot.

(32)

Tho to the castelle gonne they fare,
 To the lady fayre and bright ;
Blithe was the lady thare
 That they wold dwelle with hyr þat night ; 252

They go to that lady's castle and are well received.

hastely was there soper yare
    Off mete and drinke rychely dight.
Onne the morow gonne they dyne & fare,
    Both launcelott and þat other knight. 256

(33)

Whan they come in-to þe feld,
    Myche there was of game & play;
A while they hovid & by-held
    how Arthurs knightis Rode that day. 260
Galehodis party by-gan to held,
    On fote his knightis ar lad away;
launcelott stiff was vndyr sheld,
    Thinkis to helpe, yif that he may. 264

At the tournament on the next day they assist Galehod's party which [leaf 90] is being worsted.

(34)

Be-syde hym come þan sir Evwayne,
    Breme as Any wilde bore;
launcelott springis hym ageyne,
    In Rede armys þat he bare; 268
A dynte he yaff with mekill mayne,
    Sir Evwayne was vn-horsid thare,
That alle men wente he had bene slayne,
    So was he woundyd wondyr sare. 272

In the conflict Lancelot unhorses Evwayne.

(35)

Sir boerte thoughte no-thinge good,
    Whan Sir Evwayne vn-horsid was;
Forthe he springis as he were wode
    To launcelot, with-outen lees; 276
launcelot hytte hym on the hode,
    The nexte way to ground he chese;
Was none so stiff agayne hym stode,
    Fulle thynne he made the thikkest prees. 280

He also unhorses Boerte

(36)

Sir lyonelle be-ganne to tene
    And hastely he made hym bowne,
To launcelott with herte kene
    he rode with helme and swerd[e] browne; 284

launcelott hitte hym, as I wene,
  Throughe the helme in-to þe Crowne,
That euyr after it was sene;
  Bothe hors and man there yede adowne; 288

(37)

The knightis gadrid togedir thare
  And gan with Crafte there counselle take;
Suche a knight was neuyr are
  But it were launcelot du lake; 292
Bot, for the sleve on his Creste was thar,
  For launcelot wold they hym noght take;
For he bare nevir none suche by-fore
  But it were for the quenys sake: 296

(38)

"Off Ascolot he neuyr was
  That thus welle beris hym to-day."
Ector sayd, with-outen lees,
  What he was he wold assay. 300
A noble stede Ector hym chese
  And forthe rydis glad and gay;
launcelot he mette a-mydde þe prese,
  By-twene them was no chi[l]dis play; 304

(39)

Ector smote with herte good
  To launcelot that ilke tyde;
Throughe helme in-to his hede it yode
  That nighe loste he all his pride; 308
launcelot hytte on the hood
  That his hors felle and he be-syde.
launcelot blyndis in his blode,
  Oute of the feld full faste gan Ride; 312

(40)

Oute of the feld they Reden thoo
  To a forest highe and hore.
Whan they come by them one two,
  Off his helme he takis thore. 316

"Sir," he sayd, "me is full woo,
   I drede that ye be hurte full sore."
"Nay," he sayd, "it is not so,
   But fayne at Rest I wold we were."   320

(41)
"Sir, myne Aunte is here be-syde,
   There we bothe were all nighte;
Were it youre wille thedir to Ride,
   She wolle us helpe with all hyr might,   324
And send for lechis this ylke tyde,
   youre woundis for to hele and dight;
And I my-self wille with you abyde
   And be youre servante and youre knight."   328

*He is per-
suaded to go
again to the
castle of the
aunt of the
young knight
of Ascalot.*

[leaf 91]

(42)
To the castelle they toke the way,
   To the lady fayre and hend;
She sent for lechis, as I you say,
   That wonnyd bothe ferre and hend,   332
But by the morow that it was day
   In bed he might hym-self not wend;
So sore woundyd there he lay
   That well nighe had he sought his end.   336

*There doctors
attend him.*

(43)
Tho kinge arthur with mykell pride
   Callid his knightis all hym by
And sayd a mounth he wold there byde
   And in wynchester lye;   340
heraudis he dyd go and Ride
   Another turnamente for to Crye;
"This knight wolle be here nere be-syde,
   for he is woundyd bitterlye."   344

*King Arthur
has another
tournament
proclaimed
to draw forth
the strange
knight again.*

(44)
Whan the lettres made were
   The heraudis forth with them yede,
Throughe yngland for to fare,
   Another turnament for to bede;   348

      Bad them buske and make them yare
        Alle that stiff were on stede.
      Thus these lettris sent were
        To tho that doughty were of dede, 352

(45)

    Tille on a tyme þat it be-felle
A herald with news of the tournament comes to the castle where Lancelot is lying.
      An heraude comys by the way
      And at the castelle a night gan dwelle
        There as launcelot woundyd lay, 356
      And of the turnamente gon telle
        That shuld come on the sonday.
      launcelot sighes wondyr stille
        And sayd: "allas and well-a-way! 360

(46)

[leaf 91, back] Whan knightis wynne worship and pride,
        Som Auntre shall hold me a-way,
      As a coward for to a-byde.
Lancelot vows that he will go to the tournament,
        This turnamente, for sothe to say, 364
      for me is made this ylke tyde;
        Thoughe I shuld dye this ylke day,
      Certis I shalle thedyr Ride." 367
        [. . . . . *no gap in the MS.*] 367 b

(47)

      The leche Aunswerd also sone
though the physician says it will be his death.
        And sayd: "syr, what haue ye thought?
      Alle the Crafte that I haue done
        I wene it wille you helpe Right noght. 371
      There is no man vndir the mone,
        By hym þat all this world hath wroght,
      Might saue youre lyff to that tyme come
        That ye vpon your stede were brought!" 375

(48)

      "Certis, though I dye this day,
        In my bedde I wolle not lye;
      Yit had I levir do what I may
        Than here to dye thus cowardelye." 379

The leche anone than went his way
   And wold no lenger dwelle hym by ;
his wou*n*dis scryved and stille he lay
   And in his bedde he swownyd thrye.   383

The physician goes away, but when Lancelot's agitation causes his wounds to break open,

(49)

The lady wept as she were wode,
   Whan she sawe he dede wol*d* be,
Therlis sonne with sory mode
   The leche agayne clepis he   387
And sayd : "thou shalt haue yiftis goo*d*,
   For-why þ*a*t thou wilte dwelle w*it*h me."
Craftely than stau*n*chid he his blode
   And of good comforte bad hym be.   391

he is persuaded to return.

(50)

The heraude than wente on his way
   At morow whan the day was light
Also swithe as euyr he may
   To Wynchester that ylke night ;   395
he salued the kinge, for soth to say—
   By hym satte syr Evwayne the knight—
And sithe he told upon his playe
   What he had herd and sene w*it*h sight :   399

The herald goes back to Winchester,

[leaf 92]

(51)

"Off alle þat I haue sene w*it*h sight
   Wondir thought me nevir more
Than*n*e me dy*d* of a folyd knight
   That in his bed lay woundid sore ;   403
he myght not heve his hede vp-Right
   For alle the world haue wonne thare ;
For Angwisshe þat he ne Ride myght
   Alle his woundis scryved were."   407

and tells of the wounded knight who was so eager to ride in the tournament.

(52)

Sir Evwayne than spekis wordis fre
   And to the kynge sayd he there :
"Certis, no cowarde knight is he ;
   Allas ! that he nere hole and fere !   411

Evwayne guesses that it is the strange knight of the last tournament.

The tournament proclamation is repealed.

  Welle I wote þat it is he
   That we alle of vnhorsyd were.
  the turnament is beste lette be,
   For sothe that knight may not come there."   415

(53)

It is decided that the tournament which had been proclaimed shall not be held, and the king goes to Camelot.

  There turnement was than no more
   But this depa*r*tith alle the prese.
  knightis toke there leve to fare,
   Ichone his owne way hym chese.   419
  To kamelot the kynge went there,
   There as quene gaynore was;
  he wente haue found launcelot thar*e*;
   A-way he was, w*ith*-outen lese.   423

(54)

  Launcelot sore woundyd lay;
   knightis sought hym fuH wyde.
  Therle sonne night and day
   Was alle-way hym be-syde;   427

When Lancelot is well enough,

  Therle hym-self whan he ryde may
   Brought hym home w*ith* mykeH p*r*ide

the lord of Ascalot takes him to his castle.

  And made hym bothe game & play
   Tille he might' bothe go and Ryde.   431

(55)

[leaf 92, back] Boerte and Lyonelle go forth to seek Lancelot.

  Boerte and lyonelle than sware,
   and at the kinge ther*e* leve toke there,
  Ageyne they wold come nevir mare
   Till they wiste where launcelot were.   435

So does Ector too.

  Ector went with them thare
   To seche his brodyr þat hym was dere.
  many a land they gan*n*e through fare
   And sought hym bothe ferre and nere,   439

(56)

They come to Ascalot and find Lancelot walking on the walls.

  Tille on a tyme þat it by-felle
   That they come by that ylke way,
  And at the castelle at mete gan dweH,
   There as launcelott' woundyd lay;   443

launcelot they saw, as I you telle
 Walke on the wallis hym to play;
On knees for Ioye aʜ they felle,
 So blithe men they were that day. 447

(57)

Whan launcelott saw tho ylke thre
 That he in world[e] louyd beste,
A merier metinge might no man se,
 And sithe he ledde them to Reste. 451

All rejoice at this meeting.

Therle hym-self, glad was he,
 That he had gotten siche a geste;
So was the mayden feyre and fre
 That alle hyr loue on hym had keste. 455

(58)

Whan they were to soper dight,
 Bordis were sette and clothis spradde,
Therlis doughter and the knight
 To-gedir was sette, as he them badde, 459

At supper that night Boerte asks Lancelot where he received his wound.

Therlys sonnys. þat bothe were wight
 to serue them were nevir sadde,
And therle ħym-selfe with alle his mygh[t]
 To make them bothe blyth and glad. 463

(59)

Bot Boert, euyr in mynde he thoghte
 That launcelot had bene woundyd sore.
" Sir, were it your wille to hele it noght
 Bot telle where ye thus hurte were?" 467 [leaf 93]
" By hym þat alle this world hath wrought,"
 launcelot hym-self swore,

Lancelot vows vengeance for the wound.

" The dynte shall be fuʜ dere bought,
 yif euyr we may mete vs more!" 471

(60)

Ector ne liked that no wight,
 The wordis that he herd there;
For sorow he loste both strength & might;
 The colours changid in his leyre. 475

Ector (who had wounded him) is alarmed at this.

Boerte than sayd these wordis Right:
"Ector, thou may make yvelle chere;
For sothe it is no coward knight
That thou arte of I-manased here." 479

(61)

Lancelot now learns who gave him the wound.
"Ector," he sayd, "where thou it were
That woundid me thus wondir sore?"
Ector, aunswerd with symple chere:
Lyonelle and Boerte jest about the wounds they too had received,
"lord, I ne wiste þat ye it wore, 483
A dynte of you I had there,
felyd I nevir none so sore."
Sir lyonelle by god þan swore
That "myne wolle sene be euyr more." 487

(62)

Sir Boerte than answerd as tyte
As knight þat wise was vndir wede:
"I hope þat none of vs was quite,
I had oon þat to ground I yede. 491
Sir, your brodyr shall ye not wite,
now knowes either others dede;
now know ye how Ector can smyte
To helpe you whan ye haue nede." 495

(63)

and Lancelot reassures Ector, saying that he loves him all the better for the proof of strength he has given.
launcelot loughe with herte fre
That Ector made so mekill Sitte:
"Brother, no thinge drede thou the,
For I shalle be bothe hole and quite. 499
Though thou haue sore woundid me,
There-of I shall the nevir wite;
[leaf 93, back] Bot euyr the better loue I the,
Such a dynte that thou can smyte." 503

(64)

Lyonelle, Boerte and Ector return to court,
Than vppon the thrid day
They toke there leve for to fare,
To the courte they wille away,
For he wille dwelle a while thare. 507

"Grete welle my lorde, I you pray,
   And telle my lady how I fare,
And say I wylle come whan I may;
   And byddith hyr longe no-thinge sare." 511

taking messages from Lancelot.

(65)
They toke there leve, with-outen lees,
   And wightely wente vppon there way;
To the courte the way they chese,
   There as the quene Genure lay. 515
The kinge to the foreste is
   With knightis hym for to play;
Good space they had with-outen prese
   There erand to the quene to say. 519

When they arrive, the king is in the forest.

(66)
They knelyd downe by-fore the quene,
   The knightis þat were wise of lere,
And sayd they had launcelot sene
   And thre dayes with hym were, 523
And how þat he had woundyd bene,
   And seke he had lye full sore.
"Or ought longe ye shall hym sene;
   he bad you longe no thynge sore." 527

They give the queen news of Lancelot,

(67)
The quene loughe with herte fre
   Whan she wiste he was on lyff.
"O, worthy god, what wele is me!
   Why ne wiste my lord it also swithe!" 531
To the foreste rode these knightis thre,
   To the kinge it to kithe;
Ihesu criste þan thankis he
   For was he nevir of word so blithe. 535

and she rejoices that he is alive.

So do the king and Gawayne when they hear it.

(68)
he klepyd Sir Gawayne hym nere
   And sayd: "certis, that was he
That the rede armys bere;
   Bot, now he lyffis, welle is me." 539

[leaf 94]

Gawayne answerd w*ith* myld chere,
 As he that Ay was hend and fre :
"Was neuyr tithandis me so dere,
 Bot sore me longis launcelot to se."   543

(69)

Gawayne goes at once to Ascalot,

At the kinge and at the quene
 Sir Gawayne toke his leve that tyde,
And sithe at alle the courte by-dene,
 And buskis hym w*ith* mekyll pryde   547
Tille Ascalot, w*ith*-outen wene,
 Also faste as he might Ryde ;
Tille that he haue launcelot sene
 Night ne day ne wolle he byde.   551

(70)

but before he arrives Lancelot departs, to the great sorrow of the Maid of Ascalot.

By that was launcelot hole and fere,
 Buskis hym and makis all yare,
his leue hathe he take there ;
 The mayden wepte for sorow & Care.   555
"Sir, yif that youre willis were,
 Sithe I of the ne may haue mare,
Som thinge ye wolde be-leue me here
 To loke on whan me longith sare."   559

(71)

launcelot spake w*ith* herte fre,
 For to comforte that lady hende :

He leaves his own armour behind at Ascalot.

"Myne Armure shall I leue w*ith* the
 And in thy brothers wille I wend ;   563
loke thou ne longe not after me
 For here I may no lenger lend.
longe tyme ne shalle it noght be
 That I ne shalle eyther come or send."   567

(72)

launcelot is Redy for to Ride
 And on his way he went forth Right ;

Gawayne arrives [leaf 94, back]

Sir Gaweyn come aftir on a tyde
 And askis after suche a knighte ;   571

They reseyved hym with grete pride,   *and is hospitably treated.*
  A Riche soper there was dight,
And sayd, in herte is noght to hyde,
  A-way he was for fourtenyght.   575

(73)

Sir Gaweyne gon that mayden take,   *In conversation with Gawayne the Maid of Ascalot confesses her love for Lancelot, and says that he has taken her as his lady-love.*
  And satte hym by that swete wight,
And spake of launcelot de lake ;
  In alle the world nas suche a knight.   579
The mayden there of launcelot spake,
  Said all hyr loue was on hym light,
"For his leman he hathe me take,   *She cites the possession of his armour as proof.*
  his Armure I you shew[e] mighte."   583

(74)

"Now, damysselle," he sayd Anone,
  "And I Am glad þat it is so ;
Suche a lemman as thou haste oon
  In all this world ne be no mo ;   587
There is no lady of flesshe ne bone
  In this world so thryve or thro,
Thoughe hyr herte were stele or stone,
  That might hyr loue hald hym fro.   591

(75)

But, damysselle, I be-seche the   *At Gawayne's request,*
  his sheld that ye wold me shewe ;
launcelottis yif that it be,
  Be the coloures I it knew."   595
The mayden was bothe hend & fre,
  And ledde hym to a chambyr newe ;
launcelottis sheld she lette hym se,   *she shows him Lancelot's shield and armour.*
  And all his Armure forth she drewe.   599

(76)

hendely than syr Gawayne,
  To the mayden there he spake :
"lady," he sayd, "withouten layne,   *Gawayne recognizes the shield,*
  This is launcelottis sheld de lake,   603

and says that he is glad [leaf 95] that Lancelot has taken her for his lady-ove.

    Damesselle," he sayd, " I Am fulle fayne
        That he the wold to lemman take,
    And I with alle my myght and mayne
        Wille be thy knight for his sake."   607

(77)
    Gawayne thus spake with that swete wight
        What his wille was for to say
    Tille he was to bed I-dighte;
        Aboute hym was gamme and play.   611

He leaves the next day, and not knowing where to find Lancelot returns to court,

    he toke his leue at erle and knight
        On the morow whan it was day,
    And sithen at the mayden brighte,
        And forthe he wente vppon his way.   615

(78)
    he nyste where þat he mighte
        ne where that launcelot wold lend,
    For whan he was oute of sight,
        he was fulle yvelle for to fynd.   619
    he takis hym the way Right,
        And to the courte gon he wend;

where he is gladly received.

    Glad of hym was kyng and knight,
        For he was bothe corteyse and hend.   623

(79)
    Than it by-felle vppon a tyde,
        The kinge stode by the quene & spake,
    Sir gaweyne standis hym be-syde,[1]
        Ichone tille other there mone gan make   627
    how longe they might with bale abyde
        The comynge of launcelot du lake;
    In the courte was litelle pryde,
        So sore they sighyd for his sake.   631

(80)
    "Certis, yif launcelot were on lyff,
        So longe fro courte he nold not be."

Gawayne tells at court that Lancelot

    Sir gawayne answerd also swithe:
        "There-of no wondir thinkith me;   635

---

[1] *In the MS. this and the following line occupied the place which is filled in this edition by ll. 632-3. The scribe, however, observed his mistake and indicated the necessary correction.*

The Queen grieves at Lancelot's reported infidelity. 21

The feyrest lady that is on lyff *has chosen a lady-love.*
  Tille his le*m*man chosen hath he ;
Is noon of vs but wold be blithe
  Suche a semely for to see." 639

(81)

The kinge Arthur was fuH blythe [leaf 95, back]
  Off that tithingis for to lere,
And askid syr Gawayne also swythe *When Arthur asks who*
  What mayden that it were. 643 *it is, he says that it is the*
" Therlis doughter," he sayd as swithe, *daughter of the earl of*
  " Off Ascolot, as ye may here, *Ascalot.*
There I was made glad & blithe.
  his sheld the mayde shewid me there." 647

(82)

The quene than said wordis no mo,
  Bot to hyr chambir sone she yede,
And downe vppon hyr bed felle so
  That nighe of witte she wold wede. 651 *The queen is almost*
" Allas ! " she sayd, " and weH-a-wo ! *distraught at the news of*
  That euyr I Aught lyff in lede ; *Lancelot's supposed*
The beste body is loste me fro *infidelity.*
  That euyr in stoure by-strode stede." 655

(83)

ladyes that aboute hyr stode,
  That wiste of hyr previte,
Bad hyr be of comforte gode,
  lette no man suche semblant se. 659
A bed they made wit*h* sory mode,
  There-in they brought that lady fre ;
Euyr she wepte as she were wode,
  Off hyr they had fuH grete pite. 663

(84)

So sore seke the quene lay,
  Off sorow might she nevir lette,
Tille it felle vppon a day,
  Sir lyonelle and Ector yede 667 *Lyonelle and Ector meet*

Lancelot in the forest,

In-to the foreste, them to play,
    That floured was and braunchid swete,
And as they went by the way,
    With launcelot gonne they mete.   671

(85)

What woundyr was though they were blith
    Whan they there master saw w*ith* sight!
On knees they felle also swithe
    And aH they thankid god aH-myght;   675

[leaf 96] Ioye it was to se and lythe
    The metynge of the noble knighte.

who asks after the queen.

And sithe he freyned also swithe:
    "how fares my lady brighte?"   679

(86)

They tell him that both she and all the court are in great distress at his absence.

Than answerd the knightis fre
    And said that she was seke fuH sare:
"Grete doelle it is to here and se,
    So mekylle she is in sorow and care;   683
The kinge, a sory man ys he
    In courte for that ye come no mare;
Dede he wenys that ye be
    And alle the courte both lasse & mare.   687

(87)

Sir, were it your wille w*ith* vs to fare,
    For to speke w*ith* the quene,
Blithe I wote wele that she ware,
    yif that she had you onys sene.   691
The kynge is mekille in sorow and care,
    And so ys aH the courte by-dene;
Dede they wene welle that ye Are
    Frome courte for ye so longe haue bene."   695

(88)

Lancelot decides to return to the court with them.

he grauntis them at that ylke sythe
    home that he wille w*ith* them Ride;
There-fore the knightis were fulle blithe
    And buskcd them w*ith* mykelle p*ri*de   699

To the courte also swithe;
    Nyght ne day they nold' abyde.
The kinge and alle the courte was blithe,
    The tydandis whan they herde þat tyde.   703

(89)

The kinge stode in a toure on highe, *The king, who is on a tower, sees him approaching.*
    Be-sydes hym standis syr Gawayne;
launcelotte whan that they sighe,
    Were nevir men on mold so fayne.   707
They Ranne as swithe as euyr they might
    Oute at the gates hym Agayne;
Was nevir tidandis to them so light.
    The kinge hym kissyd' and knight & swayne;   711

(90)

To a chamber' the kynge hym lad'; *He is given a joyful reception,*
    feyre in Armys they gon hym fold',
And sette hym on A Riche bedde *[leaf 96, back]*
    That sprad' was with a clothe of gold';   715
To serve hym was there no man sad'
    Ne dight hym as hym-self wold'
To make hym bothe blithe and glad;
    And sithe Auntres he them told'.   719

(91)

Thre dayes in courte he dwellid there *but for three days he does not speak with the quene.*
    That he ne spake not with the quene:
So myche prees was Ay hym nere;
    The kyng hym lad' and courte by-dene.   723
The lady, bright as blossom on brere,
    Sore she longid hym to sene;
Wepinge was hyr moste chere,
    Thoughe she ne durste hyr to no man mene.   727

(92)

Than it felle vppon a day, *At last, when Arthur is out hunting, Lancelot goes to the queen's chamber.*
    The kinge gan on huntynge Ride
In-to the foreste hym to playe,
    With his knightis be his syde;   731

launcelot longe in bedd laye,
    With the quene he thought to byde;
To the chamber he toke the way
    And salues hyr with mekell pryde;   735

(93)

Friste he kissydd that lady shene
    And salues hyr with herte fre,
And sithe the ladyes all by-dene,
    For Ioye the teres Ranne on ther' ble.   739

She reproaches him in regard to the Maid of Ascalot.

"Well-a-way!" than sayd the quene,
    "launcelot, that I euyr the se!
The loue þat hathe be vs by-twene
    That it shall thus departed be!   743

(94)

Allas! launcelot du lake,
    Sithe thou hast all my hert in wold
Therlis doughter that thou wold take
    Off ascalot, as men me told!   747
Now thou leviste for hyr sake
    Alle thy dede of Armys bold,

[leaf 97]

I may wofully wepe and wake
    In clay tylle I be clongyn cold.   751

(95)

She begs him at least to keep their former relations secret.

But, launcelot, I be-seche the here,
    Sithe it nedelyngis shall be so,
That thou nevir more dyskere[1]
    The loue that hathe bene be-twyxe vs two,   755
Ne that she nevir be with the so dere
    Dede of Armys þat thou be fro,
That I may of thy body here,
    Sithe I shalle thus be-leve in woo."   759

(96)

launcelot fulle stille than stode,
    his herte was hevy as Any stone;
So sory he wexe in his mode,
    For Routhe hym thought it all to-torne.   763

[1] MS. discouyr.

Lancelot goes back to the forest.

"Madame," he said, "for crosse and Rode, Lancelot does not understand, and in anger
    What by-tokenyth aƚƚ this mone?
By hym þat bought me with his blode,
    Off these tydandes know I none;   767

(97)

But by these wordis thynkith me
    A-way ye wold' þat I ware;
Now haue good' day, my lady fre,
    For sothe thou seest me nevir mare."   771
Oute of the chambyr þan wendis he; he goes back to the forest.
    Now whethir his hert was fuƚƚ of Care!
The lady swownyd Sithes thre
    Almost she slew hyr-self[e] thare.   775

(98)

launcelot to his chambyr yede,
    There his owne atyre in lay,
Armyd hym in a noble wede,
    Thoughe in his hert were liteƚƚ play;   779
Forthe he spronge as sparke of glede,
    Withe sory chere, for sothe to say;
Vp he worthis vppon his stede
    And to a foreste he wendis a-way.   783

(99)

Tithyngis come in-to the halle [leaf 97, back]
    That launcelot was vppon his stede;
Oute than Ranne the knightis alle, The knights try to overtake him
    Off there witte as they wold' wede;   787
Boerte de Gawnes and lyonelle
    And Ector that doughty was of dede
Folowyn hym on horsys snelle,
    Fulle lowde gonne they blowe and grede.   791

(100)

There might no man hym ovir-take, but do not succeed.
    he Rode in-to a forest grene;
Moche mone gonne they make
    The knightis that were bold and kene.   795

The court grieves at Lancelot's departure

They blame the queen for his leaving the court again,

"Allas!" they sayd, "launcelot du lake,
That euyr shuldistow se the quene!"
And hyr they cursyd for his sake
That euyr loue was them by-twene. 799

(101)

They ne wiste nevir where to fare
Ne to what land þat he wold;
Ageyne they went with sighyng sare,
The knightis þat were kene & bold; 803

and she herself is in deep distress.

The quene they found in swownyng thare,
hyr comely tresses all vnfold;
They were so full of sorowe & Care
There was none hyr comfort wold. 807

(102)

The king hastens home and learns that Launcelot is gone.

The kynge than hastis hym for his sake
And home þan come that ylke day,
And asked after launcelot du lake,
And they sayd: "he is gone away." 811
The quene was in hyr bed all nakyd,
And sore seke in hyr chambyr lay,
So moche mone the kynge gon make,
There was no knight þat lust to playe. 815

(103)

He laments that Lancelot will never stay at
[leaf 98] court.

The kinge klepis Gawayne þat day
And alle his sorow told hym tylle:
"Now ys launcelot gone A-way
And come, I wote, he nevir wille." 819
he sayd "allas and wellaway!"
Sighed sore and gaff hym ylle:
"The lord that we have lovid all-way,
In courte why nylle he nevir dwelle!" 823

(104)

Gawayne offers to go

Gawayn spekis in that tyde
And to the kynge sayd he there:
"Sir, in this castelle shall ye byde,
Comforte you and make good chere, 827

And we shall bothe go and Ride
 In all landis ferre and nere ;
So preuely he shall hym not hyde
 Throughe happe that we ne shall of hym here." 831

in search of him.

(105)

[K]nyghtis than sought hym wide,
 Off launcelot myght they not here,
Tylle it felle vppon a tyde,
 quene Genure, bright as blossom on brere,   835
To mete is sette that ylke tyde,
 And syr Gawayne satte hyr nere,
And vppon that other syde
 A scottysshe knight þat was hyr dere.   839

(106)

A squyer in the courte hath thought,
 That ylke day, yif that he myght,
With a poyson þat he hath wrought
 To slae Gawayne, yif that he mighte ;   843
In frute he hath it forthe brought
 And sette by-fore the quene bright ;
An Appille ouereste lay on lofte,
 There the poyson was in dighte,   847

Some time after this a squire tries to poison Gawayne by means of an apple,

(107)

For he thoughte the lady bright
 Wold the beste to Gawayne bede,
But she it yaff to the scottisshe knight,
 For he was of an vnkouth stede.   851
There-of he ete a lytell wight,
 Off tresoun toke there no man hede ;
There he loste both mayne and might
 And died sone, as I you Rede.   855

but the queen, not knowing that it was poisoned, gives it to a Scotch knight [leaf 98, back] who dies from it.

(108)

They nyste what it myght by-mene,
 But vp hym sterte syr Gawayne,
And sithen all the courte by-dene,
 And ouyr the bord they haue hym drayne.   859

She laments the accident.

"Wellaway!" than sayd the quene,
"Ihesu Criste! what may I sayne!
Certis, now will all men wene
My-self that I the knight haue slayne." 863

(109)

Triacle there was anone forth brought,
The quene wende to save his lyff,
But all that myght helpe hym noght,
For there the knight is dede as swithe; 867
So grete sorow the quene than wrought,
Grete doele it was to se and lythe;
"lord, suche syttes me haue sought!
Why ne may I nevir be blithe!" 871

(110)

The dead knight is buried in a chapel in the forest, and on his tomb it is inscribed that the queen had slain him with poison.

Knyghtis done none other myght,
Bot beryed hym with doele I-noughe,
At a chapell with Riche lyghte,
In a foreste by a cloughe;[1] 875
A Riche toumbe they dyd by dight,
A Crafty clerke the lettres droughe,
how there lay the shottysshe knyght
That quene Genure with poyson slough. 879

(111)

Shortly after this, Sir Mador, the dead knight's brother, comes to court.

Aftyr thys a tyme by-felle,
To the courte ther' come a knyght,
his brodyr he was, as I you telle,
And syr mador for sothe he highte; 883
he was an hardy man and snelle,
In turnamente and eke in fight,
And mykell louyd in Courte to duelle,

[leaf 99]

For he was man of myche myght. 887

(112)

Than it felle vppon a day,

Being one day in the forest,

Sir mador wente with mekill pride
In-to the foreste, hym for to play,
That floured was and braunchid wyde; 891

---

[1] MS. swoughe. *I have adopted here Seyferth's (p. 78) conjecture. Cp. l. 893.*

he found a chapell in his way,
  As he cam by a cloughis syde,
There his owne brodyr lay,
  And there at masse he thought to abyde. 895

(113)

A Riche toumbe he found there dight
  With lettres that were fayre I-noughe;
A while he stode and Redde it Right,
  Grete sorow than to his herte droughe, 899
he found the name of the scottysshe knight
  That quene Genure with poysoun sloughe;
There he loste bothe mayne and myght
  And ouyr the toumbe he felle in swoughe. 903

he lights on his brother's tomb

and swoons when he reads the inscription.

(114)

Off swownynge whan he myght awake,
  his herte was heuy as Any lede;
he sighed for his brothers sake,
  he ne wiste what was beste Rede; 907
The way to courte gan he take,
  Off no-thinge ne stode he drede;
A lovde Crye on the quene gonne make
  In chalengynge of his brothers dede. 911

When he recovers,

he accuses the queen.

(115)

The kynge fulle sore than gan hym drede,
  For he myght not be ageyne the Right;
The quene of witte wold nyghe wede;
  thoughe¹ þat she agilte had no wight, 915
She moste there by-know the dede,
  Or fynde a man for hyr to fight;
For welle she wiste to deth she yede
  yif she were on a queste of knightis. 919

(116)

Thoughe Arthur were kynge þe land to weld,
  he myght not be agayne the Righte;
A day he toke with spere and sheld
  To fynd a man for hyr to fight, 923

[leaf 99, back] Arthur is obliged to appoint a day when the queen shall be put to death,

---

¹ *In the MS. That is written at the beginning of this line—by mistake.*

Lancelot vows that he will avenge the queen.

unless she finds a champion.

That she shalle eyther to deth hyr yeld
    Or putte hyr on a queste of knight*is*;
There-to bothe there handis vp-held
    And trewly there trouthis plighte.   927

(117)

Whan they in Certeyne had sette a day
    And that quarelle vndir-take,
The word sprange sone throw eche contrey
    What sorow that quene genure gan*ne* make;   931
So at the laste, shortely to say,

News of all this comes to Lancelot, who has been again wounded.

    Word come to launcelot du lake,
There as he seke I-woundyd lay;
    Men told hym holly all the wrake,   935

(118)

how that quene Genure the bright
    had slayne w*ith* grete treasou*n*
A swithe noble scottishe knight
    At the mete w*ith* stronge poysou*n*;   939
There-for a day was taken Right
    That she should fynd a knight full bowne
For hyr sake for to fighte
    Or ellis be brente w*ith*-oute Raunsowne.   943

(119)

Whan þat launcelot du lake
    had herd holly all this fare,
Grete sorow gon he to hym take,
    For the quene was in suche care,   947

He swears that he will avenge her on the appointed day.

And swore to venge hyr of that wrake
    That day yif þat he lyvand ware;
Than payned he hym his sorows to slake
    And wexe as breme as Any bare.   951

(120)

[leaf 100]

Now leve we launcelot there he was,
    withe the ermyte in the forest grene,
And telle we forthe of the case
    That touchith Arthur the kynge so kene.   955

Sir Gawayne on the morne to conselle he tase
    And mornyd sore for the quene ;
In-to a toure than he hym has
    And ordeyned the beste there them by-twene ; 959

As the king and Gawayne are standing in a tower one day consulting about the queen's affairs,

(121)

And as they in there talkynge stode,
    To ordeyne how it beste myght be,
A feyre Ryuer vndyr the toure yode,
    And sone there-in gonne they see 963
A lytelle bote of shappe full good
    To theyme-ward with the streme gon te ;
There myght none feyrer sayle on flode
    Ne better forgid as of tree. 967

they observe a little boat in the river which flows beneath.

(122)

Whan kynge Arthur saw þat sighte,
    he wondrid of the Riche apparrayle
That was aboute the bote I-dighte,
    So Richely was it coueryd sanzfayle, 971
In maner of a voute with clothis I-dighte,
    Alle shynand as gold as yt ganne sayle.
Than sayd Sir Gawayne the good knight:
    "This bote is of A ryche entayle." 975

They wonder at the rich furnishings of the boat,

(123)

" For sothe, sir," sayd the kynge tho,
    " Suche one sawgh I neuyr Are ;
Thedir I Rede now þat we go ;
    Som aventures shalle we se thare ; 979
And yif it be with-in dight so
    As with-oute or gayer mare,
I darre sauely say therto,
    By-gynne wille auntres or ought yare." 983

(124)

Oute of the toure adowne they wente,
    The kynge arthur & sir Gawayne ;
To the bote they yede with-oute stynte,
    They two allone, for sothe to sayne ; 987

and go down to investigate the matter.

[leaf 100, bk.]

(125)

They enter the boat,

And whan they come there as it lente,
    They by-held it faste, is not to layne;
A clothe that ouer the bote was bente
    Sir Gawayne lyfte vp, and went in bayne.   991

and on a bed in it they find a beautiful girl lying dead.

Whan they were in, w*ith*-outen lese,
    Full Richely aRayed they it found,
And in the myddis a feyre bedde was
    For Any kynge of Cristene lond.   995
Than as swithe, or they wold sese,
    The koverlet lyfte they vp w*ith* hand;
A dede woman they sighe ther' was,
    The fayrest mayde þat myght be found.   999

(126)

To Sir Gawayne than sayd the kinge:
    " For sothe dethe was to vn-hende,
Whan he wold thus fayre a thinge
    Thus yonge oute of the world do wend;   1003
For hyr biaute w*ith*-oute lesynge
    I wold fayne wete of hyr kynd,
What she was, this swete derelynge,
    And in hyr lyff where she gon*ne* lend."   1007

(127)

Gawayne recognizes her as the Maid of Ascalot.

Sir Gawayne his eyen than on hyr caste
    And by-held hyr fast w*ith* herte fre
So that he knew welle at the laste,
    That the mayde of Ascalote was she,   1011
Whiche he som tyme had wowyd faste
    his owne leman for to be,
But she au*n*sweryd hym Ay in haste,
    "To none bot launcelot wold she te."   1015

(128)

He tells Arthur who it is.

To the kinge þan sayd s*ir* Gawayne tho:
    " Thinke ye not on this endris day,
Whan my lady the quene & we two
    stode to-gedir in youre play,   1019

Her letter to Arthur and his knights.   33

Off a mayde I tolde you tho
    That launcelot louyd paramoure Ay?"
"Gawayne, for sothe," the kynge sayd tho,
    "Whan thou it saydiste wele thinke I may."   1023   [leaf 101]

(129)

"For sothe, syr," þan sayd sir Gawayne,
    "This is the mayde that I of spake;
most in this world, is not to layne,
    She lovide launcelot du lake."   1027
"For sothe," the kynge þan gon to sayne,
    "me Rewith the deth of hyr for his sake;
The inchesoun wold I wete fulle fayne;
    For sorow I trow deth gon hyr take."   1031

(130)

Than sir Gawayne, the good knight,   *They find on the Maid's*
    Sought aboute hyr with-oute stynte,   *person a purse with a*
And found a purs fulle Riche a-Righte,   *letter in it.*
    With gold and perlis þat was I-bente;   1035
Alle empty semyd it noght to sight.
    That purs fulle sone in honde he hente,
A letter there-of than oute he twight:
    Than wete they wold fayne what it mente;   1039

(131)

What there was wreten wete they wolde;
    And sir Gawayn it toke the kynge
And bad hym open yt[1] that he sholde;
    So dyde he sone with-oute lesynge;   1043
Than found he whan it was vn-folde,
    Bothe the ende and the by-gynnynge,
Thus was it wreten, as men me tolde,
    Off that fayre maydens deynge: 1047

(132)

"To kyng arthur and alle his knightis   *This letter is*
    That longe to the Rounde table,   *addressed to Arthur and*
That corteyse bene and most of myghtis,   *the knights of the Round*
    Doughty and noble, trew and stable,   1051   *Table.*

[1] MS. openyd.

34　　　*In the letter Lancelot is blamed.*

　　　　And most worshipfull in all fygh*ti*s,
　　　　　　To the nedefull helpinge & profitable,
　　　　The mayde of Ascalot to Righ*ti*s
　　　　　　Sendith gretinge, w*ith*-outen fable :　　　1055

　　　　　　　　　(133)
　　　　To you all my playnte I make
[leaf 101, bk.]　　　Off the wronge that me is wroghte,
　　　　But noght in maner to vndir-take
　　　　　　That Any of you shold mend it ought ;　　1059
　　　　Bot onely I say for this sake,
　　　　　　That, thoughe this world were throw sought,
　　　　Men shold nowhere fynd your make,
　　　　　　All noblisse to fynde that myght be sought ;　1063

　　　　　　　　　(134)
　　　　There-fore to you to vndirstand
She says that　　That, for I trewly many a day
she has died
for love　　haue lovid lelyest in lond,
　　　　　　Dethe hathe me fette of this world away ;　1067
　　　　To wete for whome yif ye will found,
　　　　　　That I so longe for in langoure lay,
　　　　To say the sothe will I noght wou*nd*,
　　　　　　For gaynes it not for to say nay ;　　　1071

　　　　　　　　　(135)
　　　　To say you the sothe tale,
　　　　　　For whome I haue suffred this woo,
　　　　I say deth hathe me take w*ith* bale
of a knight　　For the noblest knight þ*at* may go ;　　1075
who is strong
in battle　　Is none so doughty dyntis to dale,
but churlish
of manners,　　So Ryalle ne so fayre ther-to ;
　　　　But so churlysshe of maners in feld ne hale
　　　　　　Ne know I none of frende ne fo ;　　　1079

　　　　　　　　　(136)
　　　　Off foo ne frend, the sothe to say,
　　　　　　So vn-hend of thewis is ther' none ;
　　　　his gentillnesse was all a-way,
　　　　　　All churlysshe maners he had in wone ;　　1083

For for no thinge þat I coude pray,   *since he had refused to*
  Knelynge ne wepinge w*ith* Rewfull mone,   *accept her love,*
To be my leman he sayd euyr nay
  And sayd shortely he wold haue none.   1087

(137)

For-thy, lordis, for his sake
  I toke to herte grete sorow and Care,
So at the laste deth gon*ne* me take,
  So þat I might lyve na mare;   1091
¹For trew louynge had I suche wrake   [leaf 102]
  And was of blysse I-browghte All bare;
All was for launcelote du lake,   *that is to say, Lancelot.*
  To wete wisely for whom it ware."   1095

(138)

When that arthure, the noble kyng,
  had redde the lett*er* and kene the name,
he said to gawayne, w*ith*-oute lesynge,   *The king blames Lancelot.*
  that launcelott was gretly to blame,   1099
And had hym wonne a Rep*r*oovyng
  For euyr and a wikkyd fame,
Sythe she deide for gre[te] louyng,
  that he her refusyd it may hym shame.   1103

(139)

to the kyng than sayd syr gawayne:
  "I gabbyd on hym thys ȝendyr day,   *Gawayne acknowledges*
that he longede when I gon sayne   *that he was wrong in*
  W*ith* lady other with² som othyr maye;   1107 *having said that Lancelot*
bot sothe than sayde ye, is not to layne,   *had taken the Maid of*
  that he nolde nought hys loue laye   *Ascalot as his lady-love.*
In so low A place in vayne,
  But on a pryse lady and a gaye."   1111

(140)

"Syr gawayne," sayd the kyng thoo,
  "What is now thy best rede?
how mow we w*ith* thys maydyn do?"
  Syr gawayne sayd: "so god me spede,   1115

---

¹ *With this line the second hand of the MS. begins.*
² MS. whith.

The Queen upbraids Gawayne.

They determine to bury her like a duke's daughter.

  Iff' that ye wille assent ther-to,
  Worshippffully we shulle hyr lede
  In-to the palys and bery her so,
   As fallys A dukys doughter in dede."   1119

(141)

  ther-to the kyng Assentid sone;
   Syr gawayne dyd men͞ sone be ȝare,
  And worshippfully, as feH to done,
   In-to the palyse they her bare.   1123

The king tells the court how she had died on account of Lancelot.

  the kyng than͞ tolde with-out lone
   to AH hys barons, lesse and mare,
  how launcelot nolde noughte graunte hyr bone,
   ther-fore she dyed for sorow and care.   1127

(142)

Gawayne confesses to the queen too that what he had reported of Lancelot was false.

  to the quene than͞ went syr gawayne
   And gon to teH hyr AH the case:
  " For sothe, madame," he gon to sayne,
   " I yelde me gyllty of A trespas.   1131
  I gabbyd on͞ launcelot, is not to layne,
   of that I tolde you in thys place;
  I sayde that hys bydyng bayne
   the dukys doughter of Ascolote was;   1135

(143)

[leaf 102, bk.] off ascalot that m[a]yden͞ ffre,
   I sayd you she was hys leman;
  that I so gabbyd it reweth me,
   for AH the sothe now telle I can͞;   1139
  he nold hyr nought, we mowe welle se;
   For-thy dede is that white as swanne;
  thys lettere there-of' warannte wolle be;
   She playnethe on͞ launcelot to eche man͞."   1143

(144)

The queen blames Gawayne severely for what he had said.

  the quene was as wrothe as wynde
   And to syr gawayne sayd she than͞:
  " For sothe, Syr, thou were to vnkynde
   to gabbe so vppon͞ any man͞,   1147

but thou haddyst wist the sothe in mynde,
  Whether that it were sothe ore naɯ);
thy curtessy was Aℋ be-hynde,
  Whan thou thoo sawes freste begaɯ);   1151

(145)

thy worshippe thou vn-dediste gretlyche,
  Suche wronge to wite that good knyght;
I trowe he ne a-gulte the neuyr nought myche
  Why that thou oughtiste with no Ryghte   1155
to gabbe oɯ) hyɯ) so wylanlyche,
  thus be-hynde hyɯ), oute of hys syghte.
And, syr, thou ne woste not Ryght wiseliche
  What harme hathe falle there-of' and myght; 1159

(146)

I wende thou haddiste be stable and trewe
  And fuℋ of Aℋ curtessye,
bot now me thynke thy maners[1] newe,
  thay bene Aℋ tournyd to vilanye,   1163
now thou oɯ) knyghtis makeste thy glewe
  to lye vppon hem for envye;
Who that the worshippeth, it may heɯ) rewe;
  there-fore devoyede my companye."   1167

(147)

Syr gawayne thaɯ) slyghly wente awaye;
  he syghe the quene agreuyd sore;
No more to hyr thaɯ) wolde he saye
  Bot trowyd hyr wrathe haue euyr more.   1171
the quene thaɯ), as she nyghe wode were,
  wryngyd hyr handys and said : " weℋ-awaye !
Allas ! in world that I was bore !
  that I am) a wreche welle say I may !   1175

Gawayne takes leave of her, and she laments that she had believed a falsehood concerning Lancelot.

(148)

herte, Allas ! why were thou wode
  to trowe that launcelot du lake
were so falsse and fykelle of mode
  A-nother lemmaɯ) thaɯ) the to take ?   1179

---

[1] MS. meners.

nay, sertes, for Alle thys worldis goode
   he nolde to me haue wrought suche wrake." 1181

[One leaf missing in the Manuscript here between folios 102 and 103. It probably contained an account of the burial of the Maid of Ascalot, as the Vulgate-Lancelot does, and possibly also details of Lancelot's life in the forest.]

*   *   *   *   *   *   *   *

(165)

[leaf 103]
The queen is to be burnt, if she does not find a champion by the appointed day.

To fynde A man for hyr to feyghte 1318
   Or elles yeld her to be brente;
Iff she were on a queste of knyght*is*, 1320
   Wele sche wiste she shold be shente;
Thoughe that she agilte hade no wight,
   No lenger lyffe myght hyr be lente. 1323

(166)

The king and queen beg Bors, Lyonelle and Ector to aid them,

The kynge than sighed and gaffe hy*m* ylle
   And to syr gawayne than he yede,
To bors de gawnes and lyonelle,
   To estor that doughty was [in] dede, 1327
And askyd yif‘ eny were¹ in wille
   To helpe hym in that mykyll nede.
The quene one knes be-fore hem felle,
   That neyghe oute of hyr wite she yede; 1331

(167)

but they refuse, believing she is guilty.

The knyghtes answeryd w*ith* lytell p*ri*de,
   her he[r]tes was full of sorow and woughe,
Sayd: "all we saughe and satte besyde,
   The knyght when she w*ith* poyson sloughe; 1335
And sythe, in herte is nought to hyde,
   Syr gawayne ouer the bord hym droughe;
A-gayne the Ryght we wille not Ryde,
   We saw the sothe verely I-noughe." 1339

(168)

The queen makes an especial appeal to Bors,

The quene wepte and sighed sore,
   To bors de gawnes went she thoo,

¹ MS. werere.

The knights refuse to defend the Queen.

On knes by-fore hym fell she thore,
   That nyghe her hert braste in two: 1343
"lord bors," she seyde, "thyn ore!
To-day I shall to dethe goo,
Bot yiffe thy worthy wille wore
   To brynge my lyffe oute of thys woo."   1347

(169)
Bors de gawnes stille stode
And wrothe a-way hys yȝen wente.
"Madame," he sayde, "by crosse on rode
   Thou art wele worthy to be brente;   1351
The nobleste bodye of flesshe and blode
That euyr was yete in erthe lente
For thy wille and thy wykkyd mode
   Out of oure companye is wente."   1355

but he says that she ought to be burnt for driving Lancelot away.

(170)
Than she wepte and gaffe hyr ille
And to syr gawayne than she yede,
On knes downe be-fore hym felle,
   That neigh oute of hyr witte she yede;   1359
"Me[r]cy," she cryed loude and shrylle,
"Lord, as I no gilt haue of thys dede,
Yif it were thy worthy wille
   To-day to helpe me in thys nede?"   1363

She goes then to Gawayne,

[leaf 103, bk.]

(171)
Gawayne answeryd with litelle pride,
Hys hert was full of sorow and woughe:
"Dame, saw I not And sat be-syde,
   The knyght whan thou with poyson sloughe?   1367
And sythe, in hert is not to hyde,
My-selfe ouer the bord hym droughe;
A-gayne the Ryght wille I not Ryde,
   I sawghe the sothe verrye I-noughe."   1371

but he says that he was a witness of her guilt.

(172)
Than she wente to lyonelle,
   That euer had bene her owne knyght,
On knes downe be-fore hym felle
   That neyghe she lost mayne and myght.   1375

She next beseeches Lyonelle, but he answers in the same terms as Bors.

The Queen is deeply distressed.

"Mercy," she cryed loude and shrylle,
 "lord, As I ne haue gilte no wyght,
Yif^t it were thy worthy wylle
 for my lyffe to take thys fyght?"   1379

(173)

"Madame, how may thou to us take
 And wote thy-selfe so wytterly
That thou hast launcelot du lake
 Brought oute of ower companye?   1383
We may syghe and monynge make
 Whan) we se knight*is* kene in crye;
Be hym) thatt me to man) gan shape
 We ar glade that thou it a-bye!"   1387

(174)

She then goes to Estor,

Than) full sore she gan) hyr drede,
 Welle she wiste hyr lyffe was lorne;
Loude gon she wepe and grede
 And estor kneles she be-forne.   1391
"For hym) that on the Rode gon sprede
 And for vs bare the crone of thorne,
Estor, helpe now in thys nede,
 Or, certes, to-day my lyfe is lorne!"   1395

(175)

but he too refuses.

"Madame, how may thou to us take,
 Or how sholde I for the feyght?
Take the now launcelot du lake
 That euyr has bene thyn) owne knyght;   1399
My dere brother, for thy sake

[leaf 104]

 I ne shall hym) neuyr se w*ith* sight;
Cursyde be he that the batalle take
 To saue thy lyffe a-gayne the Ryghte!"   1403

(176)

Ther wolde no man) the batayle take,
 The quene wente to her chambyr soo,
So dulefully mone gon she make
 That nyghe hyr hert brast in twoo;   1407

Bors consents to fight for the Queen.

For Sorow gon she sheuer and quake
    And sayd : " Allas and wele-A-woo !
Why nade I now launcelot du lake !
    Aɫ the curte nolde me noght sloo.   1411

The queen in her distress wishes for Lancelot.

(177)

yuelle haue I be-sette the dede
    That I haue worshipped so many a knyght,
[And I haue no man in my nede¹]   1413 b
    For my lyffe darre take a fight.   1414
lord kynge of Aɫ thede !
    That aɫ the worlde shaɫ Rede and Ryght,
launcelot thou saue and hede,
    Sithe I ne shalle neuyr hym se wit*h* syght ! "   1418

(178)

The quene wepte and gaue hyr ylle ;
    Whaɲ she sawe the fyre was yare,
thaɲ mornyd she fuɫ stille ;
    To bors de gawnys went sho thare,   1422
By-sought hym, yif it were hys wille,
    To helpe hyr in hyr mekyɫe care ;
In swounynge she be-fore hym felle,
    That wordys myght sho speke no mare.   1426

She again beseeches Bors for help

(179)

Whaɲ bors saw the quene so bryght,
    Of her he hade grete pyte ;
In hys armys he helde her vpe-Ryght,
    Bade hyr of good comfort be :   1430
" Madame, but there come a better knyght
    That wolde the bataile take for the,
I shalle my-selue for the fighte,
    Whyle any lyffe may laste in me."   1434

and this time he promises to be her champion unless a better knight presents himself.

(180)

Thaɲ was the quene wonder blythe
    That bors de gawnys wolde for her feyght,

The queen rejoices.

---

¹ *A line is required here to make up the usual stanza-form. Its absence from the MS. is due, no doubt, to an oversight of the scribe. Dr. Furnivall, referring to l. 1570, has supplied the line which I have adopted in the text. There can be little doubt that the missing line had this form.*

That nere for Ioye she swounyd swythe,
   But as that he her helde vp-Ryght ; 1438
To hyr chambre he led hyr blythe,
   To ladyes and to maydens bryght,
And bad she shulde it to no man kythe,
   Tylle he were armyd and redy dyght. 1442

(181)

Bors tells the knights of his promise to the queen,

Bors, that was bolde and kene,
   Clepyd All hys other knyght*is*,
And tokyn conselle hem be-twene,
   The beste that thay couthe and myght, 1446
how that he hathe hyght the quene,
   That ilke day for hyr to feyght
A-yenste Syr mador full of tene,
   To saue hyr lyfe yife that he myght. 1450

(182)

and they are angry with him.

The knyght*is* answerd wit*h* wo and wrake,
   And sayd they wyste wetterlye
That " she hathe launcelot du lake
   Browght oute of ouere companye. 1454
Nys non that nolde thys bataile take,
   Er she hade any vylanye,
But we nylle not so glad hyr make
   By-fore we ne suffre hyr to be sorye." 1458

(183)

Bors, Lyonelle and Estor now go to the forest to say their orisons.

Bors and lionelle, the knyght,
   Estor, that doughty was of dede,
To the forest than went thay Ryght,
   There orysons at the chapelle to bede, 1462
To oure lord god All full of myght
   That day sholde lene hem wele to spede,
A grace to venquesshe the feyght ;
   Of syr mador thay hade grete drede. 1466

(184)

There they meet Lancelot.

As they came by the forest syde,
   There orysons for to make,
The nobleste knyght than saue thay Ryde
   That euer was in erthe shape ; 1470

hys loreme lemyd All with pride,
    stede and armure All was blake ;
hys name is noght to hele and hyde,
    he hyght Syr launcelot du lake.   1474

(185)
What wondyr was thoughe they were blythe,
    Whan) they ther mayster se with syght!
On knes Felle thay as swythe
    And thankyd All to god All-myght;   1478
Ioye it was to here and lythe
    The metynge of the noble knyght;
And after he askid Also swythe:
    "how now farys my lady bryght?"   1482

(186)
Bors than) tolde hym) All the Ryght,
    It was no lenger for to hyde,
How there dyed a scottysche knyght
    Atte the mete the quene besyde: 1486
"To-day, syr, is here dethe All dyght,
    It may no lenger be to byde,
And I for hyr haue take the feyght;   1489
    [. . . . . *no gap in the MS.*]   1489 *b*

(187)
Syr mador, stronge though that[1] he be,
    I hope he shall welle proue hys myght."
"To the courte now wende ye thre
    And recoumforte my lady bryghte,   1493
[. . . . .   1493 *b*
    . . . . *no gap in the MS.*]   1493 *c*
Bot loke ye speke no word of me,
    I wolle come as A strange knyght."   1495

(188)
launcelot that was mochelle of myght
    A-bydys in the forest grene ;
To the courte wente these othyr knyghtis
    For to recomforte the quene,   1499

---

[1] MS. thought tha.

The appointed day arrives.

> To make hyr glade with All theyre myght;
> Grete Ioye they made hem by-twene;
> For-why she ne sholde drede no wyght,
> Off goode comforte they bade her bene. 1503

(189)

On the appointed day the king and queen are at the table,

> Bordes were sette and clothys sprede,
> The kyng hym-selfe is gone to sytte,
> The quene is to the table lade,
> With chekys that were wanne and wete; 1507
> Off sorow were they neuyr vn-sad,
> Myght they neyther drynke ne ete;
> The quene of dethe was sore A-drade,
> That grymly terys gone she lete. 1511

(190)

> And as thay were at the thryd mese,
> The kynge and All the courte be-dene,

when Sir Mador appears and demands the execution of the covenant.

> Syr mador All redy was,
> With helme And shelde and haubarke shene; 1515
> A-monge hem All be-fore the dese
> He bloweth oute vppon the quene,
> To haue hys Ryght with-outen lese,
> As were the covenantes hem by-twene. 1519

(191)

> The kyng lokyde one All hys knyghtis,
> Was he neuere yet so woo,
> Sawhe neuyr on hym dyght

[leaf 105, bk.]

> A-yenste Sir mador for to goo; 1523
> Syr mador swore by goddys myght,
> As he was man of herte thro,
> Bot yif he hastely haue hys Ryght,
> A-monge hem All he sholde hyr slo. 1527

(192)

The king begs him to wait.

> Than spake the kynge of mekelle myght,
> That Ay was cortayse and hende:
> "Syr, lete vs ete, and sythen us dyght,
> Thys day nys nought yit gone to the ende; 1531

(193)

yet myght there come suche A knyght,
   yif' goddys wyH were hym to sende,
To fynde the thy fylle of fyghte,
   Or the sonne to grounde wende."   1535

(193)

Bors than loughe on lyonelle,   *Bors gets ready to defend the queen,*
   Wyste no man of here hertys worde ;
hys chambyr A-none he wendys tylle
   With-oute any othyr worde,   1539
Armyd hym at AH hys wille
   With helme and haubarke, spere and sworde ;
A-gayne than comys he fuH stylle
   And sette hym downe to the borde.   1543

(194)

The terys ranne on the kyngis kne   *and the king rejoices at this ;*
   For Ioye that he sawe bors adyght ;
Up he rose with hert[e] free
   And bors in armys clyppis Ryght,   1547
And sayd : "bors, god for-yelde it the,
   In thys nede that thow wolde fyghte :
Welle Acquyteste thou it me
   That I haue worshipped any knyght."[1]   1551

(195)

Than as Syr mador loudeste spake,   *but when Sir Mador again appeals,*
   The quene of treson to by-calle,
Comys syr launcelot du lake   *Lancelot rides into the hall as the champion, disguised.*
   Rydand Ryght in the halle ;   1555
hys stede and armure AH was blake,
   hys visere ouer hys yȝen falle ;
Many A man by-gonne to quake :
   A-drade of hym nyghe were they Alle.   1559

(196)

Then spake the kynge, mykelle of myght,   *The king does not at first understand,*
   That hend was in Iche A sythe :
"Syr, is it youre wille to lyghte,
   Ete and drynke and make you blythe ?"   1563

[1] MS. knytht.

launcelot spake as A strange knyght:
"Nay, Syr," he sayd as swythe,
"I herde telle here of A fight;
I come to saue A ladyes lyue; 1567

(197)
yeueɫɫ hathe the quene by-sette hyr dedys
That she hathe worsshippid many A knyght
And she hathe no man in her nedys
That for hyr lyfe dare take a fight. 1571
Thou that hyr of treson gredys,
Hastely that thow be dyghte.
Oute of thy witte þoughe that thou wedis,[1]
To-day thou shalt proue Aɫɫ thy myght." 1575

(198)
Than was Syr mador Also blythe
As foule of day after the nyght;
To hys stede he wente that[2] Sythe,
As man that was of moche myght; 1579
To the felde than Ryde thay swythe,
hem folowes bothe kyng and knyght,
The bataile for to se and lythe.
Saugh nevir no man A stronger fyght; 1583

(199)
Vn-horsid were bothe knyght*is* kene,
They metten w*ith* so myche mayne,
And sythe thay faught w*ith* swerdys kene,
Bothe on fote, for sothe to sayne; 1587
In Alle the batailles that launcelot had bene,
W*ith* hard acountres hym A-gayne,
In poynte had he nevir bene
So nyghe hande for to haue be slayne. 1591

(200)
There was so wondyr stronge A fyghte,
O fote nolde nouther fle ne founde
frome loughe none tylle late nyght,
Bot gyffen many a wofuɫɫ wounde. 1595

---

[1] MS. wendis.
[2] MS. than. *But* that *is required.* *Cp. l.* 1613.

Sir Mador is vanquished.

launcelot than gaffe A dynte with myght,
    Syr mador fallys at laste to grounde;
"Mercy," cryes that noble knyght,
    Fore he was seke and sore vnsound.   1599

but Mador is at last overcome.

(201)

Thoughe launcelot were breme as bore,
    Full stournely he ganne vp stande;
O dynte wolde he smyte no more,
    hys swerd he threwe oute of hys hande.   1603
Syr mador by god than sware;
    "I haue foughte in many A lande,
With knyghtis bothe lesse and mare,
    And neuyr yit er' my mache I founde;   1607

[leaf 106, bk.]

He praises the victor's prowess,

(202)

Bot, Syr, A prayer I wolde make,
    For thynge that ye loue moste on lyfe
And for oure swete lady sake,
    youer name that ye wolde me kythe."   1611
launcelot gan hys viser vp take
    And hendely hym shewed that sythe.
Whan he saughe launcelot du lake,
    Was neuyr man on molde so blythe: 1615

and begs to know his name.

(203)

"lord," thane said he, "welle is me,
    Myne Auauntement that I may make
That I haue stande on dynte of the
    And foughten with launcelot du lake;   1619
My brother's dethe for-geffen be
    To the quene for thy sake."
launcelot hym kyste with herte fre
    And in hys armys gan hym vp take.   1623

He congratulates himself that he could stand up at all against so famous a champion.

(204)

Kynge Arthur than loude spake
    A-monge hys knyghtis to the quene:
"Ʒa, yonder is launcelot du lake,
    Yiff I hym euyr with syght haue sene."   1627

The king now recognizes Lancelot,

48   *A squire confesses that he poisoned the apple.*

  Thay Ryden and ronne tham for hys sake,
   The kynge and Alle hys knyght*is* kene;
  In hys armys he gon hym take,
   The kynge hym kyste and courte by-dene. 1631

(205)

and the queen almost swoons for joy.

Than was the quene glade I-noghe
 Whan she saw launcelot du lake,
that nyghe for Ioy she felle in swoughe
 Bot as the lordys hyr gan vp take. 1635

The knights are now on friendly terms with Sir Mador.

The knyght*is* Alle wepte and loughe,
 For Ioye as thay to-gedyr spake;
Withe Syr mador, wit*h*-outen woughe,
 Full sone acordement gon they make. 1639

(206)

 It was no lenger for to A-byde

They all ride back to the castle,

Bot to the castelle thay Rode as swythe,
Withe trompys and wit*h* mykelle pryde,
 That Ioy it was to here and lythe; 1643
Thoughe syr mador myght not go ne Ryde
 To the curte is he brought that sythe,

[leaf 107]

And knyghtis vppon Iche A syde
 To make hym bothe glad and blythe. 1647

(207)

and under torture a squire confesses that he had slain the Scotch knight.

The squeers than were takyn Alle
 And thay ar put in harde payne,
Whiche that seruyd in the halle,
 Whan the knyght was wit*h* poyson slayne. 1651
There he grauntyd A-monge hem Alle,
 It myght no lenger be to layne,
How in an Appelle he dede the galle
 And hadde it thought to syr gawayne. 1655

(208)

Sir Mador is greatly distressed at the wrong he had done the queen.

Whan syr mador herde All the Ryght,
 That no gylte hadde the lady shene,
For sorowe he loste mayne and myghte
 And on knees felle be-fore the quene; 1659

launcelot then hym helde vppe Ryghte
    For loue that was them be-twene ;
Hym kyste bothe kynge and knyght
    And sythen all the curte by-dene.   1663

(209)

The squyer than was done to shende,
    As it was bothe lawe and Ryght,
Drawen and hongyd and for-brende
    Be-fore syr mador, the noble knyghte.   1667
In the castelle thay gan forthe lende,
    The Ioyus gard than was it hyghte ;
launcelot that was so hende
    Thay honouryd hym with Alle ther myght.   1671

The squire is executed,

(210)

A tyme be-felle, sothe to sayne,
    the knyghtis stode in chambyr and spake,
Bothe gaheriet and syr gawayne
    And mordreite that mykelle couthe of wrake :   1675
" Allas ! " than sayde syr A-grawayne,
    " How fals men schalle we vs make !
And how longe shalle we hele and layne
    The treson of launcelote du lake !   1679

One day Agrawayne is speaking to his brothers about Lancelot's intrigue with the queen.

(211)

Wele we wote, with-outen wene,
    The kynge arthur oure eme sholde be
And launcelote lyes by the queue ;
    A-geyne the kynge[1] tra[y]tor is he ;   1683
And that wote all the curte by-dene,
    And Iche day it here and see ;
To the kynge we shulde it mene,
    Yif ye wille do by the counselle of me."   1687

He thinks that they should tell the king.
[leaf 107, bk.]

(212)

" Wele wote we," sayd syr gawayne,
    " That we ar of the kyngis kynne,
And launcelot is so mykyll of mayne
    That suche wordys were better blynne.   1691

Gawayne opposes this,

[1] MS. knyke.

and says that to disclose the affair will bring on war.

Welle wote thou, brothyr agrawayne,
 There-of shulde we bot harmys wynne;
yit were it better to hele and layne
 Than werre and wrake thus to be-gynne.   1695

(213)

Welle wote thou, brother agrawayne,
 launcelot is hardy knyght and thro;
kynge and courte hade ofte bene slayne,
 Nad he bene better than we mo;   1699
And sythen myght I neuyr sayne
 The loue that has bene by-twene vs twoo;
launcelot shalle I neuyr be-trayne
 By-hynde hys bake to be hys foo.   1703

(214)

launcelot is kynges sonne full good,
 And therto hardy knyght and bolde,
And sythen and hym ned by-stode,
 Many A lande wolde *with* hym holde;   1707
Shedde ther sholde be mykelle blode
 For thys tale, yiffe it were tolde;
Syr Agrawayne he were full wode
 That suche a thynge be-gynne wolde."   1711

(215)

Just then the king comes in, and, becoming suspicious,

Than thus gatys as the knyghtis stode,
 Gawayne and All that other pres,
In come the kynge *with* mylde mode;
 Gawayne than[1] sayd: "felaus, pees";   1715

demands what they are talking about.

The kynge for wrathe was neghe wode
 For to wette what it was;
Aggrawayne swore by crosse And Rode:
 "I shalle it you telle *with*-oute lees."   1719

(216)

All the brothers leave the room except Agrawayne,

Gawayne to hys chambyr wente,
 Off thys tale nolde he noght here;
Gaheriet and gaheryes of hys A-sente
 Withe here brother went they there;   1723

[1] MS. that.

Welle they wyste that Aʆʆ was shente
 And syr gawayne by god thanͻ swere :
" here now [is] made A comsemente
 That bethe not fynysshyd many A yere."   1727

(217)

Syr Agrawayne tolde Alle be-dene
 To the kynge wit*h* symple chere,
How launcelot liggys by the quene,
 " And so has done fuʆʆ many A yere,   1731
And that wote Aʆʆ the courte by-dene
 And Iche day it se and here,
And we haue false and treytours bene
 That we ne wolde neuyr to you dyskere."   1735

who tells the king that Lancelot has been intimate [leaf 108] with the queen for many years.

(218)

"Allas!" than sayd the kynge thore,
 " Certes, that were grete pyte,
So As manͻ nad neuyr yit more
 Off biaute ne of bounte   1739
Ne manͻ in worlde was neuyr yit ore
 Off so mykylle noblyte.
Allas! fuʆʆ grete duelle it were
 In hym shulde Any treson be;   1743

The king is grieved at this,

(219)

But sythe it is so, wit*h*-outen fayle,
 Syr Agrawayne, so god the Rede,
What were now thy beste consayle
 For to take hymͻ wit*h* the dede?   1747
he is manͻ of suche Apparayle,
 Off⸱ hymͻ I haue fuʆʆ mychelle drede ;
Aʆʆ the courte nolde hymͻ Assayle
 Yiff⸱ he were Armyd vpponͻ hys stede."   1751

and wishes to know how he may catch Lancelot in the act.

(220)

" Syr, ye and Aʆʆ the courte by-dene
 Wendythe to-morowe on huntynge Ryght,
And sythen send word to the quene
 That ye wille dwelle wit*h*-oute Aʆʆ nyght,   1755

Agrawayne proposes that the king should go hunting the next day and pretend that he is to be away all night.

<small>This will give Agrawayne, with twelve knights, an opportunity to catch Lancelot.</small>

And I and other xii knyghtes kene
   Fuƚƚ preuely we shall vs dyght ;
We shaƚƚe hym haue w*ith*-outen wene,
   To-morow or Any day by lyght."   1759

(221)

<small>The next day the king acts on this proposal.</small>

On the morow w*ith* Aƚƚ the courte by-dene
   The kynge gonne on huntynge Ryde,
And sythen he sent word to the quene
   That he wolde Aƚƚ nyght oute A-byde.   1763
Aggrawayne w*ith* xii knyghtys kene
   Atte home be-lefte that ilke tyde ;
Off Alle the day they were not sene,
   So prewely thay gonne hem hyde.   1767

(222)

<small>The queen sends for Lancelot, when the king has gone.</small>

Tho was the quene wondyr blythe
   That the kynge wolde at the foreste dwelle ;
To launcelot she sente as swythe
   And bad that he shulde come her tille.   1771

<small>Bors suspects something, [leaf 108, bk.] and tries to persuade Lancelot not to go,</small>

Syr bors de gawnes be-ganne to lythe,
   Thoughe hys herte lyked ille ;
"Syr," he said, " I wolde you kythe
   A word, yifᵗ that it were your wille :   1775

(223)

Syr, to-nyght I rede ye dwelle ;
   I drede ther be som treson dight
Withe Agrawayne, that is so felle,
   That waites you bothe day and nyght ;   1779
Offᵗ Alle that ye haue gonne hyr-tylle
   Ne greuyd me neuyr yit no wight
Ne neuyr yit gaffe myn herte to ille
   So mykelle as it dothe to-nyght."   1783

(224)

<small>but he insists on going.</small>

"Bors," he sayd, "holde stylle ;
   Suche wordys ar noughte to kythe ;
I wille wende my lady tille,
   Som new tythandes for to lythe ;   1787

I ne shaH noght bote wet[e] hyr wylle,
   loke ye make youe glad and blythe;
Certenly I nelle nought dwelle
   Bot come A-gayne to youe AH swythe."   1791

(225)

For-why he wende haue comyn*ne* sone,   He did not intend stay-
   For to dwelle had he not thought,   ing long, however,
Non Armore he dyde hym vppon   so he took no armour with
   Bot A Robe AH sengle wrought;   1795   him.
In hys hand A swerd he fone,
   Off*t* tresso*n* dred he hym Ryght noght;
There was no man vndyr the mone
   he wende w*ith* harme durste hy*m* haffe sought. 1799

(226)

Whan he come to the lady shene,   He comes to the queen's
   he kissid and clypped that swete wyght;   chamber,
For sothe, they neuyr wolde wene
   That any treson was ther dyght;   1803
So mykylle loue was hem by-twene
   That they noght de-parte Myght;
To bede he gothe w*ith* the quene   and goes to bed with her.
   And there he thoughte to dwelle Alle nyght. 1807

(227)

he was not buskyd in hys bedde,   They had not been in bed
   launcelot in the quenys boure,   long, when Agrawayne
Come Agrawayne and syr mordreit   and his companions begin
   W*ith* xii knyghtys stiffe in stowre;   1811   to raise a clamour.
Launcelot of tresson they be-gredde,
   Callyd hym fals and kyngys treytoure,
And he so so strongly was by-stedde
   There-inne he hadde non Armoure.   1815

(228)

"Welaway!" than sayd the quene,   [leaf 109]
   "launcelot, what shaH worthe of vs twoo!   The queen is terribly
The loue that hathe bene vs be-twene   frightened,
   To suche endynge that it sholde goo!   1819

Withe Agrawayne that is so kene,
　That nyght And day hathe bene oure foo,
Now I wote, with-outen wene,
　That Alle oure wele is tornyd to woo." 1823

(229)

but Lancelot tries to comfort her, and asks for armour.

"Lady," he sayd, "thow moste blynne;
　Wyde I wote these wordis bethe Ryffe;
Bot is here any Armoure inne,
　That I may haue to saue my lyffe?" 1827
"Certis, nay," she sayd thenne,

There is none, however, at hand.

"Thys Antoure is so wondyr stryffe
That I ne may to none Armoure wynne,
　Helme ne hauberke, swerd ne knyffe." 1831

(230)

Agrawayne and Mordred challenge Lancelot to come forth,

Euyr Agrawayne and syr mordred
　Callyd hym Recreante fals knyght,
Bad hym Ryse oute of hys bedde,
　For he moste nedis with them fyght; 1835
In hys Robe than he hym cled,
　Thoughe he none Armoure gete myght;

and he goes to the door with sword drawn.

Wrothely oute hys swerd he gredde,
　The chamber dore he sette vp Ryght. 1839

(231)

The first knight that attempts to slay Lancelot is himself slain.

An Armyd knyght be-fore in wente,
　And wende launcelot wele to sloo,
Bot launcelot gaffe hym soche A dynte
　That to the grounde gonne he go; 1843
The other All agayne than stente;
　Aftyr hym dorste folowe no moo;
To the chambyr dore he sprente
　And claspid it with barres twoo. 1847

(232)

Lancelot now puts on the dead man's armour,

The knyght that launcelot has slayne,
　Hys Armoure founde he fayre and bryght;
Hastely he hathe hem of drayne
　And therin hym-selfe dight. 1851

He kills Agrawayne and escapes.

" Now, know thou wele, syr Agrawayne,
 Thow presons me no more to-Nyght."
Oute than sprange he with mykell mayn),
 Hym-selfe a-yenste hem) alle to fyght. 1855

and attacks his assailants.

(233)

Launcelot than smote with herte goode,
 Wete ye welle, with-outen lese ;
Syr Agrawayne to dethe yode,
 And sythen All the other presse ; 1859
Was non so stronge that hym with-stode
 Be he had made A lytelle Rese ;
Bot mordreit fled as he were wode,
 To saue hys lyff¹ full fayne he was. 1863

He slays Agrawayne, [leaf 109, bk.]

and Mordred flees.

(234)

Launcelot to hys chambre yode,
 to bors and to hys other knyghtis ;
Bors Armyd be-fore hym stode,
 To bedde yit was he noȝt dight ; 1867
The knyghtis for fere was nye wode,
 So were they drechyd all that nyght,
Bot blythe wexid they in her mode
 Whan they her mastyr sawghe with syght. 1871

Lancelot gets back to his knights,

(235)

"Syr," sayd bors, the hardy knyght,
 " Aftyr you haue we thoght full longe,
To bedde durste I ne noȝt dight,
 For drede ye hade som Aunter stronge ; 1875
Owre knyghtis haue be drechyd to-nyght,
 That som nakyd oute of bed spronge,
For-thy we were full sore a-fryght
 Leste som treson were vs Amonge." 1879

who had been uneasy about him all that night.

(236)

" Ya, bors, drede the no wight,
 Bot bethe of¹ herte good And bolde,
And swythe A-waken vp All my knyghtis
 And loke whiche wille with vs holde ; 1883

Lancelot tells them to arm themselves.

Loke they be Armyd and redy dight,
 For it is sothe that thou me tolde,
We haue be-gonne thys ilke nyght
  That shall brynge many A man full colde."   1887

(237)

Bors than) spake wit*h* drery mode:
 " Syr," he sayd, "sithe it is so,
We shalle be of hert*is* good
  Aftyr the wele to take the wo."   1891
The knyghtis sprent as they were wode
 And to there harneise gon the go;
They do so, At the morow Armyd be-fore hym stode
  An hundrethe knyght*is* and squyers mo.   1895

(238)

and ride forth to a forest, Whan they were armyd and redy dight,
 A softe pas forth gonne they Ride,
As men that were of mykelle myght,
  To A forest there be-syde;   1899
where they wait to hear what has befallen the queen. Launcelot Arrayes All hys knyght*is*
 And there they loggen hem to byde
[leaf 110] Tylle they herd of¹ the lady bryght,
  What Auntere of¹ hyr shulde be-tyde.   1903

(239)

Mordred brings the news to Gawayne, Mordreit than toke A way full gayne,
 And to the forest wente he Right,
Hys Auntures tolde, for sothe to sayne,
  That were by-fallyn that ylke nyght.   1907
"Mordreit, haue ye that treitour slayne,
 Or how haue ye wit*h* hym dight?"
"Nay, syr, bot dede is aggrawayne,
  And so Ar All oure other knyght*is*."   1911

(240)

Whan it herde syr gawayne,
 That was so hardy knyght and bolde,
"Allas! is my brother slayne?"
  Sore hys herte be-gan to colde;   1915

The Queen is about to be burnt. 57

"I warnyd wele syr Aggrawayne,
    Or euyr yit thys tale was tolde,
Launcelot was so myche of mayne,
    A-yenste hym was stronge to holde." 1919

who says that he warned Agrawayne of what would happen.

(241)

It was no lenger for to byde,
    Kynge And All hys knyghtis kene,
Toke there counselle in that tyde,
    What was beste do wi*th* the quene. 1923
It was no lenger for to byde,
    That day fo[r]-brent shuld she bene. 1925
[. . . . . 1925 *b*
    . . . . . *no gap in the MS.*] 1925 *c*

The king and his knights determine that the queen must be burnt.

(242)

The fyre than made they in the felde,
    There-to they brought that lady fre,
All that euyr myght wepene welde
    A-boute her Armyd for to bee. 1929
Gawayne, that stiffe was vndir shelde,
    Gaheryet ne gaheryes ne wold no3t see;
In there chamber they hem helde
    Off¹ hyr they had grete pyte. 1933

A fire is accordingly made,

but Gawayne and his two brothers refuse to be present at the queen's execution.

(243)

The kynge Arthure that ylke tyde
    Gawayne And gaherys for sent;
here Answeres were no3t for to hyde,
    They ne wolde no3t be of hys assente; 1937
Gawayne wolde neuyr be nere by-syde
    There Any woman shuld be brente;
Gaheriet And gaheries wi*th* lytelle pryde,
    All vn-Armyd thedyr they wente. 1941

(244)

A squeer gonne tho tythandes lythe,
    That launcelot to courte had sente;
To the foreste he wente as swithe
    There launcelot and hys folke was lente, 1945

A squire brings Lancelot news of what is impending,

[leaf 110, bk.] Bad hem come and haste blythe,
　　　The quene is ledde to be brente;
and he and his men hasten to save her. And they to hors and Armes swythe
　　　And Iche one be-fore other sprente. 1949

(245)

　　The quene by the fyre stode
　　　And in hyr smoke Aƚƚ redy was;
　　lordyngis was there many and good
　　　And grete power, with-outen lese. 1953
They get there in time, Launcelot sprente, as he were wode,
　　　Fuƚƚ sone partyd he the prees,
　　Was none so styffe a-ȝeynste hym stode,
　　　Be he had made a lytelle Rese. 1957

(246)

and overwhelm all resistance, There was no stele stode hem aȝeyne;
　　　Though faught they but A lytelle stound,
　　Lordyngys that were myche of mayne
slaying among others Gaheriet and Gaheries. 　Many goode were brought to grounde; 1961
　　Gaheriet and gaheries bothe were slayne,
　　　Wythe many A doulfuƚƚ dethes wounde;
They take the queen back to the forest with them. The quene thay toke with-oute layne,
　　　And to the foreste gonne they founde. 1965

(247)

The king laments the loss of his knights, The tythyngis is to the kynge brought,
　　　how launcelote has tane away the quene.
　　"Suche wo as there is wroughte!
　　　Slayne ar Alle oure knyghtis kene." 1969
　　Downe he felle and swounyd ofte,
　　　Grete duelle it was to here and sene;
　　So nere hys herte the sorowe sought
　　　Aƚƚ-moste hys lyffe wolde no man wene; 1973

(248)

　　"Ihesu cryste! what may I sayne?
　　　In erthe was neuyr man so wo;
　　Suche knyghtys as there ar slayne
　　　In Aƚƚ thys worlde there is no mo. 1977

Lette no man telle Syr gawayne,
  Gaheriet hys brother is dede hym fro, *and says that Gawayne must not know of Gaheriet's death.*
But weilaway! the reufulle Rayne,
  That euyr launcelote was my fo!" 1981

(249)

Gawayne gon*ne* in hys chambyr hym holde,
  Off' All the day he nolde not oute goo;
A squyer than the tythandys tolde *A squire nevertheless tells Gawayne,*
  What wondyr theighe hys herte were wo! 1985
"Allas!" he sayde, "my brother bolde,
  Where gahereit be dede me fro?" *[leaf 111]*
So sore hys hert be-gan to colde
  All-moste he wolde hym-selff sloo. 1989

(250)

The squyer spake wit*h* drery mode,
  To re-comfort syr Gawayne:
" Gaheriet eyles noght bot goode;
  he wolle sone come A-gayne." 1993
Gawayne sprent as he were wode *who goes to where his brethren lie dead.*
  To the chambre there they lay slayne;
The chambre flore All ranne on blode,
  And clothys of' golde were ouer hem drayne. 1997

(251)

A clothe he heuys than vppon hyght;
  What wondyr thoughe hys hert were sore
So dulfully to se them dight
  That ere so doughty knyghtis were! 2001
Whan he hys brother sawghe wit*h* syght,
  A word myght he speke no more;
There he loste mayne and myght *He swoons at the sight,*
  And ouyr hym felle in swounynge thore. 2005

(252)

Off' swounynge whan he myght A-wake, *but, when he recovers, he says that henceforth there will be no peace between him and Lancelot.*
  The hardy knyght, syr gawayne,
Be god he sware and loude spake,
  As man that myche was of mayne: 2009

"Be-twixte me And launcelote du lake
 Nys man in erthe, for sothe to sayne,
Shall trewes sette and pees make,
 Er outher of vs haue other slayne." 2013

(253)

A squyer that launcelot to court hadde sente
 Off the tythandys gonne he lythe;
To the foreste is he wente

Lancelot also learns of the death of Gaheriet and Gaheries.

 And tolde launcelot Also swythe, 2017
how lordy[n]ges that were Riche of rente
 Fele goode had loste hyr lyffe,
Gaheryet and gaheries sought here ende;
 Bot than was launcelot no-thynge blythe; 2021

(254)

He grieves over Gaheriet, and recognizes that reconciliation with Gawayne is now impossible.

"Lord," he said, "what may thys bene?
 Ihesu cryste! what may I sayne?
The loue that hathe be-twexte vs bene,
 That euyr gaheryet me was A-gayne! 2025
Now I wote for All by-dene,
 A sorye man Is syr gawayne;
A-cordement thar me nevyr wene,

[leaf 111, bk.]

 Tille eyther of vs haue other slayne." 2029

(255)

Lancelot begins to collect his forces for war.

launcelot gonne with hysse folke forthe wende,
 With sory hert and drery mode;
To quenys and countesses fele he sende
 And grete ladyes of gentill blode, 2033
That he had ofte here landis deffende
 And foughten whan hem nede by-stode.
Ichone her power hym lende,
 And made hys party stiffe and goode; 2037

(256)

Many ladies of noble rank whom he had assisted send him men.

quenys and countesses that Ryche were
 Sende hym erlys with grete meyne;
Other ladies that myght no more
 Sente hym barons or knyghtis free; 2041

So mykelle folke to hym gon fare,
  Hydous it was hys oste to see;
To the Ioyus gard wente he thare
  And helde hym in that stronge Cyte.

(257)

Launcelotis herte was full sore
  For the lady fayre and bryght;
A damosselle he dyd be yare,
  In Ryche Apparayle was she dyght,
Hastely in message for to fare
  To the kynge of mykelle myght,
To prove it fals (what myght he mare?)
  Bot proferys hym there-fore to fyght.

(258)

The mayden is Redy for to Ryde,
  In A full Ryche Aparaylmente,
Off Samytte grene, with mykyll pryde,
  That wroght was in the oryente;
A dwerffe shulde wende by hyr syde,
  Suche was launcelotis comaundement;
So were the manerys in that tyde,
  Whan A mayde on message wente.

(259)

To the castelle whan she come,
  In the paleise gonne she lyght;
To the kynge hyr erande she sayd sone,
  By hym satte syr gawayne the knyght,
Sayd that lyes were sayde hym vppon;
  Trewe they were by day and nyght;
To proue it as a knyght shulde done
  Launcelot proferis hym to fyghte.

(260)

The kynge Arthure spekys thore
  Wordys that were kene and thro:
"He ne myght proue it neuer more
  Bot of my men that he wold slo;

The King will not have peace.

  Be Ihesu cryste," the kynge sware,
   And Syr gawayne than Also,
  " his dedis shall be bought full sore,
   Bot yife no stele nyll in hym go."   2077

(261)

The damsel brings back the king's answer to Lancelot.

  The mayden hathe hyr answere,
   To the Ioyus garde gonne she Ryde;
  Such as the kynges wordis were
   She told launcelot in that tyde;   2081
  Launcelot Syghed wounder sore,
   Teres frome hys yȝen ganne glyde;
  Bors de gawnes by gode than sware:
   " In mydde the felde we shall hem byde."   2085

(262)

Arthur now collects his forces too,

  Arthure wolde no lenger a-byde
   Bot hastis hym *with* All hys myght;
  Messengeres dyd he go and Ryde,
   That thay ne shulde lette for day ne nyght,   2089
  Thorow-oute yngland by Iche a syde
   To erle, baroun and to knyght,
  Bad hem come that ilke tyde
   Withe hors stronge And Armure bryght.   2093

(263)

  Thoughe the knyght that were dede hem fro,
   There-of was All there mykelle kare,
  Thre hundrethe thay made mo,
   Oute of the castelle or they wold fare,   2097
  Off ynglonde A[nd] yreland Also,
   Off walys and scottis that beste were,
  Launcelot And hys folkys to slo,
   With hertis breme as Any bore.   2101

(264)

and his host sets out to besiege Joyus Gard.

  Whan thys oste was All bowne,
   It was no lenger for to byde,
  Rayses spere and gounfanoune,
   As men that were of mykelle pryde;   2105

The siege of Joyus Gard.

With helme and shelde and hauberke browne,
  Gawayne hym-selfe be-fore ganne Ryde
To the Ioyus garde that Ryche towne,
  And sette A sege on Iche A syde.   2109

(265)

A-boute the Ioyus garde they laye
  Seuentene wokys And well mare,
Tille it felle vppon A day
  launcelot home bad hem fare: 2113
"Breke youre sege! wendys a-waye!
  You to slae grete pyte it ware."
He sayd " Allas and weilawaye!
  That euyr beganne this sorewe sare!"   2117

They besiege it upwards of [leaf 112, bk.] seventene weeks, and Lancelot does not attack them.

(266)

Evir the kynge and Sir gawayne
  Calde hym fals Recreante knyght,
And sayde he had hys bretherne slayne
  And treytour was by day and nyght,   2121
Bad hym come And proue hys mayne
  In the felde with hem to fyghte.
Launcelot sighed, for sothe to sayne,
  Grete duelle it was to se with sight.   2125

The king and Gawayne challenge him to come forth.

(267)

So loude they launcelot gonne Ascrye
  With vois and hydous hornys bere,
Bors de gawnes standis hym by
  And launcelot makys yuelle chere.   2129
"Syr," he sayd, "whare-fore and why
  Shulde we these proude wordys here?
me thynke ye fare as cowardlye
  As we ne durste no man nyghe nere.   2133

At last Bors upbraids Lancelot for not accepting the challenge.

(268)

Dight we vs in Ryche Araye,
  Bothe with spere And with shelde,
As swithe as euyr that we maye,
  And Ryde we oute in-to the felde;   2137

Whyle my lyffe laste maye,
  Thys day I ne shall my wepen yelde;
There-fore my lyffe I darre wele laye
  We two shall make hem All to helde.' 2141

(269)

Lancelot is loth to fight against the king,

"Allas!" quod launcelot, "wo is me,
  That euyr shuld I se with syghte
A-ȝeyne my lord for to be,
  The noble kynge that made me knyght! 2145
Syr gawayne, I be-Seche the,
  As thou arte man of myche myght,
In the felde let not my lorde be
  Ne that thy-selfe with me not fyghte." 2149

(270)

but cannot delay the conflict any longer.

It may no lenger for to byde
  But buskyd hem and made All bowne;
Whan thay were Redy for to Ryde,
  They Reysed spere and gonfanoune; 2153

[leaf 113]

Whan these ostes gan samen glyde,
  Withe vois and hydous hornys sowne,
Grete pyte was on eyther syde,
  So fele goode ther were layd downe. 2157

(271)

In the battle Gawayne wounds Lyonelle sorely,

Syr lyonelle with myche mayne
  Withe A spere by-fore gan founde;
Syr gawayne Rydys hym A-gayne,
  hors and man he bare to grounde, 2161
That All men wende he had ben slayne,
  Syr lyonelle hade suche A wounde;
Oute of the felde was he drayne,
  For he was seke and sore vn-sounde. 2165

(272)

but no one could stand up against Lancelot.

In All the felde that ilke tyde
  Myght no man stonde launcelot a-ȝeyne,
And sythen as faste As he myght Ryde
  To saue that no man sholde be slayne. 2169

The kynge was euyr nere be-Syde
And hewe on hym with All hys mayne,
And he so corteise was that tyde   *Lancelot will not return*
O dynte that he nolde smyte a-gayne.   2173   *the king's blows.*

(273)

Bors de gawnes saughe at laste   *Bors un-*
   And to the kynge than gan he Ryde,   *horses the king,*
And on hys helme he hytte so faste
   That nere he loste All hys pryde;   2177
The stede Rigge vndyr hym braste
   That he to grounde felle that tyde,
And sythen wordys loude he caste,
   Withe Syr launcelot to chyde: 2181

(274)

"Syr, shalthou All day Suffer so   *and rebukes*
   That the kynge shall the assayle,   *Lancelot for having been*
And sethe hys herte is so thro   *so con-*
   Thy corteise may not A-vaile?   2185   *siderate.*
Batailles shall there neuere be mo,
   And thou wilt do be my consalle;
Ʒeuyth vs leue them All to slo,
   For thou haste venquesshid thys bataille."   2189

(275)

"Allas!" quod launcelot, "wo is me,   *Lancelot*
   That euyr shulde I se with syghte   *helps the king back on*
By-fore me hym vnhorsyd bee,   *his steed,*
   The noble kynge that made me knyght!"   2193
he was than so corteise and fre
   That downe of hys stede he lyghte;
The kynge ther-on than horsys he
   And bade hym fle, yiffe that he myght.   2197

(276)

Whan the kynge was horsyd there,   [leaf 113, bk.]
   Launcelot lokys he vppon,   *and the king is touched by*
How corteise was in hym more   *his chivalry.*
   Then euyr was in Any man;   2201

MORTE ARTHUR.   F

He thought on thyngis that had bene ore,
 The teres from hys yȝen Ranne;
He Sayde "Allas!" with syghynge sore,
 "That euyr yit thys werre be-gan!" 2205

(277)

The battle ceases for the day,

The parties arne with-drawen A-waye,
 Offᵗ knyghtis were they wexyn thynne;
On morow on that other daye
 Scholde the bataille efte begynne; 2209
Thay dyght hem on A Ryche Araye
 And partyd ther ostes bothe in twynne;
he that by-ganne thys wrechyd playe,
 What wondyr thoughe he had grete synne! 2213

(278)

only just at the end Bors and Gawayne have a tilt,

Bors was breme as Any bore,
 And oute he rode to syr gawayne;
For lyonelle was woundyd sore,
 Wenge hys brother he wolde full fayne; 2217
Syr gawayne gonne A-ȝeyne hym fare,
 As man that myche was of mayne;
Eyther throughe other body bare,
 That welle nere were they bothe slayne; 2221

(279)

in which both are wounded.

Bothe to grounde they Felle in fere,
 There-fore were fele folke full woo.
The kynges party Redy were
 A-way to take hem bothe two; 2225
launcelot hym-selfe come nere,
 Bors rescous he them froo;
Oute of the felde men hym bere,
 So were they woundyd bothe two. 2229

(280)

Offᵗ thys bataille were to telle,
 A man that it wele vndyrstode,
How knyghtis vndyr sadels felle
 And sytten downe with sory mode; 2233

The Pope forbids the continuance of the war.

Stedys that were bolde and snelle
  A-monge hem waden in the blode,
Bot by the tyme of euyn belle
  Launcelot party the better stode. 2237

(281)

Off' thys batayle was no more,
  Bot thus depa[r]ten they that daye;
Folke here Frendys home ledde and bare
  That slayne in the feldys laye. 2241
Launcelot' gonne to hys castelle fare,[1]
  The bataille venquesshyd, for Sothe to saye;
There was duell and wepynge sare,
  Amonge hem was no chyldys playe. 2245

The two parties withdraw their forces.

[leaf 114]

(282)

[Into] all landys northe and southe
  Off' thys werre the word spronge,
And yit at Rome it was full couthe,
  In ynglande was suche sorowe stronge; 2249
There-of' the pope had grete Routhe,
  A lettre he selid with hys hande;
Bot they accorded welle in trowthe,
  Enterdite he wolde the lande. 2253

News of the war between Arthur and Lancelot reaches the pope,

who threatens to lay the land under an interdict, if they do not stop it.

(283)

Then was A bischope at Rome,
  Off' Rowchester, with-outen lese;
Tylle ynglande he, the message, Come,
  To karllylle ther the kynge was; 2257
The popis lettre oute he nome
  In the paleis by-fore the desse,
And bade them do the popis dome
  And holde yngland in Reste and pes. 2261

The bishop of Rochester brings this message to England.

(284)

Redde was it by-fore All by-dene,
  The lettre that the pope gonne make,
How he moste haue a-ȝeyne the quene
  And a-corde withe launcelot du lake; 2265

---

[1] *The scribe by mistake began this leaf with the first seven lines of leaf 113, but afterwards struck them out.*

            Make a pes hem by-twene
              For euyr more and trews make,
            Or ynglande entyrdyted shulde bene
              And torne to sorow for ther sake.   2269

                              (285)

The king is   The kynge a-ȝeyne it wolde noȝte bene,
willing at the
pope's com-   To do the popys comaundemente,
mand to take
back his wife, Blythely A-yeyne to haue the quene;
                 Wolde he noght that ynglonde were shent;   2273
though   Bot gawayne was of herte so kene
Gawayne
opposes.   That to hym wolde he neuyr Assente
               To make A-corde hem by-twene,
                 While Any lyffe were in hym lente.   2277

                              (286)

The bishop.   Through the sente of Aħ by-dene
takes
Arthur's   Ganne the kynge A lettre make;
message to
[leaf 114, bk.] The bysschope in message yede by-twene
Lancelot,
asking for the   To syr launcelot du lake,   2281
return of the
queen.   And Askyd yiffe he wolde the quene
                 Cortessly to hym by-take,
               Or yngland enterdyt shuld bene
                 And torne to sorow for ther sake.   2285

                              (287)

               launcelot Answeryd with grete fauoure,
                 As knyght that hardy was and kene:
Lancelot is   "Syr, I haue stande in many A stoure,
at first
reluctant,   Bothe for the kynge and for the quene;   2289
               Fuħ colde had bene hys beste towre,
                 Yiff that I nadde my-selfe bene;
               he quytes it me with lytelle honoure,
                 That I haue seruyd hym Aħ by-dene."   2293

                              (288)

            The bysschope spake with-oute fayle,
              Thoughe he were nothynge A-froughte:
            "Syr, thynke that ye haue venquysshid many A bataille
              Throwgh grace that god hathe for you wrought; 2297

ye shaHe do now by my counsayle:
  Thynke on hym that you dere bought;
Wemen Ar frele of hyr entayle;
  Syr, lettes not ynglande go to noght."   2301

(289)

"Syr bysshope, castelles for to holde
  Wete you wele I haue no nede.
I myght be kynge, yifᵗ that I wolde,
  Offᵗ AH benwike, that Ryche thede,   2305
Ryde in-to my landys bolde
  Withe my knyghtes styffe on stede.
The quene, yif that I to them yolde,
  Offᵗ her lyffe I haue grette drede."   2309

and fears what may happen to the queen, if he returns her.

(290)

"Syr, be mary that is mayden floure,
  And god that AH shaH rede and Ryght,
She ne shaH haue no dyshonoure,
  There-to my trouthe I shaH you plyght,   2313
Bot boldely brought in-to hyr boure,
  To ladyes and to maydens bryght,
And holden in welle more honoure
  Than euyr she was by day or nyght."   2317

The bishop reassures him,

(291)

"Now, yifᵗ I grande suche a thynge,
  That I delyuere shaH the quene,
Syr bysshope, say my lorde, the kynge,
  Syr gawayne and hem AH by-dene,   2321
That thay shaH make me A sekerynge
  A trews to holde vs by-twene."   2323
[. . . . .   2323 b
  . . . . . *no gap in the MS.*]   2323 c

and Lancelot consents, provided the king and Gawayne will conclude a truce with him.

(292)

Then was the bysshope woundyr blythe
  That launcelot gaffe hym thys Answere;
Tylle hys palfray he wente as swythe
  And tylle karllyle gonne he fare;   2327

[leaf 115]

The bishop takes the news back to Carlisle.

                Tythandys sone were done to lythe
                    Whiche that launcelotis wordis ware;
                The kynge and courte was All full blythe,
                    A trews they sette and sekeryd thare;   2331

                                (293)
The king   Through the Assent of All by-dene
accepts
Lancelot's   A syker trews there they wrought;
conditions,   Though gawayne were of hert[e] kene,
                    There-a-yenste was he no3te,   2335
                To hald A trews hem by-twene,
                    While launcelot the quene home broght;
                Bot cordemente¹ thar hym neuyr wene,
                    Or eyther other herte haue sought.   2339

                                (294)
and a truce   A syker trews gonne they make,
is made.
                    And w*ith* ther seales they it bande;
                There-to they thre bisshopys gon take,
                    The wiseste that were in All the lande,   2343
                And sent to launcelot du lake;
                    At Ioyus gard² they hym fande;
                The lettres there they hym by-take
                    And there-to launcelot held hys hande.   2347

                                (295)
                The bisshopis than went on her way
                    To karlyll there the kynge wase;
Lancelot is   Launcelot shall come that other day
to bring the
queen back   Withe the lady proude in pres.   2351
next day.
                he dight hym I[n] a Ryche Araye,
                    Wete ye wele, w*ith*-outen les;
                An hundreth knyght*is*, for sothe to saye
                    The beste of All hys oste [he] chese.   2355

                                (296)
There is a   Launcelot and the quene were cledde
beautiful
procession,   In Robes of A Riche wede,
when the
queen is   Off¹ Samyte white, w*ith* syluer shredde,
returned.
                    yuory sadyll and white stede,   2359

¹ *In MS.* ouermente *apparently, but* cordemente *is certainly intended. Cp. ll.* 2028, 2422 *and* 2426.
² *Just after* gard *in the MS.* the *is written by mistake.*

Saumbues of¹ the same threde,
  That wroght was in the heythen thede;
launcelot hyr brydelle ledde,
  In the Romans as we Rede;   2363

(297)

The other knyght*is* euerychone
  In Samyte grene of heythen lande
And in there kyrtelles Ryde Allone,
  And Iche knyght a grene garlande,   2367 [leaf 115, bk.]
Sadillis sette w*ith* Ryche stone,
  Ichone A braunche of olyffe in hande,
All the felde A-boute hem schone;
  The knyghtis Rode full loude synghand.   2371

(298)

To the castelle when they come
  In the paleise gonne they lyghte;
Launcelot the quene of hir palfray nome,
  They Seyde it was A semly syghte;   2375   Launcelot delivers the queen to Arthur,
The kynge than salowes he full sone,
  As man that was of¹ myche myghte;
Feyre wordys were there fone,
  Bot wepynge stode there many A knyghte.   2379

(299)

Launcelot spake, as I you mene,
  To the kynge of mykelle myght:
"Syr, I haue the broght thy quene
  And sauyd hyr lyffe w*ith* the Ryght,   2383
As lady that is feyre and shene
  And trewe is bothe day and nyght;
Iffe Any man sayes she is noght clene,
  I profre me there-fore to feyght."   2387   and declares that he will fight any one who says that she is not pure.

(300)

The kynge Arthur Answerys thore
  Wordys that were kene and throo:
"Launcelot, I ne wende neuyr more
  That thow wolde me haue wroght thys woo;   2391   Arthur reproaches Lancelot.

So dere as we samen were,
There-vndyr that thou was my foo;
Bot noght for-thy me Rewis sore
That euer was werre by-twexte vs two." 2395

(301)

Lancelot replies that he has been slandered.

Launcelot than Answeryde he,
Whan he had lystenyd longe :
"Syr, thy wo thow witeste me
And welle thou woste it is w*ith* wronge; 2399
I was neuyr fer frome the,
When thow had Any sorow stronge;
Bot lyers lystenes thow to lye,
Off whome All thys word oute spronge." 2403

(302)

Gawayne vows vengeance against Lancelot for having slain his brothers,

Than by-spake hym Syr gawayne,
That was hardy knyght and free :
"launcelot, thou may it noght w*ith*-sayne
That thow haste slayne my brethrene thre; 2407
For-thy schall we proue oure mayne
In feld whether shall haue the gree;
Or eyther of vs shall other slayne
Blythe shall I neuyr be." 2411

(303)

[leaf 116]
but Lancelot asserts that he did not slay them.

Launcelot Answeryd w*ith* hert sore,
Thoughe he were nothynge A-froughte :
"Gawayne," he said, "thoughe I were there,
My-self thy brethren slow I noght; 2415
Other knyghtis fele ther were
That sythen thys werre dere han bought."
launcelot syghed wonder sore,
The terys of hys yen sowght. 2419

(304)

He begs Arthur and Gawayne to become reconciled with him,

launcelot spake, as I you mene,
To the kynge and syr gawayne :
"Syr, shall I neuyr of cordemente wene
That we myght frendys be A-ȝeyne?" 2423

Gawayne spake wit*h* hert[e] kene, — *but Gawayne vehemently refuses.*
  As man that myche was of mayne :
" Nay, cordement thar the neuyr wene
  Tylle on of¹ vs haue other slayne." — 2427

(305)

" Sythe it neuyr may be-tyde — *Lancelot then wishes to be allowed to ride into his own lands unmolested.*
  That pees may be vs by-twene,
May I in-to my landys Ryde
  Saffely wit*h* my knyghtis kene ? — 2431
Than wille I here no lenger byde,
  Bot take leue off¹ yow All by-dene ;
Where I wende in world[e] wyde,
  Engelond wolle I neuyr sene." — 2435

(306)

The kynge arthur Answered thore,
  The terys from hys yȝen Ranne :
" By Ih*es*u cryste ! " he there swore,
  " That AH thys worlde wroght and wan, — 2439
In-to thy landys whan thou willt fare, — *This the king promises.*
  The shaH lette no lyuand man."
He sayd " Allas ! " withe syghynge sare,
  " That euyr yit thys werre by-ganne ! — 2443

(307)

Sythe that I shaH wende A-waye — *Lancelot next wishes to know whether they intend to attack him in his own country,*
  And in myn Awne landys wone,
May I saffly wone ther aye,
  That ye wythe werre not come me on ? " — 2447
Syr gawayne thaᴡ sayd : " naye,
  By hym that made sonne and mone,
Dight the as welle as euyr thou may, — *and Gawayne says they do.*
  For we shaH After come fuH sone." — 2451

(308)

launcelot hys leue hathe taken thare, — *Lancelot takes his leave in sorrow.*
  It was no lenge[r] for to byde ;
hys palfray found he Redy ȝare,
  Made hym Redy for to Ryde ; — 2455

Oute of the castelle gonne they fare,
Gremly teres lette they glyde;
[leaf 116, bk.] There was dwelle and wepynge sare,
At the partynge was lytelle pryde. 2459

(309)

He first rides to Joyus Gard, To the Ioyus gard, the Ryche towne,
Rode launcelot, the noble knyghte;
Busked hem and made A bowne,
As men that were of¹ myche myght, 2463
Withe spere in hand and gonfanowne
and then to a port called Kelyon (Caerleon). (lette they nouther day *ne* nyght)
To An hauen hight kelyon;
Ryche galleys there they fande dyght. 2467

(310)

He sets sail for Benwike, Now ar thay shyppyd on the flode,
launcelot And hys knyght*is* hende;
Wederes had they feyre and goode
Wher hyr wille was for to wende, 2471
To An hauen there it stode
As men were leueste for to lende;
Off¹ benwike blythe was hyr mode,
Whan Ihesu cryst hem thedir sende. 2475

(311)

and is joyfully received there. Now ar thay Aryued on the stronde,
Off¹ hem was fele folke full blythe;
Grete lordis of the lande,
A-ʒeyne hym they come as swythe, 2479
And fellyn hym to fote and hande;
For her lord thay gonne hym kythe,
At hys domys for to stande,
And at hys lawes for to lythe. 2483

(312)

He makes Bors king of Gawnes Bors made he kynge of gawnes,
As it was bothe law and Ryght;
and Lyonelle king of France. lyonelle made kynge of fraunce,
Be olde tyme gawle hyghte; 2487

Aḻ hys folke he ganne Auance
And landys gaffe to Iche A knyghte,
And storyd hys castellys for Aḻ chance,
 For mykyḻ he hopyd more to fyght.   2491

(313)

Estor he crownys with hys hande,   *He also makes Estor king of his father's land.*
 So sayes the boke with-outen lese,
made hym kynge of¹ hys fadyr lande
 And prynce of All the Ryche prese;   2495
Bad no thynge hym shulde with-stande,
 Bot hald hym kynge as worthy was,
For ther [no] more hym-self wold fande
 Tylle he wiste to leffe in pes.   2499

(314)

Arthure wolle he no lenger A-byde,   *[leaf 117] Arthur prepares to wage war against Lancelot,*
 nyght and day hys herte was sore;
messengerys did he go And Ryde
 Throughe-oute yngland for to fare   2503
To erlys And barons on Iche A syde,
 Bad hem buske and make Aḻ ȝare,
On launcelot landys for to Ryde,
 To brenne and sle and make Aḻ bare.   2507

(315)

At hys knyghtis Aḻ by-dene   *and takes counsel with his knights as to who shall govern the realm in his absence.*
 The kynge gan hys conselle take,
And bad hem ordeyne hem by-twene
 Who beste steward were for to make,   2511
The Reme for to saue and ȝeme,
 And beste were for bretaynes sake;
Fuḻ mykelle they dred hem Aḻ by-dene
 That Alyens the land wold take.   2515

(316)

The knyghtis answeryd, with-oute lese,   *They say that Mordred is the best man,*
 And said, for sothe, that so them thought
That syr mordred the sekereste was,
 Thoughe men the Reme throw-oute sought,   2519

and he is accordingly made "steward."

To saue the Reme in trews and pees.
    Was A boke by-fore hym brought;
Syr mordreit they to steward chese;
    That many A bolde sythen A-bought.   2523

(317)

It was no lenger for to byde,
    But buskes hem And made All bowne;
Whan they were Redy for to Ryde,
    They Reised spere and gonfanowne;   2527

Arthur assembles his galleys at Kerlyonne (Caerleon),

Forthe they went wit_h_ mykelle pryde
    Tylle An hauyne hyght kerlyonne,
And graythes be the lande syde
    Galeis grete of fele fasowne.   2531

(318)

and passing over into Lancelot's country ravages it.

now are they shippid on the see
    And wendyn ouyr the water wyde;
Off¹ benwyke whan they myght se,
    Withe grete Route they gonne vp Ryde;   2535
wit_h_-stode hem neyther stone ne tre,
    Bot brente and slow on Iche A syde;
launcelot is in hys beste Cyte,
    There he batelle wolle A-byde.   2539

(319)

Lancelot gathers his [leaf 117, bk.] forces together, and holds a council.

launcelot clepis hys knyghtis kene,
    His erlys And hys barons bolde,
Bad hem ordeyne hem by-twene,
    To wete her wylle, what they wolde,   2543
To Ryde A-ȝeyne hem All by dene
    Or ther worthe walles holde;
For well they wiste, wit_h_-outen wene,
    For no fantyse Arthur nold folde.   2547

(320)

Bors urges that they should attack the invaders.

Bors de gawnes, the noble knyght,
    stornnely spekys in that stounde:
"Doughty men that ye be dyghte,
    Foundis your worship for to fownd,   2551

Withe spere and shelde and armes bryght
   A-ȝeyne your fo-men for to fownd ;
Kynge and duke, erle and knyght,
   We shall hem bete And brynge to grounde." 2555

(321)

Lyonelle spekys in that tyde,   *Lyonelle thinks it better to remain within their walls until the invaders are tired out,*
   That was of warre wyse And bolde :
"Lordyngis, yet I rede we byde
   And oure worthy walles holde ;   2559
Le[t] them pryke with All ther pryde
   Tylle they haue Caught bothe hungre and colde ;
Than shall we oute vppon them Ryde   *and then attack them.*
   And shredde them downe as shepe in folde." 2563

(322)

Syr banndemagew, that bolde kynge,   *Banndemagew says, however, that in the meanwhile the land will have been destroyed.*
   To launcelot spekys in that tyde :
"Syr, cortessye And your sufferynge
   Has wakend vs wo full wyde ;   2567
Awise you welle vppon thys thynge :
   Yiff that they ouer oure landys Ryde,
All to noght they myght vs brynge,
   Whyle we in holys here vs hyde."   2571

(323)

Galyhud, that Ay was goode,   *Galyhud is also in favour of an immediate attack,*
   To launcelot he spekys thare :
"Syr, here ar knyghtis of kynges blode
   That longe wylle not droupe And dare ;   2575
Gyffe me leue, for crosse on Rode
   Withe my men to them to fare ;
Thoughe they be wers than outlawes wode,
   I shall them sle and make full bare."   2579

(324)

Off northe gales were bretherne seuen,   *and so are the seven brothers of North Gales.*
   Ferly mekelle of strenghe and pryde ;
Not full fele that men coude neuyne
   Better dorste in bataile byde ;   2583

[leaf 118]	All they sayd w*ith* one steuen :
	"Lordyng*is*, how longe wolle ye chyde?
	Launcelot, for goddys loue in heuen
	W*ith* galehud forthe lette vs Ryde." 2587

(325)

Lancelot is in favour of staying within the walls and negotiating for peace,

Than spake the lorde that was so hende,
   Hym-Self, syr launcelot de lake :
"Lordyng*is*, A whyle I rede we lende
   And oure worthy wallys wake ;   2591
A message wlle I to them sende,
   A trews be-twene vs for to take ;
my lord is so corteise and hende
   That yit I hope A pees to make ;   2595

(326)

for enough people have been killed already.

Thoughe we myght the worshyppe wynne,
   Off A thynge myn hert is sore :
Thys land is of² folke fu*ll* thynne,
   Bataylles has it made fu*ll* bare ;   2599
Wete ye welle it were grete synne
   Crysten folke to sle thus more ;
Withe myldenesse we sha*ll* be-gynne
   And god sha*ll* wische vs wele to fare."   2603

(327)

Lancelot's counsel prevails,

And at thys Assent A*ll* they ware,
   And Sette A wacche for to wake,
knyght*is* breme as Any bare
   And derfe of drede as is the drake ;   2607

and a damsel is sent to arrange a truce, if possible.

A Damyselle thay dede be ȝare
   And hastely gon her lettres make ;
A mayde sholde on the message fare
   A trews by-twene them for to take.   2611

(328)

The mayde was fu*ll* shene to shewe,
   Vppon her stede whan she was sette,
Hyr paraylle A*ll* of one hewe,
   Off² A grene weluette,   2615

The damsel goes to the King.

In hyr hand A braunche newe,
   For-why that no man sholde her lette;
Ther-by men messangerys knewe
   In ostes whan that men them mette.   2619

(329)

The kynge was lokyd in A felde   *She approaches the king's pavilion,*
   By A ryuer brode And dreghe;
A while she houyd And by-helde;
   Pavylons were pyghte on hyghe;   2623
She saughe there many comly telde
   Wythe pomelles bryghte as goldis beghe;
On one hynge the kyngis shelde,   [leaf 118, bk.]
   That pauylon she drew hyr nyghe.   2627

(330)

The kynges baner oute was sette,
   That pauylon she drewe her nere;
With A knyght full sone she mette,   *and meets with Sir Lucan de Bottelere there.*
   hyght Syr lucan de bottelere;   2631
She hailsed hym and he her grette,
   The mayde with full mylde chere;
hyr erande was not for to lette,
   he wiste she was A messengere.   2635

(331)

Sir lucan downe gan hyr take
   And in hys Armes forthe gan lede;
hendely to her he spake,
   As knyght that wise was vndyr wede: 2639
" Thou comeste from launcelot de lake,   *He praises Lancelot,*
   The beste that euyr strode on stede;
Ihesu, for hys modyris sake,
   Yiffe the grace wele to spede!"   2643

(332)

Feyre was pight vppon a playne   *and conducts her to the king.*
   The paviloun in Ryche A-parayle;
The kynge hym-selfe and syr gawayne
   Comely sytten in the halle;   2647

Her letters are read,

The mayde knelyd the kynge A-gayne,
 So lowe to grounde gan she falle ;
here lettres were not for to layne,
 They were I-rade A-monge hem AH. 2651

(333)

hendly and feyre the mayden spake,
 FuH fayne of speche she wold be sped :
"Syr, god yow saue from wo And wrake
 And AH your knyghtis in Ryche wede ; 2655
Yow gret*is* wele, syr launcelot du lake,

and she pleads for a twelve months' truce,

 That w*ith* yow hathe bene euyr at nede ;
A xii monthe trewse he wolde take
 To lyue vppon hys owne lede, 2659

(334)

And sythen, yiffe ye make an heste,
 he wille it holde w*ith* hys honde,

and peace afterwards.

By-twene you for to make pees
 Stabully euer for to stonde ; 2663

In that event Lancelot, she says, will spend the remainder of his life in the Holy Land.

He wolle Rape hym on A Resse
 Myldely to the holy londe,
There to lyue, w*ith*-outen lese,
 Whyle he is man lyvande." 2667

(335)

The kynge than clepid hys counsayle,

[leaf 119]

 Hys douȝty knyghtis AH by-dene ;

The king is inclined to accept these terms,

Fyrste he sayde, w*ith*-outen fayle :
 " me thynke it were beste to sene ; 2671
he were A fole, w*ith*-outen fayle,
 So feyr forwardys for to fleme."
The kynge the messyngere thus did assayle :
 " It were pite to sette warre vs by-twene." 2675

(336)

but Gawayne is not.

" Sert*is*, nay," sayd syr gawayne,
 " he hathe wroght me wo I-noughe,
So traytourly he hathe my bredre*n* slayne,
 AH for your loue, sir, that is treuthe, 2679

To yngland wiH I not torne A-gayne
　Tylle he be hangid on a boughe ;
Whyle me lastethe myght or mayne,
　There-to I shaH fynd peple I-noghe." 2683

(337)

The kynge hym-self, with-owten lese,
　And Iche A lord, is nought to layne,
AH they spake to haue pese,
　But hym-self, syr gawayne, 2687
To batayle hathe he made hys hest
　Or ellys neuer to torne A-gayne.
They made hem Redy to that Rese,
　There-fore was fele folke vnfayne. 2691

All are in favour of peace except Sir Gawayne, who carries the day, however.

(338)

The kynge is comyn in-to the halle
　And in hys RoyaH see hym sette ;
He made A knyght the mayden calle,
　Syr lucane de botteler, with-outen lette : 2695
" Say to launcelot and hys knyghtis AH,
　suche an heste I haue hym hette,
That we shaH wend for no walle
　Tyll we with myghtis onys haue mette." 2699

The king sends Lancelot word that they are determined on battle.

(339)

The mayde had hyr Answere,
　Withe drery hert she gan hyr dyght ;
hyr feyr palfrey fande she yare,
　And Syr lucan ledde hyr thedyr Ryght ; 2703
So throw A foreste gan she fare
　And hasted her with AH hyr myght,
There launcelot and hys knyghtis were,
　In benwyk the browgh with bemys bryght. 2707

The damsel returns sorrowfully with this answer to Lancelot,

(340)

Now is she went with-in the walle,
　The worthy damysselle fayre in wede ;
Hendely she Cam in-to that halle,
　A knyght hyr toke downe of hyre stede ; 2711

[leaf 119, bk.

and he and his men prepare for the fight.

A-monge the prync*is* proude in palle
  She toke hyr lettres for to Rede;
There was no counsayle for to calle,
  But Redely busk*is* them to that dede; 2715

(341)

As folkys that preste were to feight,
  Frome feld wold they neuyr fle;
Arthur besieges Lancelot in his castle,
But by the morow that day was lyght
  A-boute by-segyd was All there Fee; 2719
ychone theym¹ Rayed in All Ryght*is*;
novther pa*r*ty thought to flee. 2721
[. . . . . 2721 *b*
 . . . . . *no gap in the MS.*] 2721 *c*

(342)

Erly as the day gan sprynge,
  The trompett*is* vppon the wallis went;
There myght they se a wondyr thy*n*ge,
  Off teldys Riche and ma[n]y A tente. 2725
and gets ready to make an assault.
Syr arthur than, the comely kynge,
  w*ith* hys folk*is* ther was lente,
To yeff Assaute, w*ith*-oute lesyng,
  w*ith* Alblasters and bowes bente. 2729

(343)

Lancelot restrains his men from rushing forth.
Launcelot All for-wondred was
  Off¹ the folke by-fore the walle;
But he had rather knowe*n* that rease,
  Oute had ronne hys knyght*is* All; 2733
he sayd: "prync*is*, bethe in pease,
  For folyse fele that myght by-falle;
yiff thay will not ther sege sease,
  Full sore I hope for-thynke hem shall." 2737

(344)

Gawayne offers a challenge to the knights of Lancelot's party.
Than gawayne, that was good at eu*er*y nede,
  Graythid hym in hys gode Armour,
And styffly sterte vppon A stede
  That syker was in ylke A stoure; 2741

¹ MS. theyne.

Gawayne overthrows Bors and Lyonnelle.

Forthe he sprange as sparke on glede,
  By-fore the yates a-gayne the toure;
he bad A knyght come kythe mayne,
  A cours of werre for hys honoure. 2745

(345)

Bors de gawnes buskys hym bowne *Bors accepts it, and is overthrown,*
  Vpon A stede that shuld hym bere,
With helme, sheld, And hauberke browne,
  And in hys hand A Full good spere; 2749
Owte he Rode A grete Randowne;
  Gawayn kyd he covde of werre;
hors and man bothe bare he downe,
  Suche A dynte he yaffe hym there. 2753

(346)

Syr lyonelle was All redy than *and when Lyonelle goes [leaf 120] to his brother's assistance, the same fate befalls him.*
  And for hys broder was wonder woo;
Redely with hys stede oute Ranne
  And wende gawayne for to sloo. 2757
Gawayn hym kepte as he wele can,
  As he that ay was kene and thro;
Downe he bare bothe hors and man,
  And euery day som seruyd he soo. 2761

(347)

And so more than halfe a yere, *Fighting went on thus for more than half a year, but Gawayne always escaped injury.*
  As longe as they there layne,
Euery day men myght se there
  Men woundyd and som slayne, 2765
But how that euer in world it were,
  Suche grace had sir gawayne,
Euer he passyd hole and clere;
  There myght no man stand hym Agayne. 2769

(348)

Than it by-Felle vponn A tyde, *One day he issues a challenge to Lancelot especially.*
  Syr gawayne, that was hende and free,
He made hym redy for to Ryde
  By-fore the gatis of the Cyte; 2773

Launcelot of treson he be-Cryed
    That he had slayne hys bretherne thre,
That launcelot my3te no lenger A-byde,
    But he euer A cowarde scholde be. 2777

(349)

The lord that grete was of honoure,
    Hym-selffe, sir launcelot du lake,
A-bove the gatis vppon the toure

Lancelot expresses his sorrow to the king that he has to accept,

    Comely to the kynge he spake : 2781
"My lord, god saue youre honoure !
    Me ys wo now for yowre sake,
A-gaynste thy kynne to stonde in stoure,
    But nedys I muste thys batayle take." 2785

(350)

and goes forth in full armour to meet Gawayne.

Launcelot armyd hym full wele,
    For sothe had Full grete nede,
Helme, hawberke and All of stele
    And stifely sterte vppon A stede ; 2789
Hys harneyse lacked he neuer A dele,
    To were wantyd hym no wede,
No wepyn with All to dele ;
    for-the he sprange as sparke on glede. 2793

(351)

Than was it warnyd faste on hye
    How in world that it shu[l]d fare,
That no man schold come hem nye
    Tylle the tone dede or yolden were. 2797
Folke with-drew them than bye,
    Vpon the feld was brode and bare ;

[leaf 120, bk.] The knyghtis mette, As men it sye,
    how they sette there dyntis sare. 2801

(352)

It was a peculiarity of Gawayne's that his strength always increased up to the hour of noon.

Than had syr gawayne suche a grace,
    An holy man had boddyn that bone,
Whan he were in Any place,
    There he shuld batayle done, 2805

Hys strength shulld wex in suche A space,
 From the vndyr-tyme tylle none,
And launcelot for-bare ay for that case;
 A-gayne xx strokys he yaff' not one: 2809

Lancelot, knowing this, endeavours simply to defend himself up to noon,

(353)

Launcelot saw ther was no socoure,
 nedysse muste he hys venture Abyde;
many A dynt he gan wele in-dure
 Tylle it drew nere the noon tyde; 2813
Than he straught in that stoure
 And yaffe gawayne A wond wyde;
The blode Aᚻ coueryd hys coloure
 And he felle downe vpon hys syde. 2817

but, being pressed,

he severely wounds Gawayne, who falls to the ground.

(354)

Throw the helme in-to the hede
 Was hardy gawayne woundyd so
That vnneth was hym lyfe leuyd;
 On fote myght he no ferther goo; 2821
But wightly hys swerd A-bowte he wavyd,
 For euer he was bothe kene and thro.
launcelot than hym lyAnd levyd;
 For Aᚻ the world he nold hym slo. 2825

Lancelot will not slay Gawayne,

(355)

launcelot than hym drew on dryhe;
 hys swerd was in hys hand drawen;
And syr gawayne cryed lowde on hye:
 "Traytour And coward, come A-gayne, 2829
Whan I Am hole And goynge on hye;
 Than wylle I prove with myght and mayne,
And yit A thow woldyst nyghe me nye,
 Thow shalt wele wete I am not slayn." 2833

although Gawayne continues to defy him.

(356)

"Gawayne, while thow myghtis styfflye stonde,
 many A stroke to-day of the I stode,
And I for-bare the in euery londe
 For love and for the kyngis blode; 2837

He tells Gawayne to change his mood,

Whan thou arte hole in herte and hond,
  I rede the torne and chaunge thy mode;
[leaf 121] Whyle I am launcelot and man levande,
  Gode sheld me frome werkys wode! 2841

(357)

But have good day, my lord the kynge,
  And your doughty knyght*is* Alle;
and advises the king to return home. Wendyth home A leue youre werryeng;
  ye wynne no worshyp at thys walle; 2845
And I wold my knyght*is* oute brynge,
  I wote full sore rewe it ye shalle;
My lord, there-fore, thynke on suche thynge,
  how fele folke there-fore myght falle." 2849

(358)

Lancelot's knights receive him joyfully, launcelot, that was moche of mayne
  Boldely to hys Cyte wente;
Hys good kny3t*is* [there]-of were fayne
and Gawayne is borne back to his tent.   And hendely hym in armys hente. 2853
The tother party tho toke syr gawayne,
  They wessche hys woundys in hys tente;
Or euer he coueryd myght or mayne,
  vnnethe was hym the lyffe lente. 2857

(359)

Gawayne is ill for a fortnight, A fortenyght, the sothe to saye,
  Full passynge seke and vn-sonde
There syr Gawayne on lechynge laye,
  Or he were hole All of hys wounde. 2861
but at the end of that time he again challenges Lancelot. Than it by-felle vppon A day,
  he made hym Redy for to wound;
By-fore the yat he toke the way
  And Askyd batayle in that stownd: 2865

(360)

"Come forthe, launcelot, and p*r*ove thy mayne,
  Thou traytou*r* that hast treson wroght;
my thre brethern thou haste slayne
  And falsly theym to ground[e] brought; 2869

The second combat.

Whyle me lastethe myght or mayne,
  Thys qarell leve wyll I noght,
Ne pees shall ther neuer be sayne
  Or thy sydes be throw sought." 2873

(361)

Than launcelot thoght it no thyng gode
  And for these wordis he was full wo;
A-bove the gatis than he yode
  And to the kynge he sayd so: 2877
"Syr, me rewys in my mode
  That gawayne is in hert so thro.
Who may me wyte, for corsse on Rode,
  Thouȝth I hym in bataylle sloo?" 2881

Lancelot again expresses his sorrow to the king that Gawayne should be so implacable,

(362)

Launcelot buskyd And made hym bowne,
  he will boldely the batayle A-byde,
With helme, shelde And hauberke browne,
  None better in All thys world[e] wyde, 2885
With spere in hand and gonfanowne,
  hys noble swerd by hys syde;
Oute he Rode A grete randowne,
  Whan he was Redy for to Ryde. 2889

[leaf 121, bk.] but has to ride forth for a second combat.

(363)

Gawayne grypes a full good spere
  And in he glydes glad and gay;
Launcelot kydde he coude of were
  And euyn to hym he takys the way; 2893
So stoutely they gan to-geder bere
  That marvayle it was, sothe to say;
With dyntis sore ganne they dere
  And depe wondys daltyn thay. 2897

The fight takes place,

(364)

Whan it was nyghed nere-hand none,
  Gawayne strenghe gan to in-crese;
So bitterly he hewyd hym vppon
  That launcelot All for-wery was; 2901

and Gawayne's strength, as usual, increases up to noon.

Lancelot, however, strikes, Gawayne a blow	Than to hys swerd he grypes A-none, And sethe that gawayne wyll not sese, Suche A dynte he yaffe hym one That many a Ryche Rewed that resse.	2905

(365)

	launcelot sterte forthe in that stownde, And sethe that gawayne will no sease, The helme that was Ryche and Rownde The noble swerd[e] rove that rease;	2909
on the old wound, so that Gawayne lay groaning on the ground.	he hyt hym A-pon the olde wounde That ouer the sadyll downe he wente And grysely gronyd vpon the grou*n*d, And there was good gawayne shent.	2913

(366)

He, nevertheless, continues to defy Lancelot,	yit gawayne swounynge there as he lay Gryped to hym bothe swerde And sheld; " lancelot," he sayd, " sothely to saye, And by hym that All thys world shall welde,	2917
	Whyle me lastethe lyffe to-daye, To the me shall I neu*er* yeld; But do the werste that euyr thou may, I schall defend me in the felde."	2921

(367)

[leaf 122] who answers him in a chivalrous manner.	Launcelot than full styll stoode, As man that was moche of myght: " Gawayne, me rewes in my mode, Men hald the so noble A knyght.	2925
	Wenystow I were so wode Agaynste A feble man to fyght? I wyll not now, by crosse on Rode, Nor neu*er* yit dyd by day nor nyght.	2929

(368)

Lancelot again warns the king to go home and stop the war.	But haue good day, my lord the kynge, And All youre douȝty knyght*is* by-dene, Wendyth home and leue your werrynge, For here ye shall no worshyppe wynne.	2933

yif I wolde my knyght*is* oute brynge,
  I hope full sone it shuld be sene,
but, good lord, thynke vppon A thynge,
  The loue that hathe be vs by-twene." 2937

(369)
After was it monthes two,
  As frely folke it vndyr-stode,[1]
Or eue*r* gawayne myght Ryde or go
  Or had fote vpon erthe to stonde, 2941
The thirde[2] tyme he was full thro
  To do batayle w*ith* herte and hande,
But than was word come*n* hem to
  That they muste home to yngland. 2945

Two months later Gawayne was eager for still a third combat with Lancelot,

(370)
Suche mesage was hem brought,
  There was no man that thought it goode;
The kynge hy*m*-selfe full sone it thought
  (Full moche mornyd he in hys mode 2949
That suche treson in ynglond shuld be wroght')
  That he moste nedys oue*r* the flode.
They brake sege and homward sought',
  And After they had moche Angry mode. 2953

but news from England prevents this.

(371)
That fals trayto*ur*, *sir* mordreid—
  The kynges soster sone he was,
And eke hys owne so*n*ne, As I rede—
  There-fore men hym fo[r] steward chase— 2957
So falsely hathe he yngland ledde,
  Wete yow wele, w*ith*-outen lese,
Hys Eme-is wyffe wolde he wedde,
  That many A man rewyd that rease. 2961

This news is concerning Mordred's treason, how he wished to wed the queen.

(372)
Festys made he, many and fele,
  And grete yiftys he yafe Also;
They sayd w*ith* hym was Ioye and wele
  And in Arthurs tyme but sorow and woo; 2965

He had so ingratiated himself by gifts and [leaf 122, bk.] feasts that the people now preferred him to Arthur.

---

[1] *Perhaps the mark indicating* n *over the* o *has been left out. The analogy, however, of ll. 3062 ff. speaks against this.*
[2] MS. iij.

And thus gan Ryght to wronge goo;
Aɫɫ the concelle, is noght to hele,
Thus it was, wit*h*-outen moo,
To hold mordred in londe wit*h* wele. 2969

(373)

He has false letters written to the effect that Arthur is dead, and a new king must be chosen.

False lettres he made be wroght,
And causyd messangers hem to brynge,
That Arthur was to grownde broght,
And chese they muste A-nother kynge. 2973
Aɫɫ thay sayd as hem thought:
"Arthur louyd noght but warynge
And suche thynge as hym-selfe soght.
Ryght so he toke hys endynge." 2977

(374)

The people gladly make Mordred king,

mordred let crye A pa*r*lement;
The peple gan thedyr to come,
And holly throwe there assente
They made mordred kynge wit*h* crowne; 2981

and, after holding a feast in Canterbury, he goes to Winchester.

At canturbery, ferre in kente,
A Fourtenyght held the feste in towne,
And after that to Wynchester he wente;
A Ryche brydale he lette make bowne; 2985

(375)

He has it proclaimed that he is going to marry his father's wife,

In somyr, whan it was fayr and bryght,
Hys faders wyfe than wold he wedde
And hyr hold wit*h* mayne and myght,
And so hyr brynge as byrd to bedde. 2989

and the queen is in great distress.

Sche prayd hym of leue A fourtenyght—
The lady was fuɫɫ hard be-stad—
So to london sche hyr dyght,
That she and hyr maydens myght be cledd. 2993

(376)

She shuts herself up in the tower of London,

The quene, whyte as lyly floure,
Wit*h* knyght*is* fele of her kynne,
She went to london to the towre
And speryd the gates And dwellyd therin. 2997

Mordred changed than hys coloure,
    Thedyr he went and wold not blynne;
There-to he made many A shoure,
    But the wallys myght he neuer wynne.   3001

and Mordred cannot get at her.

(377)

The Archebysshop of canterbery thedyr yode,
    And hys crosse by-fore hym broght.
he sayd: "syr, for cryste on Rode,
    What haue ye now all in your thoght?   3005
Thy faders wyffe, whether thou be wood,
    To wedd her now mayste thou noght.
Come Arthur euyr ouer the flood,
    Thow mayste be bold, it wyll be boght."   3009

The Archbishop of Canterbury rebukes him for wishing to marry his [leaf 123] father's wife,

(378)

"A nyse clerke," than mordred sayd,
    "Trowiste thow to warne me of my wille?
be hym that for vs suffred payne,
    These wordys shalt thou lyke full ylle!   3013
with wilde hors thou shalt be drayne
    And hangyd hye vpon An hylle."
The bischoppe to fle than was fayne
    And suffred hym hys folyes to fulfylle;   3017

but Mordred replies by threats against the archbishop, who takes flight.

(379)

Than he hym cursyd with boke And belle,
    At caunterbery, ferre in kente.
Sone, whan mordred herd ther-of telle,
    To seche the bisschoppe hathe he sent;   3021
The bysshop durste no lenger dwelle
    But gold And syluer he hathe hent;
There was no lenger for to spelle,
    But to A wyldernesse he is went;   3025

When the archbishop reaches Canterbury, he excommunicates Mordred, but, being pursued, has to take refuge in a wilderness.

(380)

The worldys wele ther he wyll for-sake,
    Off Ioye kepeth he neuer more,
But A chapelle he lette make
    By-twene two hye holtys hore;   3029

There he has a chapel made, and lives as a hermit.

There-in weryd he the clothys blake,
    In wode as he an ermyte ware;
Often gan he wepe and wake
    For yngland that had suche sorowis sare.   3033

(381)

Mordred cannot obtain possession of the tower of London,

Mordred had than lyen full longe,
    But the towre myght' he neuer wynne,
With strength ne with stoure stronge,
    ne with none other kynnes gynne;   3037

and in his fear of Arthur gets ready to keep him out of the kingdom.

Hys fader dred he euyr A-monge,
    There-fore hys bale he nylle not blynne;
He went to warne hem All with wronge
    The kyngdome that he was crownyd inne.   3041

(382)

Forthe to dover þan gan he Ryde,
    All the costys wele he kende;
To erlys And to barons on ylk A syde

[leaf 123, bk.]

    Grete yiftis he gaffe And lettres send,   3045
And for-sette the see on ylke A syde
    With bold men And bowes bente;
Fro yngland, that is brode And wyde,
    hys owne fader he wold deffend.   3049

(383)

Arthur returns to England, and is prevented from landing at Dover.

Arthur, that was mykelle of myght,
    With hys folke come over the flode,
An C galeyse that were welle dyght
    With barons bold And hye of blode;   3053
he wende to haue landyd, as it was Ryght,
    At Dower, ther hym thoght full gode,
And ther he fande many An hardy knyght
    That styffe in stoure A-gaynste hym stode.   3057

(384)

He lands elsewhere, however,

Arthur sone hathe take the land
    That hym was leveste in to lende;
hys fele fomen that he ther found,
    he wende by-fore had bene hys frend.   3061

The kynge was wrothe And weliney wode, *and prepares for battle.*
 And wi*th* hys men he gan vp wend;
So strong A stoure was vpon that stronde
 That many A man ther had hys end. 3065

(385)

Syr gawayne armyd hym in that stou*n*de; *In the fight Gawayne is hit on the old wound, and never speaks again.*
 Allas! to longe hys hede was bare;
he was seke And sore vnsond;
 hys woundis greuyd hym fułł sare; 3069
One hytte hym vpon the olde wounde
 Wi*th* A tronchon of An ore;
There is good gawayne gone to grou*n*de,
 That speche spake he neuyr more. 3073

(386)

Bold men, wi*th* bowes bentte, *The battle is severe,*
 Boldely vp in botes yode,
And Ryche hauberk*is* they Ryve and Rente,
 that Throw-owte braste the Rede blode; 3077
Grou*n*den gleyves throw hem wente;
 Tho games thoght theym nothynge gode;
But by that strong stoure was stente,
 The stronge stremys Ran Ałł on blode. 3081

(387)

Arthur was so moche of myght,
 Was ther none that hym wi*th*-stode;
He hewyd vppon ther helmes bryght, *but in the end Mordred's men are defeated. [leaf 124]*
 That throw ther brestes Ran the blode; 3085
By than that endyd was the fight,
 The false were feld, som wer fledde
To canterbery Ałł that nyght,
 To warne ther master, syr mordred. 3089

(388)

Mordred than made hym bowne *Mordred now goes forth himself to the battle,*
 And boldely he wylle batayle A-byde,
Wi*th* helme, scheld, And hauberke browne;
 So Ałł hys Rowte gan forthe Ryde; 3093

The battle at Barendowne.

which is renewed at Barendowne on the morrow.

They hem mette vppon barendowne,
 Full erly in the morowe tyde;
With gleyves grete And gonfanowne
 Grymly they gan to-gedyr Ryde;   3097

(389)

Arthur was of Ryche A-Raye
 And hornys blew lowde on hyght,
And mordred comyth glad and gay,
 As traytour that was false in fyght.   3101

They fight all day,

Thay faught All that longe day
 Tyll the nyght was nyghed nyghe;
Who had it sene wele myght saye
 That suche A stoure neuer he syghe.   3105

(390)

Arthur than faught with hert good—
 A nobler knyght was neuer noon;
Throw helmes in-to hede yt yoode
 And steryd knyghtis bothe blode And bone.   3109
mordred for wrathe was nye wode,
 Callyd hys folke And sayd to hem One:
"Releve yow, for crosse on Rode!
 Alas! thys day so sone is goone!"   3113

(391)

Fele men lyeth on bankys bare
 With bryght brondys throw-owte borne;

and many are slain on both sides.

Many A doughty man dede was thar,
 And many A lord hys lyfe hathe lorne;   3117
mordred was full of sorowe And care;
 At canterbery was he vpon the morne;
And Arthur All nyght he dwellyd thare,
 Hye frely folke lay hym by-forne.   3121

(392)

Arthur buries his dead,

Erely on the morow tyde
 Arthur bad hys hornys blowe,
And callyd folke on euery syde,
 And many A dede beryed on A rowe,   3125

In pittes that was depe And wyde ;
  On Iche An hepe they layd hem lowe,
So Aƚƚ that ouer gone And Ryde   [leaf 124, bk.]
  Som by there markys men myght knowe.   3129

(393)

Arthur went to hys dyner thane—
  hys frely folke hym folowed faste—
But whan he fand syr gawayne   *but when he finds Ga-*
  In A shyppe laye dede by A maste,   3133 *wayne among them, his*
Or euyr he coveryd myght or mayne,   *heart almost broke.*
  An C tymes hys hert nyghe braste.
[. . . . .   3135 *b*
  . . . . . *no gap in the MS.*]   3135 *c*

(394)

Thay layd syr gawayne vpon A bere   *They lay Gawayne's*
  And to the casteƚƚ they hym bare,   *dead body on a bier,*
And in A chapeƚƚ A-mydde the quere   *and bear it to a chapel in*
  That bold baron they beryed thare. 3139 *the castle.*
Arthur than changyd Aƚƚ hys chere ;
  What wondyr thoghe hys hert was sare !
hys sust*er* sone, that was hym dere,
  Off hym shold he here neuyr mare.   3143

(395)

Syr Arthur, he wolde no lenger A-byde ;   *Arthur goes in the direc-*
  Than had he Aƚƚ maner of euyƚƚ Reste ; *tion of Wales, and intends*
He sought aye forthe the southe syde   *to stop at Salisbury*
  And toward walys wente he weste ; 3147 *to gather together his*
At salusbury he thought to byde,   *forces there.*
  At that tyme he thought was beste,
And calle to hym by Whytesontyde
  Barons bold to batayle preste.   3151

(396)

Vnto hym came many A doughty knyght,   *Many bold*
  For wyde in worlde theyse wordys sprange, *knights join Arthur.*
That syr Arthur hade Aƚƚ the Ryght,
  And mordred warred on hym w*ith* wronge. 3155

Hydowse it was to se w*ith* syght,
  Arthur-is oste was brode And longe,
  And mordred that was mykell of myght
    W*ith* grete gyftes made hym stronge.   3159

(397)

It is fixed that there is to be a battle after the feast of the Trinity.

Sone After the feste of the trynyte
  Was A batayle by-twene hem sette,
  That A sterne batayle ther shuld be ;
    For no lede wold they it lette ;   3163
  And syr Arthur makethe game And glee
    For myrth that they shuld be mette ;
  And syr mordred can to the contre,
    W*ith* fele folke that ferre was fette.   3167

(398)

The night before the [leaf 125] battle Arthur has a vision.

At nyght whan Arthur was brought in bedd—
  He shuld haue batayle vppon the morow—
  In stronge sweu[en]ys he was by-stedde,
    That many A man that day shuld haue sorow ;   3171

He thought that he was seated crowned on a great wheel.

hym thowht he satte in gold All gledde,
  As he was comely kynge w*ith* crowne,
  vpon A whele that full wyde spredd,
    And All hys knyght*is* to hym bowne.   3175

(399)

The whele was ferly Ryche And Rownd,
  In world was neuyr none halfe so hye ;
  There-on he satte Rychely crownyd
    W*ith* many A besaunte broche And be ;   3179

Down below him there was a black water full of dragons.

he lokyd downe vpon the grownd,
  A blake water ther vndyr hym he see,
  W*ith* dragons fele there lay vn-bownde,
    That no man durst hem nyghe nyee.   3183

(400)

The wheel turned, and the dragons caught him by the limbs.

he was wondyr ferd to falle
  A-monge the fendys ther that faught ;
  The whele ou*er*-tornyd ther w*ith*-All
    And eueryche by A lymme hym caught.   3187

The kynge gan lowde crye And calle,
  As marred man of wytte vn-saught;
hys chambyrlayns wakyd hym ther with-aH
  And woodely oute of hys slepe he raught. 3191

The king cries aloud on account of his vision, and his chamberlains awaken him,

(401)
AH nyght gan he wake And wepe,
  With drery hert And sorowfuH stevyn,[1]
And A-gaynste day he felle on slepe;
  A-boute hym was sette tapers sevyn; 3195
Hym thought Syr gawayne hym dyd kepe
  With mo folke þan men can nevyn,
By A Ryuer that was brode And depe;
  AH semyd Angellys cam from heuyn. 3199

but towards day he falls asleep again and has a vision of Gawayne who is followed by angels, as it seemed.

(402)
The kynge was neuyr yit so fayne,
  hys soster sone whan that he sye;
"Welcome," he sayd, "syr gawayne;
  And thou myght leue, welle were me. 3203
Now, leue frend, with-outen layne,
  What Ar tho folke that folow the?"
"Sertis, syr," he sayd A-gayne,
  "They byde in blysse ther I motte be. 3207

Gawayne explains that these are the spirits of

(403)
lordys they were And ladyes hende,
  Thys worldys lyffe that hanne for-lorne;
Whyle I was man on lyffe to lende,
  A-gaynste her fone I faught hem forne; 3211
now fynde I them my moste Frende:
  They blysse the tyme that I was borne;
They Asked leve with me to wende
  To mete with yow vpon thys morne. 3215

lords and ladies whom he had aided in life, and who are now his best friends.

[leaf 125, bk.]

(404)
A monthe day of trewse moste ye take
  And than to batayle be ye bayne;
yow comethe to helpe lancelot du lake,
  With many A man mykeH of mayne: 3219

Gawayne exhorts Arthur to conclude a month's truce with Mordred, saying that he will then have Lancelot's assistance.

[1] MS. chere.

The King proposes a truce to Mordred.

The king is greatly disturbed,

To-morne the batayle ye moste for-sake
    Or ellys, certis, ye shall be slayne."
The kynge gan woffully wepe and wake,
    And sayd: "Allas! thys Rewffull Rayne!"   3223

(405)

hastely hys clothys on hym he dyde,
    And to hys lordys gan he saye:

and tells his lords of what Gawayne's spirit had urged.

"In stronge sweyneys I haue bene stad,
    That glad I may not for no gamys gaye.   3227
We muste vnto syr mordred sende
    And founde to take An-other day,
Or trewly thys day I mon be shende,
    Thys know I in bed as I laye.   3231

(406)

He sends Sir Lucan de Boteler and others to propose a truce to Mordred.

Goo thow, syr lucan de boteler,
    That wyse wordys haste in wolde,
And loke that thou take with the here
    Bysshopys fele and barons bolde."   3235
Forthe went they All in fere,
    in trew bokys as it is tolde,
To syr mordred and hys lordis there they were,
    And an C knyghtis All vn-tolde.   3239

(407)

The knyghtis that ware of grete valoure,
    By-fore syr mordred as they stode,

They deliver the message,

They gretyn hym with grete honowre,
    As barons bold And hye of blode: 3243
"Ryght wele the gretys kynge Arthur,
    And praythe the with mylde mode,
A monethe day to stynte thys stoure,
    For hys loue that dyed on Rode."   3247

(408)

mordred, that was bothe kene And bolde,
    made hym breme As Any bore at bay,

but Mordred rejects the proposal.

And sware by Iudas that Ih*esus*[1] sold:
    "Suche sawes Ar not now to saye;   3251

---

[1] Ihc. *in MS., i. e. Jesus Christ.*

That he hathe hyght he shall it hold;
  The tone of vs shall dye thys day;
And telle hym trewly that I tolde,
  I schall hym marre, yife that I may."   3255

(409)

" Syr, thay sayd, with-owten lese,
  Thow3 thou And he to batayle bowne,
many A ryche shall rewe that reasse,
  By All by dalte vpon thys downe;   3259
yit were it better for to sease,
  And lette [hym] be kynge and bere the crowne;
And after hys dayes, full dredelesse,
  ye to welde All yngland, towre And towne." 3263

Arthur's messengers [leaf 126] then propose a cessation of war on the condition that Arthur should rule the rest of his life, but that Mordred should be his successor.

(410)

mordred tho stode stylle A whyle,
  And wrothely vp hys eyne there wente,
And sayd: "wyste I it were hys wylle
  To yeue me cornwale And kente,   3267
lette vs mete vpon yonder hylle
  And talke to-gedyr with gode entente;
Suche forwardys to full-fylle,
  There-to shall I me sone Assent.   3271

Mordred in reply says that he is willing to discuss terms, if Cornwall and Kent be ceded him,

(411)

And yiffe we may with spechys spede,
  With trew trowthes of entayle,
hold the bode-worde that we bede,
  To yeue me kente And cornwayle,   3275
Trew loue shall ther lenge And lende;
  And, sertis, forwardys yif we fayle,
Aythur to sterte vppon A stede,
  styffely for to do batayle."   3279

but that, if these terms are violated, the war will be renewed.

(412)

"Sur, wyll ye come in suche maner,
  With xij knyghtis or fourtene,
Or ellys All your strenghe in fere,
  With helmes bryght And hauberkys shene?"   3283

Arthur's knights wish to arrange about the meeting for the discussion of terms.

The King and Mordred prepare to come together.

Mordred says that it must take place between the armies, with the hosts near at hand.

"Se[r]tys, nay," than sayd he thore,
 "Othur warke thou thare not wene,
But bothe oure hoostis shall nyghe nere
 And we shalle talke them by-twene." 3287

(413)

Arthur's messengers return to him and report what Mordred has said.

They toke ther leue, with-owten lese,
 And wyghtely vpon there way wente;
To kynge Arthur the way they chese,
 there that he satte with-in hys tente. 3291
"Syr, we haue proferyd pease,
 Yiffe ye wille ther-to Assente:
Gyffe hym the crowne After your dayes
 And in yower lyffe cornwayle and kente; 3295

(414)

To hys by-heste yiffe ye will holde,
 And your trouthe trewly ther-to plyght,
maketh All redy your men bolde,
 With helme, swerd And hauberke bryght; 3299
ye schall mete vppon yone molde
 That ayther oste may se with syght;

[leaf 126, bk.] And yiff your foreward fayle to holde,[1]
 There is no bote but for to fyght." 3303

(415)

Arthur gets ready for the meeting with all his host,

But whan Arthur herd thys nevyn,
 Trewly ther-to he hathe sworne,
And Arayed hym with batayles seuyn,
 With brode baners by-fore hym borne; 3307
They lemyd lyght As Any leuyn[2]
 Whan they shold mete vpon the morne.
There lyves no man vndyr heuyn
 A feyrer syght hath sene by-forne. 3311

(416)

but Mordred has twelve men to every one of Arthur's.

But mordred many men had mo;
 So mordred that was mykell of mayne,
he had euyr xij A-gaynste hym two
 Off barons bold to batayle bayne. 3315

---
[1] Jhu merc *at top of* leaf 126, back.
[2] MS. lemyn.

At the meeting an accident causes a misunderstanding. 101

Arthur And mordred—bothe were thro—
  Shuld mete bothe vpon A playne;
The wyse shuld come to And fro
  To make A-cord, the sothe to sayne.   3319

(417)

Arthur in hys herte hathe Caste
  And to hys lordis gan he saye:
"To yonder traytour haue I no truste
  But that he woll vs falselly be-traye,   3323
yiff we may not oure forwardys faste.
  And ye se any wepyn drayne,
presythe forthe As princes praste,
  That he & All hys hoste be slayne."   3327

Arthur tells his lords that he distrusts Mordred, and that at the least sign of treachery they must attack their enemies vigorously.

(418)

mordred, that was kene And thro,
  hys frely folke he sayd to-forne:
"I wote that Arthur is full woo
  That he hathe thus hys landys lorne;   3331
With fourtene knyghtis And no mo
  shall we mete at yondyr thorne;
yiff Any treason by-twene vs go,
  That brode baners forth be borne."   3335

Mordred expresses the same distrust of Arthur, and gives his men the same directions.

(419)

Arthur with knyghtis fully xiiij,
  To that thorne on fote they fonde,
With helme, sheld, And hauberke shene;
  Ryght so they trotted vppon þe grownde.   3339
But As they A-cordyd shulde haue bene,
  An Edder glode forth vpon the grownde;
he stange A knyght, that men myght sene
  That he was seke And full vn-sownde.   3343

Arthur, with fourteen knights, goes to the thorn-tree, where the meeting is to be, but, when they were approaching an agreement, it happened that an adder stung one of the knights,

(420)

Owte he brayed with a swerd bryght;
  To kylle the Adder had he thogh[t]e;
Whan Arthur party saw that syght,
  Frely they to-gedyr sought;   3347

who drew his sword to kill it.

Arthur's men suspect treachery at once,

The two parties engage in battle.

[leaf 127] There was no-thynge with-stande theym myght;
　　They wend that treson had bene wroghte.
That day dyed many A doughty knyght,
　　And many A bolde man was broght to noght.　3351

(421)

and the two parties assail each other.
Arthur stert vpon hys stede;
　　he saw no thyng hym with-stand myght;
mordred owte of wytte nere yede,
　　And wrothely in-to hys sadyll he lyght;　3355
Off A-corde was no-thyng to bede,
　　But fewtred sperys and to-geder sprente;
Full many A doughty man of dede
　　Sone there was leyde vpon the bente.　3359

(422)

mordred I-maryd many A man,
　　And boldely he gan hys batayle abyde;
So sternely oute hys stede Ranne,
　　many A rowte he gan throw Ryde;　3363
Arthur of batayle neuyr blanne
　　To dele woundys wykke and wyde;
The battle lasted all day,
Fro the morow that it by-ganne
　　Tylle it was nere the nyghtis tyde,　3367

(423)

There was many A spere spente,
　　And many A thro word they spake;
many A bronde was bowyd and bente
　　And many A knyghtis helme they brake;　3371
Ryche helmes they Roffe and rente;
　　The Ryche rowtes gan to-gedyr Rayke,
and a hundred thousand men were engaged in it.
An [1] C thousand vpon the bente;
　　The boldest or evyn was made Ryght meke.　3375

(424)

Sythe bretayne owte of troy was sought
　　And made in bretayne hys owne wonne,
Suche wondrys neuyr ere was wroght,
　　Neuyr yit vnder the sonne;　3379

[1] MS. And.

By evyn leuyd was there noght
   That euyr steryd wit*h* blode or bone
But Arthur and ij that he thedyr broghte,
   And mordred was levyd there Alone.   3383

By evening the only survivors were Arthur, with two of his men, and Mordred.

(425)

The tone was lucan de botelere,
   That bled at many A bale-full wound,
And hys brodyr, syr bedwere,
   Was sely seke and sore vnsounde.   3387
Than spake Arthur these wordys there :
   " Shall we not brynge thys theffe to ground ? "
A spere he gryped wit*h* fell chere,
   And felly they gan to-gedyr found.   3391

The companions of Arthur who survived were Sir Lucan de Botelere and Sir Bedwere, and both were wounded.

Arthur assails Mordred

(426)

he hytte mordred amydde the breste
   And oute At the bakke bone hym bare ;
There hathe mordred hys lyffe loste,
   That speche spake he neuyr mare ;   3395
But kenely vp hys Arme he caste
   And yaff' Arthur A wound sare,
In-to the hede throw the helme And creste,
   That iij tymes he swownyd thare.   3399

and slays him, [leaf 127, bk.] *but Arthur is himself so sorely wounded by Mordred that he swoons thrice.*

(427)

Syr lucan And syr Bedwere
   By-twene theym two the kynge vp-held ;
So forthe went tho iij in fere,
   And All were slayne that lay in feld.   3403
The doughty kynge that was hem dere,
   For sore myght not hym-self weld ;
To A chapelle they went in fere—
   Off' bote they saw no better beld.   3407

Sir Lucan and Sir Bedwere take the king to a chapel,

(428)

All nyght thay in the chapelle laye,
   Be the see syde, As I yow newyn,
To mary mercy cryand aye,
   Wit*h* drery herte and sorowfull stevyn ;   3311

and there they lay all night praying for Arthur.

And to hyr leue sonne gan they pray:
"Ihesu, for thy namys sevyn,
Wis hys sowle the Ryght way,
That he lese not the blysse of heuyn." 3415

(429)

Sir Lucan de Boteler observes people robbing the dead on the field of battle,

As syr lucan de boleter stode,
he sey folk vppon playnes hye;
Bold barons of bone and blode,
They Refte¹ theym besaunt, broche, and bee; 3419
And to the kynge Agayne thay yode,
Hym to warne with wordys slee; 3421
[. . . . . 3421 b
. . . . . no gap in the MS.] 3421 c

(430)

To the kynge spake he full styll,
Rewffully as he myght than Rowne:
"Sir, I haue bene At yone hylle,
There fele folke drawen to the downe; 3425
I note whedyr they wyll vs good or ylle,
I rede we buske And make vs bowne,

and he urges the king to go elsewhere.

yiff it be your worthy wylle,
That we wende to som towne." 3429

(431)

The king bids Sir Lucan lift him up,

"Now, syr lucan, As thow Radde,
lyfte me vp, whyle that I may laste."
Bothe hys Armes on hym he sprad
With All hys strengh to hold hym faste. 3433
The kynge was wondyd and for-bled
And swownyng on hym hys eyne he caste;

but his embrace kills Sir Lucan.

Syr lucan was hard by-stadde;
He held the kynge to hys owne herte braste. 3437

(432)

Whan the kynge had swounyd there,
By an Auter vp he stode;
Syr lucan, that was hym dere,

[leaf 128]

Lay dede and fomyd in the blode. 3441

¹ MS. Reste.

Hys bold brothyr, Sir Bedwere,   *Sir Bedwere*
  Full mykell mornyd in hys mode;   *mourns for his brother's*
For sorow he myȝte not nyghe hym nere,   *death.*
  But euyr wepyd As he were wode.   3445

(433)

The kynge tornyd hym there he stode,
  To syr Bedwere *with* wordys kene:
"Have Excalaber, my swerd[e] good;   *The king commands*
  A better brond was neuyr sene;   3449 *Bedwere to cast his good*
Go, Caste it in the salt flode   *sword, Excalaber,*
  And thou shalt se wonder, as I wene.   *into the sea and report*
hye the faste, for crosse on Rode,   *to him what happens.*
  And telle me what thou haste ther sene." 3453

(434)

The knyght was both hende and free,   *Sir Bedwere,*
  To save that swerd he was full glad,   *reflecting that it is a*
And thought "whethyr I better bee,   *pity to throw away the*
  yif neuyr man it After had;   3457   *sword,*
And I it caste in-to the see,
  Off mold was neuyr man so mad."
The swerd he hyd vndyr A tree,   *hides it under a tree,*
  And sayd: "syr, I ded as ye me bad." 3461 *but tells Arthur that he has done his bidding.*

(435)

"What saw thow there?" than sayd the kynge, *The king wishes to*
  "Telle me now, yif thow can."   *know what Sir Bedwere*
"Sertes, syr," he sayd, "nothynge   *saw, but when*
  But watres depe And wawes wanne." 3465 *he replies, "nothing but*
"A! now thou haste broke my byddynge!   *waters deep and waves*
  Why haste thou do so, thow false man? *wan," Arthur re-*
A-nother bode thou muste me brynge."   *proaches him and sends*
  Thanne careffully the knyght forthe Ranne 3469 *him forth again.*

(436)

And thought the swerd yit he wold hyde, *This time*
  And keste the scauberke in the flode. *Sir Bedwere casts the*
"yif Any Aventurs shall be-tyde,   *sheath into*
  There-by shall I se tokenys good." 3473 *the flood,*

In-to the see he lette the scauberke glyde;
A whyle on the land hee there stode,
and again reports to the king that he has fulfilled his command. Than to the kynge he wente that tyde,
And sayd: "syr, it is done, by the Rode." 3477

(437)

The king recognizes the false-hood and reproaches him a second time. "Saw thou Any wondres more?"
"Sertys, syr, I saw nought."
"A! false traytor," he sayd thore,
"Twyse thou haste me treson wroght; 3481
That shall thou rew sely sore;
And, be thou bold, it shal be bought."
The knyght than cryed: "lord, thyn ore!"
And to the swerd sone he sought. 3485

(438)

Sir Bedwere now goes a third time and throws the sword into the sea. [leaf 128, bk.] Syr bedwere saw that bote was beste,
And to the good swerd he wente;
In-to the see he hyt keste;
Than myght he se what that it mente. 3489
A hand comes up out of the water, seizes the sword, brandishes it and disappears. There cam An hand with-outen Reste
Oute of the water And feyre it hente,
And brandysshyd As it shuld braste,
And sythe, as gleme, A-way it glente. 3493

(439)

When Sir Bedwere tells the king of what he has seen, Arthur bids him help him to the strand. To the kynge A-gayne wente he thare,
And sayd: "leve syr, I saw An hand;
Oute of the water it cam All bare,
And thryse brandysshyd that Ryche brande." 3497
"helpe me sone that I ware there."
he lede hys lord vnto that stronde;
There they find a rich ship full of ladies, A ryche shyppe, with maste And ore,
Full of ladyes, there they fonde. 3501

(440)

The ladyes, that were feyre and free,
who receive the king, one of them, who calls him "brother," weeping sorely. Curteysly the kynge gan they fonge,
And one that bryghtest was of blee
wepyd sore and handys wrange. 3505

"Broder," she sayd, "wo ys me!
  Fro lechyng hastow be to longe.
I wote that gretely greuyth me,
  For thy paynes Ar full stronge." 3509

(441)

The knyght kest A rewfull rowne,
  There he stode, sore and vnsownde,
And say[dc]: "lord, whedyr Ar ye bowne?
  Allas! whedyr wyll ye fro me fownde?" 3513
The kynge spake with A sory sowne:
  "I wylle wende a lytell stownde
In-to the vale of Avelovne,
  A whyle to hele me of my wounde." 3517

When Sir Bedwere asks the king whither is he bound, he replies that he will go a little while to the vale of Aveloune to be healed of his wound.

(442)

Whan the shyppe from the land was broght,
  Syr bedwere saw of hem no more;
Throw the forest forthe he soughte,
  On hyllys and holtys hore. 3521
Of hys lyffe Rought he Ryght noght,
  All nyght he went wepynge sore;
A-gaynste the day he fownde ther wrought
  A chapelle by-twene ij holtes hore. 3525

The ship disappears, and Bedwere goes through the forest in great sorrow.

Towards daylight he comes upon a chapel,

(443)

To the chapell he toke the way;
  There myght he se A woundyr syght;
Than saw he where an ermyte laye
  By-fore A tombe that new was dyghte; 3529
And coveryd it was with marboll graye
  And with Ryche lettres Rayled Aryght;
There-on An herse, sothely to saye,
  With an C tappers lyghte. 3533

where he finds a hermit lying before a new tomb, lighted up with a hundred tapers.

(444)

vnto the ermyte wente he thare
  And Askyd who was beryed there.
The ermyte Answeryd swythe yare:
  "There-of can I tell no more. 3537

He asks the hermit who is buried there,

[leaf 129]

but the hermit only knows that the body in the tomb was brought there about midnight by ladies,

A-bowte mydnyght were ladyes here,
 In world ne wyste I what they were;
Thys body they broght vppon a bere
 And beryed it with woundys sore;   3541

(445)

who offered him a hundred pounds and bad him pray for the dead man to Our Lady.

Besavntis offred they here bryght,
 I hope an C povnd and more,
And bad me pray bothe day and nyght
 For hym that is buryed in these moldys hore   3545
Vnto ower lady bothe day And nyght,
 That she hys sowle helpe sholde."
The knyght redde the lettres A-ryght;
 For sorow he fell vn-to the folde.   3549

(446)

Sir Bedwere reads the letters on the tomb and exclaims that it is Arthur.

"Ermyte," he sayd, "with-oute lesynge,
 here lyeth my lord that I haue lorne,
Bold arthur, the beste kynge
 That euyr was in bretayne borne.   3553

He begs the hermit to let him live with him as a hermit also.

yif me som of thy clothynge,
 For hym that bare the crowne of thorne,
And leue that I may with the lenge,
 Whyle I may leve, And pray hym forne."   3557

(447)

It turns out that the hermit is the Archbishop of Canterbury whom Mordred drove away.

The holy ermyte wold not wounde—
 Some tyme Archebishop he was,
That mordred flemyd oute of londe,
 And in the wode hys wonnyng chase—   3561
he thankyd Ihesu All of his sound
 That syr bedwere was comyn in pease;

He receives Sir Bedwere gladly.

he resayved hym with herte And honde,
 To-gedyr to dwelle, with-outen lese.   3565

(448)

When the queen hears of all these misfortunes, she goes to Amesbury to become a nun.

Whan quene Gaynor, the kynges wyffe,
 Wyste that All was gone to wrake,
A-way she went with ladys fyve
 To Avmysbery, A nonne hyr for to make.   3569

Ther-in she lyvėd An holy lyffe,
  In prayers for to wepe And wake;
neuyr After she cowde be blythe;
  There weryd she clothys whyte And blake. 3573

(449)

Whan thys tydyng*is* was to launcelot broght,   Lancelot,
  What wondyr thowgh hys hert were sore!   in the mean-
hys men, hys frendys, to hym sought   while, had set
                                                out to help
  And A‍ll the wyse that w*ith* hym were. 3577 Arthur.
her gallayes were A‍ll Redy wroght,
  They buskyd theyme And made yare;
To helpe Arthur was ther thoght
  And make mordred of blysse fu‍ll bare. 3581

(450)

lancelot had crownyd kyng*is* sevyn,
  Erlys fele And barons bold;   [leaf 129, bk.]
The nombyr of knyght*is* I can not nevyn,
  The squyres to fele to be told;   3585
They lemyd lyght as Any levyn¹
  The wynde was as hem-self wold,
Throw the grace of god of' hevyn;
  At douer they toke hauyn And hold; 3589 When he
                                           reaches
                                           Dover,
(451)

There herd telle lancelot in that towne,   he hears all
  In lond it is not for to layne,   about the
how they had faught at barendowne,   war and the
                                               final battle at
  And how beryed was s*yr* gawayne, 3593   Salisbury.
And how mordred wold be kynge w*ith* crowne,
  And how ayther of theym had other slayn,
And All that were to batayle bowne
  At salysbery lay dede vpon the playne; 3597

(452)

Also in londe herd hyt kythe,   He hears,
  That made hys hert wonder sare,   moreover,
                                               that the
quene Gayno*ur*, the kyng*is* wyffe,   queen with
                                               five ladies
                                               has gone no
  Myche had levyd in sorow and care; 3601   one knows
                                               where.

¹ MS. leme.

A-way she went wit/h ladyes fyve,
  In lond they wyste not whedyr whar,
Dolwyn dede or to be on lyve;
  That made hys mornyng moche the mare.   3605

(453)

Lancelot tells his lords that he is going away and that they must wait for him fifteen days.

lancelot clepid hys kyng*is* wit/h crowne,
  Syr bors stode hym nere be-syde;
he sayd: "lordyng*is*, I wyH wend to-forne,
  And by these bankys ye shaH A-byde   3609
Vnto fyftene dayes at the morne.
  In lond what so euyr vs be-tyde,
To herkyn what lord hys lyffe hathe lorne,
  loke ye Rappe yow not vp to Ryde."   3613

(454)

There had he nouther Roo ne Reste,
  But forthe he went wit/h drery mode,

For three days he went westward,

And iij dayes he went euyn weste,
  As man that cowde nother yveH nor good;   3617
Than syghe he where A towre by weste
  Was byggyd by A burnys flode;
There he hopyd it were beste
  For to gete hym som lyves stode.   3621

(455)

till by chance he came to the nunnery where the queen was.

As he cam throw A cloyster clere—
  AH-moste for wepynge he was mad—
he see A lady bryght of lere,
  In nonnys clothyng was she clad.   3625

The queen swoons at the sight of him, and has to be taken to her chamber.

Thryse she swownyd swyftely there,
  So stronge paynes she was in stad
That many A man[1] than) nyghed hyr nere,
  And to hyr chambyr was she ladde.   3629

(456)

The nuns do not understand the queen's trouble; [leaf 130]

"Mercy, madame," they sayd AH,
  For Ihesu, that is kynge of blysse,
Is there Any byrd in boure or halle
  hathe wrathed yow?" she sayd: "nay, I-wysse." 3633

[1] nonne?

The Queen implores Lancelot to return to his kingdom. 111

lancelot to hyr gan they calle,
   The Abbes and the other nonnys I-wysse,
They that wonyd wit*h*-in the walle;
   In covnselle there than sayd she[1] thus: 3637

they ca Lancelot before her, however,

(457)

"Abbes, to you I knowlache here
   That throw thys ylke man And me,
For we to-gedyr han loved vs dere,
   All thys sorowfull werre hathe be;   3641
my lord is slayne, that had no pere,
   And many A doughty knyght And free;
There-fore for sorowe I dyed nere,
   As sone As I euyr hym gan see—   3645

and she tells the abbess and the other nuns that she and this man have been the cause of all the war,

(458)

Whan I hym see, the sothe to say,
   All my herte by-gan to colde,
That euyr I shuld A-byde thys day,
   To se so many barons bolde   3649
Shuld for vs be slayne A-way;
   Oure wylle hathe be to sore bought sold;
But god, that All myght*is* maye,
   Now hathe me sette where I wyll hold;   3653

but that now she has no thought except for the salvation of her soul.

(459)

I-sette I am In suche A place,
   my sowle hele I wyll A-byde,
Telle god send me som grace,
   Throw mercy of' hys woundys wyde   3657
That I may do so in thys place
   my synnys to A-mende thys ilke tyde,
After to haue A syght of' hys face
   At domys day on hys Ryght syde.   3661

(460)

There-fore, syr lancelot du lake,
   For my loue now I the pray,
my company thow Aye for-sake
   And to thy kyngdome thow take thy way;   3665

She accordingly begs Lancelot to leave her for ever, and return to his kingdom

[1] MS. they.

And kepe thy Reme from werre and wrake,
And take A wyffe with her to play,
And loue wele than thy worldys make,
God yiffⁱ yow Ioye to-gedyr, I pray! 3669

(461)
Vnto god I pray, All-myghty kynge,
he yeffe yow to-gedyr Ioye And blysse,
But I be[se]che the in All thynge
That newyr in thy lyffe After thysse 3673
Ne come to me for no sokerynge,
Nor send me sond, but dwelle in blysse;
I pray to god euyr lastynge
To¹ Graunte me grace to mend my mysse." 3677

(462)
"Now, swete madame, that wold I not doo,
To haue All the world vnto my mede²;
So vntrew fynd ye me neuyr mo;
It for to do cryste me for-bede! 3681

(463)
For-bede it god that euyr I shold
A-gaynste yow worche so grete vnryght,
Syne we to-gedyr vpon thys mold
haue led owre lyffe by day And nyght! 3685
Vnto god I yiffe a heste to holde,
The same desteny that yow is dyghte
I will Resseyve in som house bolde,
To plese here-After god All-myght; 3689

(464)
To please god All that I maye
I shall here-After do myne entente,
And euyr for yow specyAlly pray,
While god wyll me lyffe lente." 3693
"A! wylte thow so," the quene gan say,
"Full-fyll thys forward that thou has ment?"
lancelot sayd: "yiffⁱ I sayd nay,
I were wele worthy to be brent; 3697

---
¹ *From the top of leaf* 130, *back, to the end the initial letter of each line is stained with red.*
² MS. mode.

The parting of Lancelot and the Queen.

(465)

Brent to bene worthy I were,
  Yiff⁼ I wold take non suche A lyffe,
To byde in penance, as ye do here,
  And suffre for god sorow and stryffe ;   3701
As we in lykynge lyffed in fere,
  By mary moder, made and wyffe,
Tyll god vs departe with dethes dere,
  To penance I yeld me here As blythe.   3705

Lancelot declares that he is going to lead a life of penance as a hermit.

(466)

All blyve to penance I wyll me take
  As I may fynde Any ermyte
That wyll me Resseyue for goddys sake,
  me to clothe with whyte And blake."   3709
The sorow that the tone to the tother gan make
  myght none erthely man se hytte.
" madame," than sayd launcelot de lake,
  " kysse me, And I shall wende as-tyte."   3713

At parting Lancelot wishes to kiss the queen,

(467)

" nay," sayd the quene, " that wyll I not ;
  launcelot, thynke on that no more ;
To Absteyne vs we muste haue thought,
  For suche we haue delyted in ore ;   3717
lett vs thynk on hym that vs hathe bought
  And we shall please god ther-fore ;
Thynke on thys world how there is noght
  But warre And stryffe And batayle sore."   3721

but she says that they must abstain now and think only of God and the troubles of the world.

(468)

What helpeth lenger for to spelle ?
  With that they gan departe in twene,
But none erthely man covde telle
  The sorow that there by-gan to bene ;   3725
Wryngyng ther handis and lowde they yelle,
  As they neuyr more shuld blynne,
And sythe in swonne bothe downe they felle ;
  Who saw that sorow euyr myght it mene.   3729

[leaf 131] Lancelot and the queen part in great sorrow,

(469)

<small>and the attendants of each try to comfort them.</small>

But ladyes than with mornyng chere,
   In-to the chambyr the quene they bare,
And All full besy made theym there
   To cover the quene of hyr care.   3733
many Also that with lancelot were,
   They comforte hym w[ith] rewfull care;
Whan he was coveryd, he toke hys gere
   And went frome thense with-outen mare;   3737

(470)

<small>Lancelot hastens away to a forest,</small>

hys hert was hevy As Any lede,
   And leuer he was hys lyffe haue lorne;
he sayd: "Ryghtwosse god! what is my Rede?
   Allas! for-bare, why was I borne?"   3741
A-way he went, as he had fled,
   To A foreste that was hym by-forne;
hys lyffe fayne he wold haue leuyd;
   hys Ryche A-tyre he wold haue of-torne.   3745

(471)

All nyght gan he wepe And wrynge
   And went A-boute As he were wode;

<small>in which at dawn he comes upon a chapel where a priest is about to hold mass.</small>

Erely, As the day gan sprynge,
   Tho syghe he where A chapell stode;   3749
A belle herd he rewfully Rynge;
   he hyed hym than And thedyr yode;
A preste was Redy for to synge,
   And masse he herd with drery mode.   3753

(472)

<small>It is the Archbishop of Canterbury who is singing mass, and Sir Bedwere is there.</small>

The Arshebysshoppe was ermyte thare,
   That flemyd was for hys werkys trew;
The masse he sange with syghyng sare,
   And ofte he changyd hyde and hewe;   3757
Syr bedwere had sorow And care
   And ofte mornyd for tho werkys newe;

<small>They recognise each other.</small>

Aftyr masse was morny[n]ge mare,
   Whan Iche of hem othyr knewe.   3761

(473)

Whan the sorow was to the ende,
  The byshope toke hys obbyte thare,
And welcomyd launcelot as the hend,
  And on hys knees downe gan he fare: 3765
"Syr, ye be welcome as oure frende
  Vnto thys byggying in bankys bare;
Were it yower wyll with vs to lende
  Thys one nyght, yif¹ ye may [no] mare!" 3769

The archbishop welcomes Lancelot, [leaf 131, bk.]

(474)

Whan they hym knew at the laste,
  Feyre in Armys they gan hym folde,
And sythe he askyd frely faste
  Off¹ Arthur And of other bolde; 3773
An C tymes hys hert ne[re] braste,
  Whyle syr Bedwere the tale told.
To Arthur-is tombe he caste,
  Hys carefull corage wexid All cold; 3777

who is filled with sorrow when Sir Bedwere tells him of Arthur's end.

(475)

He threw hys armys to the walle,
  That Ryche were and bryght of blee;
By-fore the e[r]myte he gan downe falle,
  And comely knelyd vpon hys knee; 3781
Than he shrove hym of¹ hys synnes Alle
  And prayd he myght hys broder be,
To serue god in boure and halle,
  That myght-full kynge of¹ mercy free. 3785

Lancelot is shriven of his sins, and begs the archbishop to accept him as a brother-hermit.

(476)

That holy bisshope nold not blynne,
  But blythe was to do hys boone;
He resseyuyd hym with wele and wynne
  And thankyd Ihesu trew in trone, 3789
And shroffe hym ther of hys synne,
  As clene as he had neuyr done none;
And sythe he kyste hym cheke and chynne
  And an Abbyte there dyd hym vpon. 3793

The archbishop gladly consents, and puts an appropriate habit on him.

(477)

All this time Lancelot's host lay at Dover, expecting his return. Finally with fifty lords Lyonell goes in search of Lancelot, but is slain at London.

hys grete hooste at dover laye,
   And wende he shuld have comyn A-gayne,
Tylle After by-felle vpon A day,
   Syr lyonell, that was mekyll of mayne, 3797
With fyffty lordys, the sothe to saye,
   To seche hys lord he was full fayne ;
To london he toke the Ryght way ;
   Alas for woo ! there was he slayne. 3801

(478)

Bors despatches Lancelot's host home, and goes also in search of his lord.

Bors De gawnes wold no lenger Abyde,
   But buskyd hym And made All bowne,
And bad All the oste homeward Ryde—
   God send theym wynd and wedyr Rownd— 3805
To seke lancelot wyll he Ryde.

He and Ector go different ways.

Ector and eche dywerse wayes yode,
   And bors sowght forthe the weste syde,

[leaf 132]

   As he that cowde nowther yvell nor gode. 3809

(479)

Full Erly in A morow tyde
   In A foreste he fownd A welle ;
he Rode euyr forthe by the Ryver syde,

Bors comes to the chapel, and wishing to hear mass there finds Lancelot.

   Tyll he had syght of A chapelle ; 3813
There at masse thought he A-byde ;
   Rewfully he herd A belle Rynge ;
Ther lancelot he fand with mekelle pryde
   And prayd he myght with hym there dwelle. 3817

(480)

In the space of half-a-year seven of the friends had gathered together at this chapel.

Or the halfe yere were comen to the ende,
   There was comyn of there felowse sevyn,
Where ychone had sought there frend,
   With sorowfull herte And drery stevyn ; 3821
had neuyr none wyll A-way to wend,
   Whan they herd of launcelot nevyn,
But All to-gedyr there gan they lend,
   As it was goddys wyll of heuyn. 3825

(481)

holyche Aƚƚ tho sevyn yerys
   lancelot was preste and masse songe;
In penance and in dyverse prayers
   That lyffe hym thought no-thyng longe;   3829
Syr bors And hys other ferys
   On bokys Redde and bellys Ronge;
So lyteƚƚ they wexe of lyn And lerys,
   Theym to know it was stronge.   3833

For seven years they all led a life of penance and prayer,

until they were so thin that one could scarcely recognise them.

(482)

hytte felle A-gayne an euyn-tyde
   That launcelot sekenyd sely sare;
The bysshop he clepyd to his syde
   And Aƚƚ hys felaws lesse and mare;   3837
he sayd: "bretherne, I may no lenger A-byde,
   my baleffuƚƚ blode of lyffe is bare;
What bote is it to hele And hyde?
   my fowle flesshe wiƚƚ to erthe fare.   3841

At last Lancelot falls sick,

and tells his companions that he is about to die.

(483)

but, bretherne, I pray yow to-nyght,
   To-morow, whan ye fynde me dede,
vpon A bere that ye wyƚƚ me dyght
   And to Ioyes garde than me lede;   3845
For the loue of god Aƚƚ-myght,
   Bery my body in that stede;
Some tyme my trowthe ther-to I plyght,
   Allas! me for-thynketh that I so dyd."   3849

He entreats them, when he is dead, to take his body back to Joyus Gard.

(484)

"mercy, *syr*," they Sayd Aƚƚ three,
   "for hys loue that dyed on Rode,
yif Any yveƚƚ haue greuyd the,
   hyt ys bot hevynesse of yower blode;   3853
To-morow ye shaƚƚ better be.
   Whan were ye but of comforte gode?"
merely spake Aƚƚ men but he,
   But streyght vnto hys bed he yode,   3857

They do not believe that he is so near death,

[leaf 132, bk.]

but he goes straight to his bed,

(485)

and gets the archbishop to come and shrive him.

And clepyd the bysshope hym vntylle,
 And shrove hym of^t hys synnes clene,
Off^t Aƚƚ hys synnes loude and stylle,
 And of^t hys synnes myche dyd he mene ;   3861
Ther he Resseyved with good wylle
 God, mary-is sonne, mayden clene.
Than bors of wepyng had neuyr hys fylle ;
 To bedde they yede than Aƚƚ by-dene.   3865

(486)

A little while before day the archbishop frightens every one by laughing in his sleep.

A lyteƚƚ whyle by-fore the day,
 As the bysshop lay in hys bed,
A laughter toke hym there he laye,
 That Aƚƚ they were Ryght sore A-dredt.   3869
They wakenyd hym, for sothe to saye,
 And Askyd yif he were hard by-sted.

He is sorry when they awaken him,

he sayd : "Allas And wele A-way !
 Why ne had I lenger thus be ledd ?   3873

(487)

Allas ! why nyghed ye me nye,
 To A-wake me in word or stevyn ?

and tells them that he has had a beautiful vision of an angelic host bearing Lancelot to heaven.

here was launcelot bryght of blee
 With Angellis xxx thousand and sevyn ;   3877
hym they bare vp on hye ;
 A-gaynste hym openyd the gatys of hevyn ;
Suche A syght Ryght now I see,
 Is none in erthe that myght it nevyn."   3881

(488)

They refuse to believe that Lancelot is dead,

"Syr," thay sayd, "for crosse on Rode,
 Dothe suche wordys clene A-way.
Syr lancelot eylythe no-thynge but gode ;
 he shaƚƚ be hole by pryme of day."   3885

but when they go to his bed, they find that he is.

Candeƚƚ they lyght And to hym yode,
 And fownde hym dede, for sothe to saye,
Rede and fayer of^t flesshe and blode,
 Ryght As he in slepynge laye.   3889

(489)

"Allas! syr bors, that I was borne!
  That euyr I shuld see thys in dede!
The beste knyght hys lyffe hathe lorne
  That euyr in stoure by-strode A stede.   3893
Ihesu that crownyd was with thorne,
  In heuyn hys soule foster and fede!"[1]
Vnto the fyfty day at the morne
  They lefte not for to synge And Rede,   3897

The archbishop laments Lancelot's death,

and they hold services for his soul,

(490)

And After they made theym A bere,
  The bysshop and these other bold,
And forthe they wente, All in fere
  To Ioyes garde, that Ryche hold.   3901
In A chapell a-myddys the quere
  A graue they made as thay wold,
And iij dayes they wakyd hym there,
  In the castell with carys cold.   3905

and afterwards they [leaf 133] bear the body to Joyus Gard, and bury it in a chapel there.

(491)

Ryght as they stode A-boute the bere
  And to bereynge hym sold haue browght,
In cam syr Ector, hys brodyr dere,
  That vij yere A-fore had hym sought.   3909
he lokyd vp in-to the quere;
  To here A masse than had he thought;
For that they All Ravysshyd were,
  They knew hym and he hem nought.   3913

Just as they were burying him, Ector, who had been looking for Lancelot for seven years, comes in.

No one recognises him at first.

(492)

Syr bors bothe wepte And songe,
  Whan they that feyre faste vnfold;
There was none but hys handys wrange,
  The bysshop nor none of the other bold.   3917
Syr Ector than thought longe;
  What thys corps was feyne wete he wolde;
An C tymes hys herte nye sprange,
  By that bors had hym the tale tolde.   3921

He inquires whose corpse it is, and his heart is almost broken when Bors tells him that it is Lancelot's.

---

[1] *In the MS. this line follows l. 3897.*

(493)

Full hendely s*yr* bors to hym spakke
  And sayd: "welcome, syr Ector, I-wysse;
here lyethe my lord lancelot du lake,
  for whome that we haue mornyd thus." 3925
Than In Armys they gan hym take,
  The dede body to clyppe And kysse,
And prayed All nyght he myght hym wake,
  For Ihe*s*u love, kynge of blysse. 3929

They all embrace Lancelot's dead body,

(494)

Syr Ector of hys wytte nere wente,
  Walowed and wronge as he were wode;
So wofully hys mone he mente,
  hys sorow myngyd All hys mode; 3933
Whan the corps in Armys he hente,
  The terys owte of hys yen yode;[1]
At the laste they myght no lenger stent,
  But beryed hym w*ith* drery mode. 3937

and Ector is almost crazed with grief.

At last the burial is completed,

(495)

Sythen on there knees they knelyd downe—
  Grete sorow it was to se w*ith* syght—
"Vnto Ihe*s*u cryste Aske I A boone,
  And to hys moder, mary bryght. 3941
lord, As thow madyste bothe sonne and mone,
  And god And man arte moste of myght,
Brynge thys sowle vnto thy trone,
  And euyr thow Rewdyste on gentyll knyght." 3945

and Lancelot's companions pray to Jesus Christ and his mother on behalf of the soul of their lord.

[leaf 133, bk.]

(496)

Syr Ector tent not to hys stede,
  Whedyr he wold stynt or Renne Away,
But w*ith* theym to dwelle and lede,
  For lancelot All hys lyffe to pray. 3949
On hym dyd he armytes wede,
  And to hyr chapell went hyr way;
A fourtenyght on fote they yede,
  Or they home come, for sothe to say. 3953

Ector also resolves to become a hermit,

and after a fortnight's journey they reach their chapel again.

---

[1] went *was written before* yode *and then struck out.*

The Queen dies and is buried by Arthur's side.

(497)

Whan they came to Avmysbery,
  Dede they faunde Gaynour the quene,
With Roddys feyre and Rede as chery;
  And forthe they bare hyr theym by-twene, 3957
And beryed hyr with masse full merry
  By syr Arthur, as I yow mene.
Now hyght there chapell glassynbery,
  An Abbay full Ryche, of order clene. 3961

When they come to Amesbury, they find the queen dead also.

They take her body to their chapel, which is now called Glastonbury,' and bury it by the side of Arthur.

(498)

Off lancelot du lake telle I no more,
  But thus by-leve these ermytes sevyn;
And yit is Arthur beryed thore,
  And quene Gaynour, as I yow nevyn; 3965
With monkes that ar Ryght of lore.
  They Rede and synge with mylde stevyn:
"Ihesu, that suffred woundes sore,
  Graunt vs All the blysse of hevyn!" 3969
    Amen.

Thus the seven companions remain there as hermits,

and pray with their monks that Jesus may grant them the bliss of heaven.

Explycit le morte Arthur.[1]

---

[1] Explycit le morte Arthur *is repeated in diffcrent ink, but apparently the same hand.*

NOTES.

1. *Lordingis.* This term is very commonly employed by the minstrels in addressing their audiences. That it did not necessarily imply noble birth on the part of those who are thus addressed is evident from passages like the Preamble of the 'Pardoner's Tale,' l. 329, where the Pardoner uses it in speaking to the Canterbury Pilgrims, or again 'Havelok,' l. 1401, where the hero addresses as "Louerdinges" the sons of the fisherman, Grim. In his note to 'Athelston,' l. 7 ('Englische Studien,' xiii, 345), Zupitza has brought together a great many instances of the occurrence of this term in the romances.

5. This uninflected genitive form recurs in l. 3346. On the other hand, we have the usual form *Arthurs*, l. 260. The alliterative 'Morte Arthure' (Thornton MS.) shows the same variation. So *Thus endys the emperour of Arthure hondes* (= by Arthur's hands), l. 2225, but *Me angers ernestly at Arthures knyghte3*, l. 2838. In Middle English generally the genitives of proper names often appear without an inflexional ending. So frequently in the case of the name of Philip of Macedon in the 'Wars of Alexander,' *e.g.* Alexander begins a letter : *I, kyng Philipp soñ þe ferce & hys fayre ladys*, l. 2415. Cp. the same poem ll. 2535, 2961, 4711. So also in the 'Destruction of Troy,' *Andromaca . . . . . Worthy Ector wyfe was a we faire*, ll. 3982 f. In this poem we have also *Agamynon* as a genitive, l. 5403. In the 'Holy Grail,' ch. xiii, l. 739, we have *And whanne kyng Ewalach steward this beheld . . . . To him ward Rod he A ful gret pas.* On this whole subject of uninflected genitives in Middle English see 'Anglia,' xxiv, pp. 211 f., and especially Paul's 'Grundriss der Germanischen Philologie,' i, pp. 1086 f. (2nd edition).

14. *For.* This is no doubt the preposition.

18. For a similar scene where Arthur and his consort, as they lie in bed together, discuss questions that concern the glory of the former, see the Latin romance 'De Ortu Waluuanii' ('Publications of the Modern Language Association of America,' xiii, 424). One may compare with these scenes the "bolster-conversation" between Ailell and Meave which begins the long train of incidents in the famous Irish epic of Táin Bó Cuailgne' (see the 'Cuchullin Saga in Irish Literature' by Eleanor Hull, London, 1898, pp. 111 ff.). It is under similar circumstances that Gornoille, the eldest daughter of King Lear, proposes to her husband in Layamon's 'Brut' (ll. 3285 ff.) that they should deprive the old king of a fourth of his knights. Cp. also the conversation between Darius and Atossa in Herodotus, Book iii, chap. 134.

36. *To dede of Armys for to Ryde* = by riding to deeds of arms. This construction seems to be repeated in l. 2123. Cp. 'Foure Sonnes of Aymon,' p. 60, *for ye knowe well the offence that your broder hadde doon to me, for to haue slayne soo cruelly Lohier.* For examples of the infinitive thus used as the gerund see Kellner's edition of Caxton's 'Blanchardyn and Eglantine' (E. E. T. S.), Introduction, p. 65.

63. *with the dede* = in the act, cp. l. 1747. Also 'Erl of Tolous,' l. 526 : *Thou schalt take us wyth the ded* ; 'Romaunt of the Rose,' l. 7634 : *That ye shulde take him with the dede* ; 'Octavian' (Southern version), l. 229 :   *For sche was founde with þe dede* ;

'Sir Tristrem,' l. 3182 :
> And Brengwain þretned ay
> To take hem in her dede.

79. *ya swithe that thou Armyde be.* Cp. ll. 211, 1573, 2550, 3335. Cp. 'Richard Coer de Lion,' ll. 3066 ff. :
> Takes a Sarezyne yonge and fat;
> In haste that the theff be slayn,
> Openyd and hys hyde off flayn.

Also ll. 3238, 3507. 'Seuyn Sages,' ll. 649 ff. :
> Goht he seigh to the prisone
> And fechcheth forht mine sone,
> And quik that he war an-honge
> On heghe galewes and on stronge.

Also l. 3974. 'Destruction of Troy,' ll. 3610 ff. :
> Þerfore wackon þi wille into wight dedis,
> And þere as sikyng & sorow slees the within
> Þat þe harme þat þou has and hethyng with all
> Pas noght vnponisshed for pité ne other.

'Emare,' ll. 1004 f. :
> And sayde : Lord, for þyn honour
> My worde þat þou wyll here.

Cp. moreover, 'Athelston,' l. 374, 'Libeaus Desconus,' l. 608, 'Sir Beues of Hamtoun,' l. 2286. In this construction a verb of wishing is, no doubt, to be understood. The influence of the French *que* + the subjunctive in expressing a wish or command is evident here.

99. *Wyth his shuldres gonne he fold.* See under *fold* (4) in the 'New English Dictionary' : " To bend, bow (oneself, the body, or limbs)" and the examples given in illustration, *e. g.* from the 'Cursor Mundi,' 8965 (Cott.) : *To þe tre sco can hir fold.* Cp. besides 'Octavian' (Lincoln MS. of the Northern version), ll. 891 ff. :
> The childe hym hitt one þe schuldir bone,
> That to þe pappe þe swerde gan gone,
> And þe geaunt to þe grounde gane folde.

The word is applied even to the heart in 'Sir Eglamour of Artois,' l. 726, in the sense of " sink."
> Of that worme when he had a syght
> Hys herte began to folde.

105. *The kinge stode on a toure on highte.* Cp. 'Sir Triamore,' l. 1420 : *high on a tower stood that good Ladye*; 'Generydes,' l. 2598 : *Clarionas was on the towre on hye*; 'Sir Beues,' l. 3357 : *Saber stod on is tour an hiȝ*—also ll. 3033 ff, 4082 ; 'Ipomedon,' B, l. 1897 : *The lady lay in an hye towre.*

110. *is not to hyde.* This formula is more frequent in this romance than in any other. Cp. 'Ipomedon,' A, ll. 3955 f. :
> Yesturday juste I here in white,
> To-day in rede, ys not to hyde ;

'Ywain and Gawain,' 806 f. :
> And soght him in þe maydens hall,
> In chambers high (es noght at hide);

'Octavian' (Lincoln MS. of the Northern version), l. 1277 : *In herde es noghte to hide.* This last formula is particularly common in 'Horn Childe,' cp. ll. 39, 57, 669, 751. For examples of this and kindred expressions (*ys not to layne*, etc.), see Breul's 'Sir Gowther,' pp. 175 f.

124   *Notes. Lines* 117–315.

117. *braundisshid yche a bone.* S. under *brandish* (l. c.) in 'N. E. D.' "To flourish about, move vigorously (the limbs, the head, etc.)." The verb is commoner used absolutely without direct object, and with the sense of "to swagger." Cp. 'Babees Book,' How the Good Wyfe taught her Daughter, 38 : *Braundische not with þin heed.*

165. *Sir, the semys a noble kn[i]ght.* Cp. 'Morte Arthure' (Lincoln MS.), l. 139 : *By lukynge withowttyn lesse, a lyon the semys.* 'Rowlande and Ottuell,' l. 862, *þam semes bothe felle and ferse.* 'Wars of Alexander,' l. 2000 : *Bot þaim semys to be softe, as þees sedis preuez*—also ll. 3036, 5399. It will be noticed that the construction is impersonal. For other curious impersonal constructions of the Middle English observe ' Libeaus Desconus ' (Cotton MS.), l. 566 : *þe ne askapeth so away* ; 'Ipomedon,' A, l. 5182 : *Sertus, syr, me owethe to wete.* For *seem* and *must* in the impersonal construction see L. Kellner, 'Englische Studien,' xviii, 287 f.

179. *hyr Rode was rede as blossom on brere.* Cp. 'Seege of Troye,' l. 1416 : *Here rode rede as blosom on the brere* ; 'King of Tars,' ll. 13 f. :
  Chaast heo was & feir of chere
  Wiþ rode red so blosme on brere.

'Syre Gawene and the Carle of Carelyle,' l. 367 : *Her roode was reede, her chek rounde.* 'Death and Liffe,' ll. 65 f. :
  shee was brighter of her blee then was the bright sonn,
  her rudd redder then the rose, that on the rise hangeth.

'Eger and Grine,' l. 217 : *her rud was red as rose in raine.* In the Northern version of 'Octavian' (Lincoln MS.), l. 41, we have *whyte so blossome on þe brere.* For the expressions *her rode was red* and *as bryȝt as blosme on brere,* see still further respectively Kaluza's note to 'Libeaus Desconus,' 938, and Zupitza's to 'Athelston,' 72.

190. *other mo.* Cf. 'Beues of Hamtoun,' l. 3410 : *Wel ten þosend oþer mo* ; 'Sir Eglamour of Artois,' l. 480 : *On us and odur moo* ; 'Seuyn Sages,' ll. 3645 :
  The steward wendes, the childe alswa,
  And with tham other many ma.

202. *For me ne giff the no thynge Ille.* See 821, 1324. Cp. 'Ysumbras,' l. 109 : *They wepede alle and gafe þam ill* ; ibid. 304 : *þe lady grete and gafe hir ill* ; 'Emare,' l. 778 : *Bothe they wepte and yaf hem ille* ; 'Octavian' (Lincoln MS. of the Northern version), l. 75 : *Gyffe ȝow no thynge ille.* For *give* in the sense of to "make account of," out of which the above formula has developed, see Zupitza, 'Guy of Warwick,' l. 4459.

266. *Breme as Any wilde bore.* The formula *breme as bore* is very frequent in this romance. Cp. 951, 1600, 2101, 2214, 2606, 3249. Cp. 'Cursor Mundi,' l. 4899 : *þe sargantz þat ware brem als bare.* 'Golagros and Gawane,' l. 822 : *He wourdis brym as ane bair* ; Malory's 'Morte Darthur,' p. 820 : *Soo vpon the morne there came syre Gawayne, as brym as ony bore.* Cp. also 'Ferumbras,' l. 545, 'Sege of Melayne,' l. 969, 'Romance of Duke Rowlande and of Sir Ottuell of Spayne,' l. 166. The expression is even found in sixteenth century English, 'Roister Doister,' iv, 6 : *Never bore so brymme nor tost so hot.*

315. *by them one two.* So 'Octavian' (Lincoln MS. of the Northern version), ll. 1347 ff. :
  Lady, we one two
  By þe reuer banke salle go
  That he may vs see.

Cp. also ' William of Palerne,' l. 1415 : *non knew here cunseile but þei þre one.* 'Morte Arthure' (Lincoln MS.), l. 3195 : *Alle the senatours are sette sere be thame one.* 'Wars of Alexander,' l. 755*: *And stighillys hym in som stede, by hym one.*

389. *For why þat* = provided that. This use is exceptional.

399. *What he had herd and sene with sight.* The second member of this clause has frequent parallels in our poem. So ll. 673, 1476, 1627, 1871, 2002, 2143, 2191, 3301. Cp. 'Ferumbras,' l. 193: *þat y so longe scholde lyue alas, to sen hit with my siȝte.* 'Sege of Melayne,' ll. 893 f.:

> *And a fayre oste of brede þer appon he fande*
> *þat euer he sawe with syghte.*

'Libeaus Desconus,' ll. 1447 ff.:

> *What? wenest þou fendes fere,*
> *Uncristened þat I were,*
> *Till I siȝ þe wiþ siȝt?*

402. *a folyd knight.* For the verb "to fool" in the intransitive sense see under *fool* (1) in the 'N. E. D.' "To be or become foolish or insane," and the examples, 'Cleanness,' l. 1422: *al waykned his wyt & wel neȝe he foles.* Barbour's 'Bruce' (Edinburgh MS.), iv, 222 f.:

> *Bot he fulyt, forouten weir,*
> *That gaf treuth to that creature.*

411. *hole and fere.* For examples of this phrase see Hall's note to 'King Horn,' l. 149.

426. For the uninflected genitive cp. 'Beues of Hamtoun,' l. 3193:

> *Sire, ȝhe seide to þat erl sone*
> *'Ich bidde, þow graunte me a bone.'*

For such uninflected genitives in the case of proper names and titles see note to l. 5, above. The want of inflection in such cases is due no doubt to the influence of the Old French uninflected genitive very largely.

480. "*Ector,*" *he sayd,* "*where thou it were,*
> *That woundid me thus wondir sore?*"

So ll. 3006, 3456. For *where* (= whether) introducing a direct question cp. 'Piers Plowman,' C. xvii, 336: "*Wher clerkus knowe hym nat*" quath ich "*that kepen holy churche?*"—also C. xx, 25. 'House of Fame,' iii, 1779 ff.:

> *What? false theves! wher ye wolde*
> *Be famous good, and nothing nolde*
> *Deserve why?*

'Syre Gawene and the Carle of Carlyle,' ll. 509 f.:

> *Uher I schaƚƚ se enny mor þis knyȝt*
> *That hathe ley my body so ner.*

Cp. also 'Wars of Alexander,' ll. 2910, 3810, 'Cleanness,' l. 717, 'York Plays,' xxi, 259:

486. *Syr lyonelle by god þan swore*
> *That myne wolle sene be ewyr more.*

For direct discourse introduced by *that* compare the 'Anglo-Saxon Gospel of St. John,' i, 32: *Johannes cydde gewitnesse cweðende þaet ic geseah nyðercumendne Gast of heofenum.* This construction is frequent in the Anglo-Saxon Gospels owing to the influence of the Latin original which derived it in turn from the Greek. See Gorrell, 'Publications of the Modern Language Association of America,' x, 350. Many examples for the French are given by Tobler in 'Vermischte Beiträge zur französischen Grammatik,' i, 218 ff., e. g. Robert de Clary's 'Prise de Constantinople,' 88: *et apres dist Agolanz que "se ma gent est vaincue, je prendre*

baptesme." The construction is not frequent in Middle English, but cp. 'Seuyn Sages,' ll. 3740 f.:
> *The yonger sais that " myne sho ys ;*
> *For I haue wond with hir alway."*

Caxton's 'Blanchardyn and Eglantine,' 184 : *He sayd full angerly to the styward that to an ewyll owre hath your lady ben so madde as to mary her self to a ladde.* Cp. Kellner's 'Introduction to Blanchardyn and Eglantine,' p. 90, and for the whole subject of abrupt changes from indirect to direct discourse in Middle English, ibid. 98 ff., and Zupitza's note to 'Guy of Warwick,' l. 1785.

556. *Sir yif that youre willis were.* Cp. Barbour's 'Bruce,' i, 618 : *Tharfor giff that ʒour willis wer*—also ibid. xix, 158. 'Towneley Plays,' xxii, 277 :
> *Dere lady, if thi will were,*
> *I must tell tythyngys playn.*

'Ipomedon,' B, l. 270 : *yff your wille be.* 'Richard Coer de Lion,' ll. 5234 ff. :
> *To Kyng Richard forth he wente*
> *And prayed, yiff his wylle be,*
> *Off batayle betwen thre.*

So 'Sir Emare,' l. 919 : 'Horn Childe,' l. 979 ; 'Seuyn Sages,' ll. 123, 133, etc.; 'Octavian' (Northern version, Lincoln MS.), l. 417. Cp. also Hall's note to 'King Horn,' l. 193.

589. *so thryve or thro.* Cp. 'Pearl,' ll. 867 ff. :
> *I seghe, says Iohan, þe loumbe hym stande,*
> *On þe mount of syon ful þryuen & þro.*

'Cursor Mundi,' ll. 14806 ff. :
> *fast es he throd and thriuen*
> *And mikel grace ai es him giuen ;*

'Destruction of Troy,' l. 6537 : *With þre thowsaund þro men þriuond in armys.*

595. *Be the coloures I it knew.* knew here is subjunctive.

651. *That nighe of witte she wold wede.* So ll. 787, 914. Cp. 'Octavian' (Northern version, Lincoln MS.), l. 1511 : *Of witt als he wolde wede.* 'Wars of Alexander,' l. 1410 : *Went wode of þaire witt.* For similar expressions see Hall's note to 'King Horn,' l. 1084.

657. *That wiste of hyr priuete.* Cp. 'Arthour and Merlin,' l. 12 :
> *For þai mo witen & se*
> *Miche of godes priuete.*

'Eger and Grine,' l. 362 : *shee shall know nothing of our priuitye.* 'Sir Eglamour of Artois,' l. 62 : *Ye haue tolde me yowre prevyte.* Handlyng Synne, ll. 397 f. :
> *And sum beyn goddys pryuyte*
> *Þat he shewyþ to warne þe.*

'Squyr of Lowe Degre,' ll. 511 f. :
> *He wende in the worlde none had bene*
> *That had knowen of his pryuite*

—also l. 990 ; cp. besides 'Wars of Alexander,' ll. 255, 2878, 3613.

751. *In clay tylle I be clongyn colde.* Cp. 'Hymns to the Virgin,' (E. E. T. S. 1867), l. 85 : *In coold clay now schal y clinge* ; Böddeker's 'Altenglische Dichtungen des MS. Harl. 2253,' p. 211 : *clingeþ so þe clai.*

764. *for crosse and Rode.* Cp. 'Athelston,' l. 169 : *Þanne swoor þe kyng be cros and roode.* The usual formula in our poem is *crosse on Rode.* So ll. 2576, 2880, 2928, 3112, 3452, 3882. This last is probably the

Notes. Lines 770–1083.

original form of the expression, in which case the word *crosse* would mean the horizontal cross-piece on the cross.

770. *Now haue good day, my lady fre.* This common formula of parting is illustrated by Hall in his note to 'King Horn,' ll. 727 f. For formulas of leave-taking in general see Kaluza to 'Libeaus Desconus,' l. 1051, and Kölbing to 'Ipomedon,' l. 298.

782. *Vp he worthis vppon his stede.* Cp. 'Sowdone of Babylone,' l. 1163 : *Thai worthed vp on here stedes*: 'Ipomedon,' B, l. 1489 : *Anon he worthyd vppon his stede.* 'Torrent of Portyngale,' ll. 627 f.:

*On he dyd hys harnes ageyne
And worthe on hys sted, serteyne.*

For expressions for mounting in general in Middle English see Zupitza, 'Athelston,' l. 381.

933. For the apparent inconsistency in the narrative here see Introduction under the head of Source, pp. xvii f.

983. *By-gynne wille auntres or aught yare.* *yare* here is the adverb = *quickly* as in 'King Horn,' ll. 468 f. :

*& tolde him ful ȝare
Hu he hadde ifare.*

991. *bayne* here of course does not mean "both," as Seyferth (p. 36) assumes, but "readily"—i. e. it is derived from O.N. *beinn*, not O.E. *bégen*.

1017. *Thinke ye not on this endris day.* Cp. l. 1105. See *ender* in 'N. E. D.' "Only in phrase, This ender day, night, year, indicating a day, etc., recently past." Cp. also the examples there given. 'Confessio Amantis,' v. 7400 f. :

*This ender day as I gan fare
To hunte vnto the grete hert.*

'Thomas of Erceldoune,' l. 25 (Thornton MS.) :

*I me went þis Endres daye
ffast on my way makyng my mone.*

'Guy of Warwick,' ll. 2827 f. :

*He slewe my lordys sone þe emperoure
Thys endurs day in a stowre.*

'Sir Lambewell,' l. 282 : *I shall die this yenders night.* 'Ipomedon,' B, ll. 849 f. :

*"I am" he sayd "þe strange squyere
That servyd my lady þis endris yere."*

1019. *Stode togedir in youre play.* As J. Hall has remarked ('K. Horn,' l. 32), the verb *to play* means usually to ride out by wood or water. The meaning of the noun often corresponds to this, but not in the present instance.

1063. Notice the concessive force of the infinitive clause here. Cp. note to l. 36.

1083. *Alle churlysshe maners he had in wone.* The word *wone* here means 'abundance.' Cp. 'Legend of Good Women,' ll. 1651 f. :

*Now hath Iasoun the flees and home is went
With Medea and tresor ful gret won.*

'Piers Plowman,' C. xxiii, 171 : *And gaf hym gold, good won.* 'Golagros and Gawane,' ll. 36 f. :

*And all thair vittalis war gone
That thay weildit in wone.*

'Richard Coer de Lion,' l. 5125 : *Off tresore they hadde so mekyl wonne.*
'Horn Childe,' ll. 778 f. :
> Þer Horn seiȝe þe mest þrang
> In he rides hem amang
> & lays on wel gode won.

'Seuyn Sages,' ll. 2817 ff. :
> The emperowre and his men ilkane
> Of the Sarezins slogh gode wane.

For other examples see Kittredge, 'Authorship of Romaunt of Rose,' p. 37. For the derivation of this word from Icelandic *ván* see Zupitza's note to 'Guy of Warwick,' l. 10329.

1093. *And was of blysse I-browghte Alle bare.* Cp. 'Libeaus Desconus,' l. 2088 : *Of bliss he was all bare.* 'Amis and Amiloun,' l. 2338 : *For me of blis þou art al bare.* 'Ipomedon,' A, l. 2204 : *Off blis I were full bare.* Cp. also 'Seuyn Sages,' 1788 ; 'Ferumbras,' 225 ; 'Sege of Melayne,' 198.

1134 f. *I sayde that hys bydyng bayne the dukys doughter of Ascolote was.* Cp. Horstmann's 'Nordenglische Legendensammlung, St. Andrew,' l. 117 : *To do his biding war þai bayne.* 'Turke and Gowin' (Percy Folio, i, 94) : *I will be att thy bidding baine* ; 'John de Reeve,' l. 504 (Percy Folio, ii, 578) : *att your bidding wee will be baine* ; 'York Plays,' xx, 284 : *And to þer bidding baynely bowe.* The spelling with one *d* is frequent in the York and Towneley Plays. Cp. 'Towneley Plays,' xx, 616 : *and bow to thi bydyng as bachlers shold.* So also xxii, 1.

1141. *dede is that white as swanne.* The phrase is used of the male sex as well. Cp. 'Seuyn Sages,' ll. 77 f. :
> The thrid maister was litel man,
> Fair of chere and white as swan.

'Octavian' (South English version), ll. 553 ff. :
> A tygre þey seye þer yn her dan,
> And a manchyld whyt as swan
> Sok of her as of a woman.

Examples of similar phrases are the following : 'Sir Triamore,' l. 649 : *shee was as white as lilye flower* (see also 'Le Morte Arthur,' 2994). 'Sir Degree,' ll. 15 f. :
> The King had no more Children but one,
> a daughter white as whales bone.

For a very full enumeration of such comparisons in the romances, see Hall's note to 'King Horn,' l. 15.

1144. *The quene was as wrothe as wynde.* For examples of this formula, cp. 'Piers Plowman,' C. iv, 486 : *As wroth as the wynd wex Mede therafter*, and so again 'Richard the Redeless,' iii, 153. 'Patience,' l. 410: *He wex as wroth as þe wynde towarde oure lorde.* Other examples are 'Sir Gawain and the Green Knight,' l. 318; 'Golagros and Gawane,' l. 770 ; 'Coventry Mysteries' (Prologue), p. 8. As will be observed, the formula was not Langland's property, as M. Jusserand seems to think (' L'Epopée mystique de William Langland,' p. 185).

1380. *Madame, how may thou to us take.* Here *take to* = betake oneself to, consult. Cp. 'Piers Plowman,' C. vii, 154 :
> And yf ich telle eny tales, thei taken hem to-geders
> And don me faste Fridaies to bred and to water,

where, however, the verb is reflexive.

1412. *yuelle haue I be-sette the dede.* Cp. 'Sir Triamore,' ll. 339 f. :
> Then waxed he wrath, I weene,
> & held his Iourney euill besett.

Notes. Lines 1537–1904.

'Octavian' (Northern version, Lincoln MS.), ll. 870 ff. :
> Now thynke me righte in my mode
> That þou hase wele bysett our gude.

1537. *here hertys worde* = the words they had spoken privily together.
1557. *hys visere ouer hys yȝen falle.* N. b. *falle* here is the preterite.
1576 f. *Also blythe As foule of day after the nyght.* Cp. 'Sir Degree,' ll. 802 ff. :
> & shee was glad to see that sight
> as euer the bird was of daylight.

'Octavian' (Northern version, Lincoln MS.), ll. 490 ff. :
> Als blythe were þay þane of þat syghte
> Als es þe foulles, whene it es lighte,
> Of þe dayes gleme.

'Beues of Hamtoun,' ll. 148 ff. :
> Gladder icham for þat sawe
> Þan þe fouel, whan hit ginneth dawe.

'Horn Childe,' ll. 754 ff. :
> & þan was Horn as fain o siȝt
> As is þe foule of þe liȝt,
> When it ginneth dawe.

Cp. also 'Genesis,' l. 16. Other examples are given by Kölbing, 'Beues of Hamtoun,' l. 148.

1644. *Thoughe syr mador myght not go ne Ryde.* Cp. 'Seuyn Sages,' ll. 3535 ff. :
> Nay, sertes, it sal noght be swa,
> Whils that I may ride and ga.

'Seege of Troye,' ll. 1223 f. :
> Shuld y, wheder I may go or ryde,
> Se my fader swyche shame betyde?

For other examples see Kittredge, 'Authorship of the English Romaunt of the Rose,' p. 17 (Boston, 1892).

1893. *the* = they. For this spelling of *they* cp. 'Destruction of Troy,' l. 4361: *And þe sun the saidon sothely a god.* 'Sir Iohn Butler' (Percy Folio MS.), l. 37: *thé sought that hall then vp and doune.* 'Young Cloudeslie,' Percy Folio MS., l. 399: "*bring her, for gods loue*" *said thé all.* The spelling is particularly common in Bishop Percy's Folio MS., but is found throughout Middle English. More surprising perhaps is the spelling *they* for the definite article *the*. This likewise is frequent in the Percy MS. Cp. 'Sir Degree,' ll. 105 f. :
> yett peradventure they time may come
> that I may speake with my owne sonne.

So ll. 25, 119. 'Eger and Grine,' l. 37: *they Ladye granted her good will.* 'Sir Triamore,' ll. 502 ff. :
> when they Lords were sett at meate, soone
> the grayhound into the hall runn
> amonge the knights gay.

Cp. also Louelich's 'Holy Grail,' chap. 35, l. 423 et passim.

1904. *Mordreit than toke A way full gayne.* Cp. 'William of Palerne,' l. 4189, *þe geynest gatis.* 'Rauf Coilȝear,' l. 201, *Quhair gangis thow, gedling, thir gaitis sa gane?* Lidgate, 'Thebes,' l. 2148 : *At a posterne forth they gonne to ride By a gein paþ.* Much commoner is the phrase *at þe gaynest* = by the shortest road possible. 'Morte Arthure' (Lincoln MS.), l. 3114 : *To þe cete vnsene thay soghte at þe gayneste.* 'Sir Gawayne and the Green Knight,' l. 1973: f[e]rk þurȝ þe fryth & fare at þe gaynest. For the parallel expressions, take the redy way, etc., see Zupitza, 'Guy of Warwick,' l. 10078, and Kölbing's 'Ipomedon,' l. 8731.

1957. *Be he had made a lytelle Rese.* Be as a conjunction = by the time that, is not recorded in Mätzner's ' Altenglisches Wörterbuch,' Stratmann-Bradley, or the 'N. E. D.' The above, however, is an evident example. Cp. also 'Sir Eglamour,' ll. 682 ff.:

   Be xij wekys were comyn and gone,
   Crystyabelle as whyte as fome,
   Alle pale was hur hewe.

'Towneley Plays,' xxi, 13 f.:

   Bot at last shall we be out of hart langing,
   Be thou haue had two or three hetys worth a hanging.

' Destruction of Troy,' l. 814: *By the renke hade hym restid ryses the sun.* 'Merline' (Percy Folio), ll. 2132 ff.: *& by they had rydden a stonde . . . he mett with Merlyn on the playne.* 'Wars of Alexander,' l. 3900: *Be þai had fyneschid þis fiȝt, was ferre in with euyn.* So also ll. 4437, 5163. For examples of *be þat* in the same sense cp. ' Lay le Freine,' l. 232. 'Octavian' (Northern version, Cambridge MS.), l. 1639.

1979. *Gaheriet hys brother is dede hym fro.* Similarly in 'York Plays,' xxxviii, ll. 189 ff.:

   My sorowe is all for þat sight
   Þat I gune see,
   Howe Criste my maistir, moste of myght,
   Is dede fro me.

Cp. likewise, 'York Plays,' vi, 6: *Þe joie of heuen þat thaym was lent is lost thaym froo.* Also in this romance, l. 654.

1992. *Gaheriet eyles noght but goode.* Cp. 'Triamour,' A, l. 909: *Me eylyth nothyng but gode.* 'Guy of Warwick,' B, 6184: *Tyrrye schall eyle noþyng but gode.* For other examples see Kölbing's note to 'Ipomedon,' 1215.

2104. *Rayses spere and gounfanoune.* Phrase often used to denote the beginning of an expedition or battle. Cp. ll. 2153, 2527. For *gounfanoune* cp. 'N. E. D.' "In the middle ages chiefly applied to the small flag or pennon suspended immediately beneath the steel head of a knight's lance"—also such examples as 'Sir Tristrem,' l. 173: *He bad his kniȝtes . . . Com Wiþ hors and wepenes fele And rered goinfaynoun.* 'Horn Childe,' ll. 65 f.:

   Alle were þai redi to fiȝt
   and rered gonfeynoun.

'Romaunt of the Rose,' l. 2018:

   I bere of Love the gonfanoun,
   Of curtesye the banere.

2108. *that Ryche towne.* Cp. 'Guy of Warwick,' B, l. 8317: *To Alysawndur he went, þe ryche towne.* For many examples of *riche cite,* etc. see Kölbing, 'Ipomedon,' l. 2031.

2133. *As we ne durste no man nyghe nere.* 'Sir Ferumbras,' l. 350, *þe knyȝt him neȝede þanne neer & spak til him þat tide.* 'Rowlande and Ottuell,' ll. 283 ff.:

   Lete Duke Naymes lenge at hame
   To kepe pareche walles fro schame
   Þat no gledes neghe þam nere.

'York Plays,' v. 36 ff.:

   For oure Lord god forbeedis vs itt,
   The frute þer of, Adam nor I,
   to neghe it nere.

'York Plays,' iii, 370: *Yei, water nyghys so nere that I sit not dry.*

2256. *Tylle ynglande he, the message, Come.* Here *messag e* = *messenger.* Cp. Chaucer's 'Tale of Melibee,' § 71: *And therfore I conseille that ye sende your messages, swiche as been discrete and wyse, unto your adversaries.* 'Troylus and Cryseyde,' ii, 936 f.: *Two or three of his messages yeden For Pandarus.*

2300. *Wemen Ar frele of hyr entayle. Entayle* meant originally *cut, form,* and then *quality*. So 'Richard Coer de Lion,' l. 5669: *An helme he hadde off ryche entayle.* 'Confessio Amantis,' l. 1087 ff.:

An Hors of Bras thei let do forge
That in this world was nevere man
That such an other werk began.

In the present passage the word means *nature, disposition.* Cp. 'Confessio Amantis,' i, ll. 1252 ff.:

Forthi, my Sone, of such entaile
If that thin herte be disposed,
Tell out and let it noght be glosed.

2338. *thar* here is impersonal. Cp. 'Wars of Alexander,' ll. 5377 ff.:

Þe thare bot graunt me to geue quat guds as I craue
And I sall prestly þat prince present into þi handis.

So also 'Destruction of Troy,' l. 2080.

2369. *Ichone A braunche of olyffe in hande.* For the olive branch as a sign of peace cp. 'Kyng Alisaunder,' ll. 1700 ff.:

Theose comen, hond by hond,
Tofore Alisaundre in Tirelond,
And eche with a braunche of olyve
That was tokenyng of pes and lyue.

'Sege of Melayne,' ll. 1213 ff.:

Þe Messangere bare a wande
Of ane Olefe in his hande
In takynnynge he come of pece.

'Generydes,' ll. 3144 ff.:

Anon these lordes went on ther message,
Eche man A braunche of Olyve in his hande
In token of pece for ther viage.

'Octavian' (Northern version, Lincoln MS.), ll. 1173 ff.:

For þat was þat tym messangere lawe
A braunche of olyue for to schewe
And it in hand to bere;
For the ordynaunce was so,
Messengerys schulde sauely come and go,
And no man do them dere.

2457. *Gremly teres lette they glyde.* Cp. l. 1512, 2083, 2457. For *glyde* in the sense of *fall* see 'Kynge Roberd of Cysille,' ll. 384 f.:

And thorow that worde y felle in pryde,
As the aungelle that can of hevyn glyde (= Lucifer).

'Sir Perceval of Galles,' ll. 2115 f.:

Righte there appone the faire molde
The ryng owte glade.

For other curious expressions for weeping cp. l. 1544: *The terys ranne on the kyngis kne.* 'Destruction of Troy,' l. 865: *Sho brast out bright water at hir brode een*; ibid. ll. 1286:

Pité of þat pert knight persit his hert
Þat the shire water shot ouer his shene chekys.

Also ibid. l. 3300. The expression above in l. 2457 does not appear among the expressions for weeping given by Zupitza, 'Athelston,' l. 275, and Breul, 'Sir Gowther,' l. 228.

2537. N. b. the omission of the subject. Similarly in l. 3598. Cp. also 'Seege of Troy,' ll. 1469 ff.:
> Now shull ye here of Achilles:
> Whenne of bed arysyn was
> Toward the batayle he came rydyng.

'Beues of Hamtoun,' ll. 829 f.:
> Þanne a sette horn to mouþe
> And blew þe pris ase wel kouþe.

'Sir Ferumbras,' l. 222:
> By-þenk þe how þy blod ys schad & hast a grislich wounde.

Cp. P. de Reul's 'Language of Caxton's Reynard the Fox' (Ghent, 1901), pp. 30 f. for instances of the same thing. For omission of the subject in Old English see A. Pogatscher, 'Anglia,' xxiii, 261 ff.

2575. *That longe wylle not droupe And dare.* Cp. L. Minot's 'Poems,' i, 9:
> In þis dale I droupe and dare
> For dern dedes þat done me dere.

So 'Awntyrs of Arthure' (Ireland MS.), l. 52: *Thay droupun and daren.* See also 'Morte Arthure' (Lincoln MS.), l. 4007, and 'Seege of Troy,' l. 1413. The word *dare* here, which means "to tremble with fear," is of obscure origin, and of course not identical with the common verb of that form. According to the 'N. E. D.' it does not appear in the documents until about 1200. It is still in dialect use, not only in North Britain but in the Midland and South and South-western districts. Cp. Wright's 'English Dialect Dictionary.'

2592. Such spellings as *wlle* (= *wolle*) are particularly common in Robert of Brunne's 'Handlyng Synne,' e. g. *wrdys* (= *wordys*), l. 545: *wlde* (= *wolde*), l. 693, *wrlde* (= *worlde*), l. 829, *wnt* (= *wont*), l. 914.

2750. *Owte he Rode A grete Randoune.* Cp. 'Sowdone of Babylone,' ll. 200 f.:
> Forth than rode þat faire Ooste
> With right goode chere and randon.

'Beues of Hamtoun,' ll. 4499:
> He armede him in yrene wede
> And lep vpon a sterne stede
> And rod forth wiþ gret randoun.

'Libeaus Desconus,' 338 f.:
> Togeder þey gonne ride
> Wiþ well greet raundoun.

'Sir Degree,' l. 445: *They rode together then with great randome.* 'Kyng Alisaunder,' ll. 2483 ff.:
> Kyng and duyk, eorl and baroun,
> Prikid the stedis with gret raundoun.

'Sir Ferumbras,' l. 890:
> Þan cam til him a sarsyn prout
> prikyng wiþ rendoun.

Also 'Richard Coer de Lion,' l. 4815.

2751. *Gawayn kyd he covde of werre.* So l. 2892. Cp. 'Seege of Troye,' ll. 1045 f.:
> Dyademades was here name,
> Moche she cowd of gle and game.

Notes. Lines 3166–3613.

'York Plays,' xxxi, l. 148: *Nay, my lorde, he can of no bourdyng.*
'Libeaus Desconus,' ll. 1513 ff.:
> *For þis fair lady
> Couþe more of sorcery
> þen oþer swiche five.*

'Ipomedon,' A, l. 319: *The burgays cowth of curtessye.* 'Sir Degree,' l. 681: *Sir Degree cold of curtesye.* 'Ipomedon,' B, l. 792: *All men konne not of justynge.*

3166. *And syr mordred can to the contre.* can = *gan*, and the verb of going is omitted after the auxiliary as frequently in Modern German.

3172. Seyferth (pp. 18 f.) suggests here the substitution of *cled "anstatt des sinnlosen *gledde*." The alliteration, however, evidently demands a form with *g*, so I have adopted the view of the 'N. E. D.' (see *gled*) that we have here a variant form of *cled*. Dr. Furnivall's gloss to this word, viz. *burning, glowing*, is certainly not correct.

3339. *Ryght so they trotted vppon þe grownde.* For *trot* in the general sense of *advance* cp. 'Wars of Alexander,' l. 2610: *Trottis him on to Tigre & þare his tentis settis.* Cp. also ibid. l. 2988.

3407. *Off bote they saw no better beld.* Cp. 'Sir Tristrem,' l. 1323: *Of bot sche was him beld.* 'Bone Florence of Rome,' ll. 1718 f.:
> *But as a woman dyscownfortyd sare
> Wythowten bote or belde.*

3422 f.:
> *To the kynge spake he fult stytt,
> Rewffully as he myght than Rowne.*

Cp. 'Octavian' (Southern version), ll. 939 ff.:
> *Ech day he sente to towne
> Þat fowle þyng to aske batayle with rufull roune
> Ayens þe kyng.*

3498. *helpe me sone that I ware there.* Cp. 'Holy Grail,' ch. 55, ll. 347 f.:
> *but helpeth me hens Owt Anon
> that Owt Of this Chambre I were gon.*

'Generydes,' l. 3784: *helpe that I were Armyd anon.* 'Eger and Grine,' ll. 234 f.:
> *helpe that I were sounded with one sleepe
> & some Easment for me and my hackney.*

'Libeaus Desconus,' ll. 660 f.:
> *Helpe Libeaus Desconus
> Þat he wer nouȝt y-schent.*

'Sir Triamore,' ll. 443 f.:
> *helpe me, Sir, out of this Mischeefe!
> att some towne that I were.*

'Beues of Hamtoun,' l. 1627: *And help þat þis þef wer ded.* The same construction occurs with *that* omitted. 'Sir Ferumbras,' l. 217:
> *Do þat myn armes sone be heer
> & help me y were a-rayde.*

We have a curious extension of this construction in instances like the following. 'Beues of Hamtoun,' ll. 1080:
> *Iosian, þe faire maide,
> Vn-arme Beues, he wer at mete
> And serue þe self him þer ate.*

3613. *loke ye Rappe yow not vp to Ryde.* Cp. 'Cursor Mundi,' l. 25439: [*R*]*ape þe lauerd nu forto ren.* 'Piers Plowman,' C. ii, 90 f.: *Kynges and knyȝtes shoulde . . . Ryden and rappe adowne in reames aboute.* 'Destruction of Troy,' l. 818: *And now rapis hym to ryse & rom from his bede.* 'Rowlande and Ottuell,' l. 255:
> *Nay, sir, we witt our batells guy*

>   And rape vs for to ryde
>   Agayne þe Emperour, sir Garcy.

3733. *To cover the quene of hyr care.* Cp. 'Sir Ysumbras,' ll. 487 ff.:
>   þe kyng sware
>   When he were couerde of his care
>   That he wolde dubbe hym knyghte.

'Athelston,' ll. 331 f.:
>   God may couere hem off here care
>   Or þat I slepe a wynke.

'Morte Arthure' (Lincoln MS.), l. 859: *The care of þat creatoure couer sall I neuer.* 'Erl of Tolous,' ll. 382 ff.: *Myght y oght get of that free . . . . Hyt wold covyr me of care.* Horstmann's 'Nordenglische Legendensammlung, St. Nicholas,' l. 137: *And out of care so covered he.* Cp. also 'Athelston,' l. 41; 'Octavian' (Northern version, Lincoln MS.), l. 525.

3757. *And ofte he changyd hyde and hewe.* 'Squyr of Lowe Degre,' ll. 387 f.:
>   I woulde not for my crowne so newe
>   That lady chaunge hyde or hewe.

'Death and Liffe,' ll. 157 f.:
>   & shee the ffoulest ffreake that formed was euer
>   both of hide & hew.

'Richard Coer de Lion,' ll. 675 f.:
>   He was Ynglysch and wel trew
>   Be speche and syghte, hyde and hew.

'Eger and Grine,' l. 263: *The Ladye fayre of Hew & hyde.* 'Destruction of Troy,' ll. 3908 f.:
>   Þo freikes were fourmet of feturs [a]like
>   Bothe of hyde & of hew to hede of a mykell.

'York Plays,' viii, 22: *And fordone hoyly, hyde and hewe.* 'Rowlande and Ottuell,' l. 1230: *Full fayre of hewe & hyde.*

3764. *And welcomyd launcelot as the hend.* 'St. Edmund the Confessor,' l. 102: *Þis holi child ne wornde hire noȝt ac dude as þe hende;* 'Emare,' l. 84: *He wellcomed hym as þe hende;* 'Sir Eglamour of Artois,' l. 124: *Aftur mete do ye as hynde;* 'Kyng Alysaunder,' l. 6324: *Ther [he] dude noght as the wise!*

3832. *So lyteH they wexe of lyn And lerys.* Cp. 'Eger and Grine,' ll. 597 ff.:
>   for there is neither Lin nor light
>   that Egeking my sword meeteth with
>   but gladlye it will through itt gone.

'Golagros and Gawane,' ll. 81 f.:
>   Schir Kay ruschit to the roist and reft fra the swane,
>   Lightly claught, throu lust, the lym fra the lyre.

Similarly 'Hali Meidenhad,' p. 21: *Se ferliche ha driuen dun to þe eorthe, þat al ham is to-limet, liȝ ba & lire.* 'St. Juliana,' p. 59: *As þat istelede irn to-limede hire & to-leac liȝ ba & lire.* As Mätzner ('Altenglisches Wörterbuch') remarks, this *lire* (*lyre*) = Ags. *lira*, meaning *flesh, muscle*, was easily confounded with *lire* (*lere*) = Ags. *hléor*, meaning *cheek, face*. Cp. also Amours' note to the above passage from 'Golagros and Gawane.'

3940. *Vnto Ihesu cryste Aske I A boone.* By analogy to the expression "make a boon." Cp. 'Sir Eglamour of Artois,' l. 101: *To Jhesu Cryste he made a boone.*

EDITIONS OF MIDDLE ENGLISH TEXTS
REFERRED TO IN THE NOTES.

Altenglische Dichtungen des MS. Harl. 2253, herausgegeben von K. Böddeker. Berlin, 1878.
Altenglische Legenden, Neue Folge, herausgegeben von Carl Horstmann. Heilbronn and Leipsic, 1878–81.
Amis and Amiloun, herausgegeben von E. Kölbing. Heilbronn, 1884 ('Altenglische Bibliothek').
Arthour and Merlin, herausgegeben von E. Kölbing. Leipsic, 1890 ('Altenglische Bibliothek').
Athelston, herausgegeben von J. Zupitza, 'Englische Studien,' vol. xiii.
Awntyrs of Arthure at the Tarnewathelan, in 'Scottish Alliterative Poems,' ed. F. J. Amours (Scottish Text Society). Edinburgh, 1897.
Babees Book, ed. F. J. Furnivall. London, 1868 (E. E. T. S.).
Beues of Hamtoun (The Romance of Sir), ed. E. Kölbing. London, 1885–94 (E. E. T. S.).
Blanchardyn and Eglantine (Caxton's), ed. L. Kellner. London, 1890 (E. E. T. S.).
Bone Florence of Rome (Le), herausgegeben von Wilhelm Vietor, 1893.
Bruce (The), by John Barbour, ed. W. W. Skeat. London, 1870 et seq. (E. E. T. S.).
Cleanness, ed. Richard Morris, in 'Early English Alliterative Poems.' London, 1864 (E. E. T. S.).
Confessio Amantis. Complete Works of John Gower, ed. G. C. Macaulay. Oxford, 1899 et seq., vols. ii. and iii.
Coventry Plays (published under the name of Ludus Coventriae), ed. J. O. Halliwell. London, 1841, Shakespeare Society.
Cursor Mundi, ed. Richard Morris. London, 1874 et seq. (E. E. T. S.).
Death and Lyffe, in Bishop Percy's Folio MS., ed. J. W. Hales and F. J. Furnivall. London, 1868, vol. iii.
Degree (Sir), in Percy's Folio MS., ed Hales and Furnivall, vol. iii.
Destruction of Troy, ed. Panton and Donaldson. London, 1869 (E. E. T. S.).
Eger and Grine, in Percy's Folio MS., ed. Hales and Furnivall, vol. i.
Eglamour of Artois (Sir), in 'The Thornton Romances,' ed. J. O. Halliwell for the Camden Society. London, 1844.
Emare, edited by A. B. Gough, London, 1901 (Morsbach and Holthausen's 'Old and Middle English Texts').
Erl of Toulous, herausgegeben von G. Lüdtke. Berlin, 1881.
Ferumbras (Sir), ed. S. J. Herrtage. London, 1879 (E. E. T. S.).
Floris und Blauncheflur, herausgegeben von E. Hausknecht. Berlin, 1885.
Foure Sonnes of Aymon, ed. O. Richardson. London, 1885 (E. E. T. S.).
Gawayne and the Green Knight (Sir), ed. Richard Morris. London, 1864 (E. E. T. S.).
Gawene and the Carle of Carelyle (Sir), in 'Syr Gawayne,' ed. Sir F. Madden, 1839 (Bannatyne Club).
Generydes, ed. W. A. Wright. London, 1879 (E. E. T. S.).
Golagros and Gawane, in 'Scottish Alliterative Poems,' ed. F. J. Amours (Scottish Text Society). Edinburgh, 1897.

Gowther (Sir), herausgegeben von K. Breul. Oppeln, 1886.
Guy of Warwick (The Romance of), ed. J. Zupitza. London, 1875-76 (E. E. T. S.).
Handlyng Synne, Part I., ed. F. J. Furnivall. London, 1903 (E. E. T. S.).
Havelok (The Lay of), ed. W. W. Skeat. Oxford, 1902.
Holy Grail, by H. Louelich, ed. F. J. Furnivall. London, 1874-78 (E. E. T. S.).
Horn Childe, ed. J. Hall as Appendix to his edition of King Horn. Oxford, 1901.
Ipomedon, herausgegeben von E. Kölbing. Breslau, 1889.
King of Tars, herausgegeben von F. Krause, 'Englische Studien,' vol. xi.
Kyng Alisaunder in 'Metrical Romances,' ed. H. Weber, 1810, vol. i.
Lambewell (Sir), in Percy's Folio MS., vol. i.
Lay le Fraine, herausgegeben von H. Varnhagen. Anglia, vol. iii.
Laȝamon's Brut, ed. Sir F. Madden. London, 1847.
Libeaus Desconus, herausgegeben von M. Kaluza. Leipsic, 1890 ('Altenglische Bibliothek').
Merline, in Percy's Folio MS., vol. i.
Morte Arthure (Lincoln MS.), ed. M. M. Banks. London, 1900.
Morte Darthur, by Sir Thomas Malory, ed. H. O. Sommer. London, 1889-91.
Octavian, herausgegeben von G. Sarrazin. Heilbronn, 1885 ('Altenglische Bibliothek').
Patience, ed. Richard Morris in 'Early English Alliterative Poems.' London, 1864 (E. E. T. S.).
Pearl, ed. I. Gollancz. London, 1891.
Perceval of Galles (Sir), in 'The Thornton Romances,' ed. J. O. Halliwell. London, 1844.
Piers Plowman (The Vision of William concerning), ed. W. W. Skeat. Oxford, 1886.
Rauf Coilȝear (Taill of), herausgegeben von M. Tonndorf, 1894.
Richard Coer de Lion, in 'Metrical Romances,' ed. H. Weber. Edinburgh, 1810, vol. ii.
Roberd of Cisyle, herausgegeben von R. Nuck. Berlin, 1887.
Romans of Partenay, ed. W. W. Skeat. London, 1866 (E. E. T. S.).
Romaunt of the Rose, in 'The Complete Works of Geoffrey Chaucer,' ed. W. W. Skeat. Oxford, 1894-97, vol. i.
Rowlande and Ottuell (Romance of Duke), ed. S. J. Herrtage. London, 1880 (E. E. T. S.).
Seege of Troye, ed. C. H. A. Wager. Boston, 1899.
Sege of Melayne, ed. S. J. Herrtage. London, 1880 (E. E. T. S.).
Seuyn Sages, in 'Metrical Romances,' ed. H. Weber, vol. iii.
Sowdone of Babylone, ed. E. Hausknecht. London, 1881 (E. E. T. S.).
Squyr of Lowe Degree, in 'Remains of the Early Popular Poetry of England,' ed. W. C. Hazlitt. London, 1866, vol. ii.
Torrent of Portyngale, ed. E. Adam. London, 1887 (E. E. T. S.).
Towneley Plays, ed. G. England. London, 1897 (E. E. T. S).
Triamore (Sir), in Percy's Folio MS., vol. ii.
Tristrem (Sir), herausgegeben von E. Kölbing. Heilbronn, 1882.
Wars of Alexander, ed. W. W. Skeat. London, 1886 (E. E. T. S.).
William of Palerne, ed. W. W. Skeat. London, 1867 (E. E. T. S.).
York Plays, ed. L. T. Smith. Oxford, 1885.
Ysumbras (Sir), herausgegeben von J. Zupitza und G. Schleich. Berlin, 1901 (Palaestra, xv).
Ywain and Gawain, herausgegeben von G. Schleich, Oppeln and Leipsic, 1887.

GLOSSARY.

A, *adj.* all, 2462.
A, *conj.* and, 2844.
A, *conj.* if, 2832.
ABBYTE, *s.* habit, robe, 3793.
ABYDE, *v.* wait for, 162.
ABYE, *subj.* 2 *s.* pay for, suffer for, 1387; *pret.* 3 *s.* ABOUGHT, 2523.
ACORDEMENT, *s.* agreement, composition of differences, 1639.
ACOUNTRES, *s. pl.* encounters, 1589.
ADYGHT, *p.p.* prepared, 1545.
A-FROUGHTE, *p.p.* afraid, 2295, 2413.
AGAYNE, *prep.* towards, to meet, 709; opposite to, before, 2648.
AGILTE, *p.p.* sinned against, wronged, 915, 1322; *pret.* 3 *s.* AGULTE, 1154.
ALBLASTERS, *s. pl.* cross-bows, 2729.
ALL-MYGHT, *adj.* almighty, 675.
ALSO, *adv.* as, 1576.
AND, *conj.* if, 161, 239, 1706, 2846, 3945.
ANTOURE, 1829. See AUNT(E)RE.
APARAYLMENTE, *s.* dress, apparel, 2055.
APPAR(R)AYLE, *s.* furnishings, 969; accomplishments in arms, 1748.
ARE, *adv.* before, 291, 977.
ARMYTES, *s. gen.* hermit's, 3950.
AS, *conj.* as if, 220.
ASCRYE, *v.* call upon, 2126.
ASSENT(E), *s.* opinion (in common with others), 1722, 1937, 2604.
AS-TYTE, *adv.* quickly, 488, 3713.
AUAUNTEMENT, *s.* boast, 1617.
AUGHT, *pret.* 1 *s.* owned, possessed, 653.
AUNT(E)RE, *s.* adventure, fortune, 33, 362, 1903; *pl.* AUNTRES, 719, 983.
AUNTUR(E)S, *s. pl.* 3, 6, 11, 19, 1906. See AUNT(E)RE.
AWAYTES, *pres.* 3 *s.* watches, 64.
AWISE, *imperat.* 2 *s.* (*reflexive*), bethink oneself, reflect, 2568.
AYTHUR, *indef. pron.* either, each, 3278.

BALE, *s.* sorrow, 628, 1074.
BARE, *s.* boar, 229, 951.
BATAYLES, *s. pl.* battalions, divisions, 3306.
BAYNE, *adj.* straight, ready, obedient, 991, 1134, 3217, 3315.
BE, *conj.* by the time that, when, 1861, 1957.
BE(E), *s.* ring, 3179, 3419.
BE-CRYED, *p.p.* accused, 2774.
BEDE, *v.* offer, 849, 1462, 3356; proclaim, 32, 41, 348; *pres.* 1 *pl.* 3274.
BEDENE, BYDENE, *adv.* together, 24, 70, 546, 723, 1513, 1663, 1760, 2278; well, completely, 1684, 1728.
BEGHE, *s.* ring, 2625. See BE(E).
BEGREDDE, *pret.* 3 *pl.* accused, 1812.
BELD, *s.* comfort, 3407.
BELEUE, BELEVE, *v.* remain, 759, 3963; leave, 558; *pret.* 3 *s.* BE-LEFTE, BY-LEFTE, 60, 1765.
BEMYS, *s. pl.* trumpets, 2707.
BENE, *v.* be, 1503.
BENTE, *s.* field (of battle), 3359, 3374.
BENTE, *p.p.* stretched, 990.
BERE, *s.* bray, sound, 2127.
BERE, *pret.* 3 *s.* bore, 538.
BESAUNT(E), *s.* a gold coin of Byzantian origin, 3179, 3419; *pl.* BESAVNTIS, 3542.
BESETTE, BYSETTE, *p.p.* employed, applied, 1412, 1568.
BETHE, *pres.* 3 *s.* (*in future sense*), will be, 1727; *pres.* 3 *pl.* are, 1825; *imper.* 2 *pl.* be, 1881.
BETTE, *pret.* 3 *pl.* beat, 13.
BLANNE. See BLYNNE.
BLE(E), *s.* complexion, countenance, 739, 3504, 3779, 3876.
BLOO, *adj.* blue, 151.
BLYNDIS, *pres.* 3 *s.* becomes blind, 311.
BLYNNE, *v.* decline, cease, stop, 37,

Glossary.

1691, 1824, 2999, 3039, 3727; pret. 3 s. BLANNE, 3364.
BLYVE, adv. quickly, 3706.
BODDYN, p.p. prayed, 2803.
BODE, s. message, report, 3468.
BODE-WORDE, s. promise, 3274.
BOGHT, p.p. paid for, redeemed, requited, 470, 3009, 3483, 3718.
BOLD, adj. sure, 3009, 3483.
BOLDE, adv. surely (?), 3688.
BONE, s. limb, 117.
BO(O)NE, s. prayer, request, 2803, 3787, 3940.
BORD, s. table, 859.
BOTE, s. remedy, help, amends, 3303, 3407, 3486, 3840.
BOTHIS, adj. gen. both, 176.
BOUGHT. See BOGHT.
BOUNTE, s. valour, knightly qualities, 125, 1739.
BOWNE, adj. ready, prepared, 941, 2151, 2525, 2882, 3427, 3803.
BOWNE, v. make ready, 3257.
BRAST(E), v. break, burst, 3492; pret. 3 s. 188, 1343, 2178, 3077, 3135, 3774.
BRAYED, pret. 3 s. drew suddenly, 3344.
BRAUNDISSHID, pret. 3 s. flourished about, moved vigorously, 117.
BREME, adj. fierce, 229, 951, 1600, 2214, 2606, 3249.
BRENNE, v. burn, 2507; pret. 3 pl. BRENTE, 2537; p.p. BRENT(E), 943, 1319, 1939, 3697.
BRERE, s. briar, wild rose, 179, 724, 835.
BROWGH, s. town, 2707.
BUSK(E), v. get ready, hasten, betake oneself, 349, 2505, 3427; pres. 3 s. BUSKES, -IS, 547, 2525, 2715; pret. 3, BUSKED, -YD, 699, 2151, 2882, 3579, 3803; p.p. BUSKYD, 1808.
BUSKYD. See BUSK(E).
BY, v. be, 34, 876; pres.subj. 3 s. 1759.
BY-CALLE, v. accuse, impeach, 1553.
BY-DENE. See BEDENE.
BYDYNG, s. bidding, 1134.
BYGGYD, p.p. built, 3619.
BYGGYNG, s. building, dwelling, 3767.
BY-HESTE, s. offer, 3296.
BY-KNOW, v. confess, 916.
BY-LEFTE. See BELEUE.
BY-MENE, v. mean, 856.
BYRD, s. bride, lady, 2989, 3632.

BY-SETTE. See BE-SETTE.
BY-SPAKE, pret. 3 s. spoke to, 2404.
BY-TAKE, v. deliver, hand over to, 2283; pres. 3 pl. 2346.

CASTE, pret. 3 s. looked, 3776.
CHASE. See CHESE.
CHERE, s. countenance, manner, 477, 540, 781.
CHESE, v. choose, 2973; pret. 3, CHESE, 419, 514, 2355, 2522, 3290; pret. 3, CHASE, 2957, 3561.
CLEPIS, pres. 3 s. calls, summons, 106, 387, 2540; pret. 3 s. CLEPID, CLEPYD, 1444, 2668, 3606, 3858.
CLONGYN, p.p. withered, shrunk up, 751.
CLOUGHIS, s. gen. ravines, 893.
CLYPPE, v. embrace, 3927; pres. 3 s. CLYPPIS, 1547; pret. 3 s. CLYPPED, 1801.
COLDE, v. grow cold, 3647.
COLOURE, s. hue, countenance, 2816.
COMSEMENT, s. commencement, 1726.
CORAGE, s. heart, 3777.
CORDEMENT, s. agreement, reconciliation, 2422, 2426.
CORSSE, 2880. See CROSSE.
CORTESSLY, adv. courteously, 2283.
COUDE, COVDE, COWDE, pret. 3 s. knew, 3617, 3809; had knowledge, was skilled, 2750, 2892.
COUTH(E), pret. could, knew, 104, 223, 1446, 1675; p.p. known, 2248.
COVER, v. recover, heal, 3733; pret. 3 s. COUERYD, 2856, 3134, 3736.
CRYE, s. company (of contestants at a tournament), 44.
CRYE, v. proclaim, 342.
CRAFTELY, adv. skilfully, 390.

DALE, v. deal, 1076; pret. 3 pl. DALTYN, 2897; p.p. DALTE, finished, 3259.
DARE, v. crouch in fear, be afraid, 2575.
DEDE, s. death, 911.
DEDE, s. capacity, 493.
DEFFEND, v. exclude, 3049.
DEPARTE, v. part, 1805, 3704; subj. 3 s. divide, 3704; p.p. DEPARTED, come to an end, 743.
DERE, s. harm, 3704.
DERE, v. harm, 2896.
DERFE, adj. terrible, 2607.

Glossary.

DESSE, s. daïs, 2259.
DEVOYEDE, imperat. 2 s. get out of, 1167.
DEYNGE, s. dying, 1047.
DIGHT v. (intrans.), get ready (especially of arming), 167, 1874; dress, 326; attend to, 717; imperat. 1 pl. 2134, 2 s. 2450; p.p. got ready, prepared, 142, 456, 573, 876, 1884, 1896; put, 847; disposed of, 1909; conditioned, 2000.
DO, v. cause to, 1003; pret. 3 s. DID, DYD, 341, 1121, 2502; p.p. DONE, 370, 2328; imperat. 2 pl. DOTHE, put, 3883.
DOEL(L)E, s. sorrow, 682, 873.
DOLWYN, p.p. buried, 3604.
DOME, s. command, 2260; pl. DOMYS, 2482.
DONE, infin. 1122. See DO.
DORE, v. endure, 238.
DRAKE, s. dragon, 2607.
DRAYNE, p.p. drawn, 859, 1997, 2164, 3014, 3325.
DRECHYD, p.p. disturbed, troubled, 1869.
DREGHE, adj. great, 2621.
DROUPE, v. sink down (from fear), 2575.
DRYHE, in ON DRYHE, aside, apart, 2826.
DUELLE, DWELLE, s. sorrow, mourning, 2244, 2458; pity, 1742, 1971, 2125.
DUL(E)FULLY, adv. pitiably, 1406, 2000.
DUOGHTY, adj. doughty, 24.
DWELLE, v. stay, stop, 1769, 1790, 1793; subj. pl. 1776.
DWELLE, s. See DUELLE.
DWELLYNGE, s. staying, 80.
DYGHT. See DIGHT.
DYNT(E), s. blow, 484, 503, 2173, 2753, 2812; pl. DYNTIS, 1076, 2801.
DYSKERE, v. disclose, 1735.

EDDER, s. adder, 3341.
ELLIS, adv. else, 943.
EME, s. uncle, 1681; gen. EME-IS, 2960.
ENDRIS, adj. other, 1017.
ENTAYLE, s. fashion, quality, character, 975, 2300; good form, 3273.
ENTENTE, s. assiduous effort, endeavour, 3691.
ENTERDITE, v. lay under an interdict, 2253; p.p. ENTERDYT, ENTYRDYTED, 2268, 2284.
EUYN, adv. straight, 3616.
EUYN, s. evening, 2236.
EYNE, s. pl. eyes, 3265, 3435.

FALLYS, pres. 3 s. befits, 1119; pret. 3 s. FELL, was suitable, 1122.
FANTYSE, s. vain thing, 2547.
FARE, s. matter, business, 945.
FARE, v. go, journey, 156, 222, 249, 688.
FASOWNE, s. fashion, kind, 2531.
FASTE, v. make fast, confirm, 3324.
FAYNE, adj. happy, 3200; eager, 3799.
FEE, s. possessions, 2719.
FELE, adj. many, 6, 2019, 2032, 2157.
FELLY, adv. fiercely, cruelly, 3391.
FER, adv. far, 2400.
FERE, adj. sound, in good condition, 411, 552.
FERE, s. company, 2222, 3402, 3702, 3900; pl. FERYS, companions, 3830.
FERLY, adv. wonderfully, 6, 3176.
FERRE, adv. far, 2982, 3019, 3167.
FETTE, p.p. fetched, taken, 1067.
FEYGHT, s. fight, 1489.
FEYGHT(E), v. fight, 1318, 1397, 1436.
FEWTRED, pret. 3 pl. put into "fewter," the felt-lined rest for the spear attached to the saddle, 3357.
FLEME, v. reject, 2673; pret. 3 s. FLEMYD, banished, 3560; p.p. FLEMYD, banished, 3755.
FOLDE, s. ground, 3549.
FOLDE, v. bend, 99; yield, 2547; clasp, 3771.
FOLE, s. fool, 2672.
FOLYD, p.p. foolish, 402.
FONDE, pret. 3 pl. advanced, 3337. See FOUND.
FONE, adj. few, 2378.
FONE, pret. 3 s. took, 1796.
FONE, s. pl. foes, 3211.
FONGE, v. receive, 3503.
FORBARE, pret. 1 s. spared, 2836.
FORBARE, p.p. miscreated creature? 3741.
FORBEDE, 3 pres. subj. forbid, 3681.
FORBLED, p.p. weakened by loss of blood, 3434.

140 *Glossary.*

FORBRENDE, FORBRENT, *p.p.* put to death by burning, 1666, 1925.
FORLORNE, *p.p.* lost, 3209.
FORNE, *prep.* for, 3211.
FORSETTE, *pret.* 3 *s.* set round with a guard, 3046.
FOR-THY, *conj.* therefore, 104, 1088, 1141, 2394, 2408; because, 1878.
FOR-THYNKE, *v.* rue, repent, 2737; *pres.* 3 *s.* FOR-THYNKETH, 3849.
FOR(E)WARD, *s.* offer, agreement, 3302; *pl.* FORWARDYS, 2673, 3270, 3324.
FOR-WERY, *adj.* very weary, tired out, 2901.
FOR-WONDRED, *p.p.* full of wonder, 2730.
FOR-WHY (THAT), *conj.* wherefore, 33, 2617; because, 97; on condition that, 389.
FORYELDE, 3 *pres. subj.* reward, 1548.
FO(U)NDE, FOWND(E), *v.* thrust, 2159; advance (*trans.*) 2551; advance (*intrans.*) 2553; go, 3513; strive, 3229; *imperat.* 2 *pl.* FOUNDIS, 2551.
FRE(E), *adj.* noble, open, generous, 75, 90, 242, 408, 454, 1009, 3643.
FRELE, *adj.* frail, 2300.
FRELY, *adj.* noble, 2939, 3121, 3329.
FRELY, *adv.* very, 3772.
FRESTE, *adv.* first, 1151.
FREYNED, *pret.* 3 *s.* asked, 678.
FRISTE, *adj.* first, 149; *adv.* 736.
FRO, *prep.* from, 633, 1979, 1987.
FYFTY, *adj.* fiftieth, 3895. Probably a mistake for FYFTE.

GAB, *v.* tell lies, 1147, 1156; *pret.* 1 *s.* GABBYD, 1105, 1132, 1138.
GAME, *s.* delight, mirth, 96, 430, 611; *pl.* GAMYS, 3227.
GATYS, *s. gen.* thus gatys = in this way, 1712.
GAYNE, *adj.* straight, 1904.
GERE, *s.* gear, things, 3736.
GESTE, *s.* guest, 453.
GILTE, *p.p.* wronged, 1377.
GLAD, *v.* be glad, 3227.
GLEDDE, *p.p.* clothed, dressed, 3172.
GLEDE, *s.* a live coal, fire, 780, 2742, 2793.
GLENTE, *pret.* 3 *s.* glinted forth, 3493.
GLEWE, *s.* jokes, 1164.
GLEYVES, *s. pl.* spears, 3078, 3096.

GLODE, *pret.* 3 *s.* glided, 3341.
GON(NE), *pret.* 3, began, 1390; did, 99, 139, 1031; *p.p.* done, 1780.
GOODE, *adj. pl.* good, brave men, 2157.
GO(U)NFANOUNE, GONFANOWNE, *s.* small flag or pennon attached to the lance just below the steel head, 2104, 2153, 2464, 2886, 3096.
GRANDE, *pres.* 1 *s.* grant, 2318.
GRAYTHES, *pres.* 3 *pl.* get ready, 2530; *pret.* 3 *s.* GRAYTHID, 2739.
GRE(E), *s.* prize, preëminence, 48, 2409.
GREDDE, *pret.* 3 *s.* drew, 1838.
GREDE, *v.* cry, 791, 1390; *pres.* 2 *s.* GREDYS, accusest, 1572.
GRETE, *adj.* great, 682.
GYNNE, *s.* device, stratagem, 3037.

ȜARE, *adj.* ready, 2505, 2608; *s.* YARE.
ȜEME, *v.* take care of, 2512.

HALD, *v.* hold, consider, 2336, 2497; *pres.* 3 *pl.* 2925; *pres.* 3 *s.* HALDYS, 89.
HALE, *s.* hall, 1078.
HAILSED, *pret.* 3 *s.* saluted, 2632.
HAN, HANNE, *pres.* 3 *pl.* have, 2417, 3209.
HELDE, *v.* incline, 184; yield, 261, 2141.
HELE, *s.* salvation, 3655.
HELE, *v.* conceal, 143, 466, 1678, 2967, 3840.
HEM, *person. pron.* them, 1464, 2123.
HEND(E), *adj.* gentle, courteous, 110, 330, 541, 623, 1529, 2469, 3764.
HENDE, *adv.* near, at hand, 332.
HENDELY, *adv.* courteously, gracefully, with good manners, 600, 1613, 2638, 2710, 3922.
HENTE, *pret.* 3 *s.* seized, laid hold of, took, 1037, 2853, 3491, 3934; *p.p.* HENT, 3023.
HERSE, *s.* a frame designed to carry the candles lighted in honour of the dead, 3532.
HEST(E), *s.* promise, vow, 2660, 2688, 2697, 3686.
HETTE, *p.p.* promised, 2697.
HIGHT(E), HYGHT(E), *pres.* 3 *s.* is called, 3960; *pret.* 3 *s.* was called,

Glossary.

93, 883, 1474; *p.p.* called, 2487; promised, 1447, 3252.
HOLLY, *adv.* entirely, wholly, 935, 945, 2980.
HOLTYS, *s. pl.* groves, 3029.
HOLYCHE, *adv.* wholly, 3826.
HOPE, *pres.* 1 *s.* think, 490, 1491, 2737, 3543; *pret.* 3 *s.* HOPYD, 2491, 3620.
HORE, *adj.* grey (from lichen, perhaps), ancient, 314, 3029.
HORSYD, *pret.* 3 *s.* mounted, 87.
HOUYD, HOVID, *pret.* lingered, 259, 2622.
HYE, *s.* haste, 2830.
HYE, *imperat.* 2 *s.* haste, 3452.
HYGHT, *s.* HIGHT.
HYTTE, *pers. pron.* it, 3711, 3834.

I-BENTE, *p.p.* adorned, 1035.
ICHE, *indef. pron.* each, 1685, 2109, 2367, 2504, 3761.
ICHONE, *indef. pron.* every one, 627, 2036, 2369.
I-DIGHTE, *p.p.* got ready, 610.
ILKE, YLKE, *adj.* same, 1765, 1886, 1907, 2092, 2166.
I-MANASED, *p.p.* menaced, 479.
I-MARYD, *pret.* 3 *s.* marred, 3360.
INCHES(S)OUN, *s.* occasion, 56, 1030.
I-RADE, *p.p.* read, 2651.
I-WOUNDYD, *p.p.* wounded, 934.
I-WYSSE, *adv.* surely, 3633, 3635, 3923.

KENE, *adj.* bold, 803, 955, 1921, 1969, 3248.
KENNE, *v.* know, recognize, 175; *p.p.* KENE, 1097.
KEPETH, *pres.* 3 *s.* pays attention to, 3027; *pret.* 3 *s.* KEPIT, 102.
KEST(E), *pret.* 3 *s.* uttered, 3510; *p.p.* fixed, 455.
KITHE, 533. See KYTHE.
KLEPIS, *pres.* 3 *s.* calls, summons, 816; *pret.* 3 *s.* KLEPITTE, 191, KLEPYD, 536.
KNOWLACHE, *pres.* 1 *s.* acknowledge, 3638.
KYNNES, *s. gen.* kind of, 3037.
KYTHE, *v.* make known, display, declare, 1441, 1611, 1774, 2481, 2744, 3598; proclaim, 1785; *pret.* 3 *s.* KYD(DE), 2751, 2892.

LAD(E), *pret.* 3 *s.* led, 712, 723; *p.p.* 1506.
LAYNE, *s.* concealment, 602, 1964, 3204.
LAYNE, *v.* conceal, 989, 1026, 1108, 2650, 3591.
LAYNE, *pret.* 3 *pl.* lay, 2763.
LECHE, *s.* leech, physician, 368, 380, 387; *pl.* LECHIS, 325, 331.
LECHYNG, *s.* medical treatment, 3507.
LEDE, *s.* man, 3163; land, 653, 2659.
LEDE, *v.* live? 3948.
LEES, LES(E), *s.* falsehood, 276, 423, 992, 1719, 2255, 2353, 2959, 3565.
LEFF, *adj.* dear, 1.
LEFFE, *v.* live, 2499.
LEFTE, *pret.* 3 *s.* remained, 53; *s.* LEUE.
LELYEST, *adv.* most loyally, 1066.
LEME (miswritten for LEUYN), *s.* light, 3586.
LEM(M)AN, *s.* lover (male or female), 586, 605, 637, 1086, 1137, 1179.
LEMYD, *pret.* shone, 1471, 3308, 3586.
LEMYN (miswritten probably for LEUYN), *s.* bright flame, lightning, 3308.
LEND(E), *v.* stay, tarry, 565, 617, 1007, 3276, 3768; *pres.* 1 *pl.* 2590; *pret.* 3 *s.* LENTE, 988; *p.p.* LENTE, 1353, 1945, 2277, 2727.
LENDE, *v.* land, 2473.
LENE, *v.* lend, grant, 1464.
LENGE, *v.* stay, dwell, 3276, 3556.
LENGER, *adv.* longer, 40, 162, 381, 565, 1484, 3802.
LENTE, *v.* lend, 3693.
LERE, *s.* learning, 521.
LERE, *s.* cheek, countenance, 3624; for the *pl.*, 3832, cp. note.
LERE, *v.* learn, 641.
LESE. See LEES.
LESE, *subj.* 3 *pres.* lose, 3415.
LESYNG(E), *s.* falsehood, lying, 1004, 1043, 1098, 2728, 3550.
LET(TE), LETT, *pret.* 3 *s.* caused (to be made), 41, 2978, 2985, 3028.
LETTE, *v.* cease (*intrans.*), 201, 665; hinder, prevent, 205, 2441.
LEUE, LEVE, *adj.* dear, 3204, 3412, 3495.
LEUE, *v.* stay, 3203.
LEUE, *imperat.* 2 *s.* permit, 3556.
LEUYD, *pret.* 3 *s.* left, 2824; *p.p.* 2820, 3744.

LEVANDE, *pres. part.* living, 2840.
LEVYD, *p.p.* lived, 3601.
LEYRE, *s.* countenance, 475. See LERE,
LIGGYS, *pres.* 3 *s.* lies, 1730.
LIGHT, *p.p.* settled, 581.
LOGGEN, *pres.* 3 *pl.* lodge, arrange, 1901.
LOKYD, *p.p.* enclosed, lodged, 2620.
LONE, *s.* concealment, 1124.
LORE, *s.* learning, doctrine, 3966.
LOREME, *s.* bridle-reins, 1471.
LORNE, *p.p.* lost, 3551.
LOUGHE, *adj.* flaming, full, 1594.
LOUGHE, *pret.* laughed, 496, 1536, 1636.
LOVDE, *adj.* loud, 910.
LYKYNGE, *s.* love, 3702.
LYTHE, *v.* listen to, hear, 676, 1479, 1582, 1643, 1772, 1787, 1942.
LYVAND, 949. See LEVANDE.

MAKE, *s.* match, 1062; mate, spouse, 3668.
MAY(E), *s.* maiden, 196, 1107.
MAYNE, *s.* strength, 3797.
MEKELLE, MEKYLLE, *adj.* great, 1424, 1528, 3816. See MYKELLE.
MENE, *v.* complain, mourn, 727, 3861.
MENE, *v.* discourse, tell, indicate, 22, 1686; remember, 3729; *pres.* 1 *s.* 2420, 3959; *pret.* 3 *s.* 3932; *p.p.* 3695.
MERELY, *adv.* merrily, cheerfully, 3856.
MESE, *s.* course, 1512.
MEYNE, *s.* company, 2039.
MO, *adv.* more, 198, 648.
MOCHE, MYCHE, *adj.* great, 1960, 2219, 2850, 2923, 3082; *adv.* much, 96.
MOCHELLE, *adj.* great, 1496.
MODE, *s.* mind, 3679.
MOLD(E), *s.* earth, ground, 707, 3300, 3459, 3684; *pl.* MOLDYS, 3545.
MON, *pres.* 1 *s.* must, shall, 3230.
MORROW, *s.* morning, 3366, 3810.
MOSTE, *adj.* greatest, 3212.
MOTTE, *pres.* 1 *s.* am permitted to, 3207.
MOW(E), *pres.* 1 *pl.* may, 1114, 1140.
MYCHE. See MOCHE.
MYCHELLE, MYKELLE, MYKYLLE, *adj.* great, 1560, 1642, 1690, 1749, 3313; *adv.* much, 1675, 1708, 1783, 2042. See MEKELLE, MOCHELLE.
MYNGYD, *pret.* 3 *s.* disturbed, confused, 3933.
MYNNE, *v.* remind, 169.
MYSSE, *s.* sin, 3677.

NADE, *pret.* 1 *s.* had not, 1410.
NE, *adv.* not, 76, 98, 566.
NEDELYNGIS, *adv.* necessarily, 753.
NERE, *pret. subj.* 3 *s.* were not, 411.
NEUYN(E), NEVYN, NEWYN, *v.* name, tell, 2582, 3304, 3584, 3823, 3881; *pres.* 1 *s.* 3409, 3965.
NO, *adv.* not, 37.
NOLD(E), *pret.* would not, 633, 701, 1455, 2825, 3786.
NOME, *pret.* 3 *s.* took, 2258, 2374.
NONE, *adj.* no, 89.
NOTE, *pres.* 1 *s.* know not, 3426.
NYE(E), *v.* draw nigh to, 2832, 3183.
NYLLE, *pres.* 3 *s.* will not, 823, 2077, 3039; *pres.* 1 *pl.* 1457.
NYSE, *adj.* foolish, 3010.
NYSTE, *pret.* knew not, 616, 856.

O, *numeral*, one, 1593, 1602.
OBBYTE, *s.* habit, dress, 3763.
OF, *adv.* off, 1850.
OF-SHERE, *v.* cut off, 213.
ONE, *adv.* alone, 315.
ONYS, *adv.* once, 2699.
ORE, *s.* mercy, 1344, 3484.
OR(E), *adv.* before, 1740, 2202, 3717; *conj.* 1535, 1917, 2856, 3134, 3953; *prep.* 526, 3375.
OSTE, *s.* host, 2043, 2102; *pl.* OSTES, 2154, 2211, 2619.
OUERESTE, *adv.* uppermost, 846.
OUTHER, *indef. pron.* either, 2013.

PALLE, *s.* a costly cloth, 2712.
PARAYLLE, *s.* apparel, 2614.
PIGHT, PYGHTE, *p.p.* pitched, 2623, 2644.
PLAY(E), *s.* sport, amusement, 398, 779, 1019.
PLAY(E), *v.* amuse oneself, 445, 517, 730, 815, 890.
POMELLES, *s. pl.* apple-shaped ornaments on top of tent-poles, 2625.
PRASTE, 3326. See PRESTE.
PREES, PRES, PRES(S)E, *s.* press, 518;

throng, company, 417, 1713, 1859, 1955, 2351.
PRESONS, *pres.* 2 *s.* imprisonest, 1853.
PRESTE, *adj.* ready, eager, 2716, 3151, 3827.
PREVITE, *s.* private affairs, secret counsels, 657.
PREWELY, *adv.* privately, 1767.
PRYDE, *s.* splendour, 630, 1940.
PRYSE, *adj.* prize, choice, 1111.

QUERE, *s.* choir, 3138, 3902, 3910.
QUEST(E), *s.* judicial inquiry, 919, 925, 1320.
QUITE, *adj.* free, 490.
QUYTES, *pres.* 3 *s.* requites, repays, 2292.

RADDE. See REDE.
RANDOWNE, *s.* onrush, pace, 2750, 2888.
RAP(P)E, *v.* hasten, 2664; *pres. subj.* 2 *pl.* 3613.
RAUGHT, *pret.* 3 *s.* started, 3191.
RAYED, *pret.* 3 *s.* arrayed, 2720, 3306.
RAYKE, *v.* charge, rush, 3373.
RAYLED, *p.p.* adorned, 3531.
RAYNE, *s.* kingdom, 1980, 3223.
REAS(S)E, RES(S)E, *s.* rush, attack, 1861, 1957, 2690, 2905, 3258; expedition, pilgrimage, 2664.
REDE, *s.* counsel, advice, 907, 1113.
REDE, *pres.* 1 *s.* counsel, say, direct, 168, 232, 233, 855, 978, 2839, 3427; *pres. subj.* 3 *s.* 1745; *pret.* 2 *s.* RADDE, 3430; rule, 1416, 2311 (*infin.*); read, 2956 (*pres.* 1 *s.*).
RELEVE, *imperat.* 2 *pl.* recover, 3112.
REME, *s.* realm, kingdom, 2512, 3666.
RENNE, *v.* run, 3947.
RESCOUS, *pres.* 3 *s.* rescues, 2227.
RE(S)SEYVE, *v.* receive, 3688, 3708; *pret.* 3 *s.* RESSEYUYD, RESSEYVED, 3788, 3862; *pret.* 3 *pl.* RESEYVED, 572.
RIGGE, *s.* back, 2178.
RIGHT, *adj.* and *adv.* straight, 161, 620.
RODE, *s.* rood, cross, 3851, 3882.
RODE, *s.* redness, rosy colour, 179; *pl.* RODDYS, 3956.
ROFFE, ROVE, *pret.* rived, split, 2909, 3372.

ROMANS, *s.* romance, 2363.
ROO, *s.* quiet, rest, 3614.
ROUGHT, *pret.* 3 *s.* recked, 3522.
ROWND, *adj.* favourable, 3805.
ROWNE, *s.* speech, 3510.
ROWNE, *v.* speak, 3423.
RYCHE, *adj.* mighty (one), 2905, 3373.
RYFFE, *adj.* rife, 1825.
RYGHTWOSSE, *adj.* righteous, 3740.

SAD(D)E, *adj.* tired, 461, 716.
SALOWES, SALUES, *pres.* 3 *s.* salutes, 68, 735, 737, 2376.
SAMEN, *adv.* together, 2154, 2392.
SAMYTE, *s.* samite, a rich silk stuff, 2358.
SANGRAYLE, *s.* Holy Grail, 10.
SANZFAYLE, *adv.* surely, indeed, 971.
SARE, *adv.* sorely, 158, 272.
SAUMBUES, *s. pl.* housings, 2360.
SAWES, *s. pl.* speeches, sayings, 1151, 3251.
SAYNE, *v.* say, 3319; *p.p.* said, declared, 2872.
SCAUBERKE, *s.* scabbard, 3471, 3474.
SCRYVED, *pret.* 3 *pl.* burst, 382; *p.p.* 407.
SE(E), SEY, *pret.* saw, 741, 1476, 3181, 3417, 3624.
SECHE, *v.* seek, 437, 3021, 3799.
SEE, *s.* seat, 2693.
SEKE, *adj.* sick, 54, 158, 173, 525, 664, 2165.
SEKERESTE, *adj.* most trustworthy, 2518.
SEKERYD, *pret.* 3 *pl.* confirmed, 2331.
SEKERYNGE, *s.* assurance, guarantee, 2322.
SELY, *adv.* very, 3387, 3835.
SEMBLANT, *s.* appearance, 659.
SEMELY, *adj.* beautiful (one), 639.
SENGLE, *adv.* uniquely, 1795.
SENTE, *s.* opinion, consent, 2278.
SETHE, *conj.* since, 2903. See SITHE.
SEY. See SE(E).
SHENDE, *s.* shame, 1664.
SHENDE, SHENT(E), *p.p.* put to shame, disgraced, 1321, 2273, 2913, 3230; lost, 1724.
SHENE, *adj.* bright, beautiful, 51, 68, 1515, 1657, 1800, 2384, 2612, 3338.
SHO, *pers. pron.* she, 1426.
SHORE, *p.p.* taken, 84.
SHOURE, *s.* attack, 3000.

Glossary.

SHREDDE, *v.* cut, 2563.
SHYNAND, *pres. part.* shining, 973.
SIGHE, *pret.* saw, 706, 998.
SITHE, SYTHE, *adv.* afterwards, 398, 451, 546, 1336, 3792.
SITHE, *conj.* since, 126, 209, 234, 557, 745, 753.
SITHEN, *adv.* afterwards, then, 614.
SITTE, *s.* unhappiness, 497; *pl.* SYTTES, calamities, 870.
SLAE, SLE, *v.* slay, 843, 2115, 2507, 2579, 2601.
SLEE, *adj.* sly, cunning, 3421.
SLO(O), *v.* strike, slay, 1411, 1527, 1841, 2100, 2188, 2825. See SLAE.
SNELLE, *adj.* quick, active, 884, 2234; *adv.* quickly, 790.
SOKERYNGE, *s.* comforting, 3674.
SO(U)ND, *s.* message, that which is sent, 3562, 3675.
SONE, *adv.* soon, 930, 963.
SOTH(E), *s.* truth, 60, 93, 226, 396, 771, 3798.
SOUGHT, *pret. pl.* went, journeyed, 2952; *p.p.* pierced, 870, 2873.
SOUND. See SO(U)ND.
SOWNE, *s.* speech, utterance, 3514.
SPELLE, *v.* talk, 3024, 3722.
SPERYD, *pret.* 3 *s.* shut, 2997.
SPILLE, *v.* become empty, 23.
SPRENT(E), *pret.* sprang, 1846, 1892, 1949, 1954, 1994, 3357.
STAD, *p.p.* placed (with sense of discomfort, oppression), 3226, 3627.
STEDE, *s.* place, 851.
STENT(E), *v.* delay (*intrans.*), 3936; *pret.* 3 *pl.* stopped, 1844; *p.p.* 3080.
STERT(E), *v.* spring, 3278; *pret.* 3 *s.* 2740, 2789, 3352.
STEUEN, STEVYN, *s.* voice, 2584, 3411, 3821, 3875, 3967.
STODE, *s.* support, sustenance, 3621.
STOMELYD, *pret.* 3 *s.* stumbled, 115.
STORNNELY, *adv.* sternly, 2549.
STOUND(E), STOWND, *s.* time, short while, 1959, 2549, 2865, 3066.
STOURE, STOWRE, *s.* conflict, struggle, battle, 236, 655, 1811, 2288, 2741, 3036, 3893.
STRAUGHT, *pret.* 3 *s.* stretched himself, put forth his strength, 2814.
STRONGE, *adj.* difficult, 3833.
STRYFFE, *adj.* sharp, keen, 1829.

STYNT(E), *v.* stop, 3246 (*trans.*), 3947 (*intrans.*). See STENTE.
SWEUYS, SWEYNEYS, *s. pl.* dreams, 3170, 3226.
SWITHE, SWYTHE, *adv.* very, 246; quickly (frequently with pleonastic *as, also*), 79, 394, 531, 674, 700, 996, 1477, 1481.
SWONNE, *s.* swoon, 3728.
SWOUGHE, *s.* swoon, 903, 1634.
SWOUGHE? 875.
SWYTHE. See SWITHE.
SY(GH)E, *pret.* saw, 2800, 3105, 3201, 3618, 3749.
SYKER, *adj.* assured, 2333; safe, 2741.
SYNE, *conj.* since, 3684.
SYTHE, *s.* time, 696; occasion, 1561; *pl.* SITHES, 774.
SYTHE, *adv.* afterwards. See SITHE.
SYTHEN, *adj.* afterwards, then, 1530, 1700, 2660. See SITHEN.
SYTTES. See SITTE.

TASE, *pres.* 3 *s.* takes, 956.
TE, *v.* draw, come, 965, 1015.
TELDE, *s.* tent, 2624; *pl.* TELDYS, 2725.
TELLE, *conj.* till, 3656.
TENE, *s.* anger, 1449.
TENE, *v.* become vexed, 281.
TENT, *pret.* 3 *s.* paid attention to, 3946.
THAN, *adv.* then, 1461, 2876, 2944, 3528.
THAR(E), *pres.* 3 *s.* need (*impersonal*), 2028, 2338, 2426; *pres.* 2 *s.* (*personal*), 3285.
THE, *person. pron.* they, 1893.
THEDE, *s.* people, 1415; country, 61, 2305, 2361.
THEDYR, *adv.* thither, 3751.
THEIGHE, *conj.* though, 1985.
THEREOF, *adv.* therefrom, 1038.
THEWIS, *s. pl.* manners, 1081.
THINKITH, THYNKITH, *pres.* 3 *s.* seems, 635, 768; *pret.* 3 *s.* THOUGHT, 3829.
THO(O), *demonstr. pron. pl.* those, 352, 448, 1151, 1942, 3079, 3402.
THO(O), *adv.* then, 186, 249, 313, 976, 1020, 1112, 1341, 2854, 3749, 1526.
THORE, *adv.* there, 2005, 2388, 3284, 3480.
THOUGHT TO, *p.p.* intended for, 1655.

Glossary. 145

THRO(O), *adj.* hard, bold, fierce, 589, 1526, 2184, 2389, 2879, 2942, 3328.
THRYE, *adv.* thrice, 383.
THRYVE, *p.p.* excellent, strong, 589.
TIDANDIS, TYDANDIS, -ES, *s. pl.* tidings, 703, 710, 767.
TILLE, TYLLE, *prep.* to, 191, 637, 817, 1771, 1780, 1786.
TITHANDIS, TYTHANDIS, -YS, *s. pl.* tidings, 542, 1984, 2015, 2328.
TITHINGIS, *s. pl.* tidings, 641.
TO, *conj.* until, 374, 3437.
TO-FORNE, *adv.* before, 3608.
TOKE, *pret.* 3 *s.* gave, 2713.
TONE, *def. art.* + *numeral*, the one, 2797, 3253, 3384, 3710.
TRIACLE, *s.* antidote to poison, sovereign remedy, 864.
TRONCHON, *s.* handle, 3071.
TRONE, *s.* throne, 3789, 3944.
TWIGHT, *pret.* 3 *s.* twitched, took, 1038.
TWYNNE, *numeral*, two, 2211.
TYDE, *s.* time, 54, 241, 365, 834, 2081, 3834.
TYLLE. See TILLE.

VNDYR-TYME, *s.* morning, 2807.
VNFAYNE, *adj.* unhappy, 2691.
VN-HEND(E), *adj.* ungentle, unkind, 1001, 1081.
VNKOUTH, *adj.* unknown, foreign, 851.
VNNETH(E), *adv.* hardly, 2820, 2857.
VN-SAD, *adj.* not satiated, 1508.
VNSAUGHT, *p.p.* insane, 3189.
VNSO(U)NDE, VNSOWNDE, *adj.* ill, 2859, 3343, 3387.
VNTYLLE, *prep.* to, 3858.
VOUTE, *s.* vault, dome, 972.

WAITES, WAYTES, *pres.* 3 *s.* watches, 74, 1779.
WAKE, *v.* keep vigils, 3571 ; watch, 2605 ; *pres. subj.* 1 *pl.* 2591.
WARNE, *v.* prevent, 3011, 3040 (?).
WARYNGE, *s.* warring, 2975.
WAWES, *s. pl.* waves, 3465.
WEDE, *s.* apparel, armour, 83, 176, 778, 2639.
WEDE, *v.* rave, be mad, 651, 787, 914.
WEDRES, *s. pl.* weather, 2470.
WELDE, *v.* wield, control, 101 ; rule, 920, 2917.
WELE, *s.* joy, 3788.

MORTE ARTHUR.

WELLUETTE, *s.* velvet, 2615.
WENE, *s.* doubt, question, 548, 1680, 1758, 1822, 2546.
WENGE, *v.* avenge, 2217.
WENTE. See WENYS.
WENTE, *pret.* 3 *s.* turned, 1349.
WENYS, *pres.* 3 *s.* weens, thinks, 686 ; *pret.* 3 *s.* WENDE, WENTE, 422, 865, 3054, 3795.
WERE, *v.* wear, 2791 ; *pret.* 3 *s.* WERYD, 3030.
WERRYNGE, 2932. See WARYNGE.
WESSCHE, *pret.* 3 *pl.* washed, 2855.
WET(T)E, *v.* know, 1005, 1039, 1717, 2543, 3919 ; *imperat.* 2 *s.* 2303 ; *imperat.* 2 *pl.* 2600.
WETTERLYE, WYTTERLY, *adv.* surely, 1381, 1452.
WEXE, *pret.* 3 *s.* grew, 762, 951 ; *p.p.* WEXYN, grown, 2207.
WHAN, *conj.* when, 1367, 3304.
WHEDYR, *adv.* whither, 3512, 3513, 3603.
WHERE, *conj.* whether, 1987.
WIGHT, WYGHT, *s.* person, 577, 608 ; thing (especially strengthening the negative = not at all), 107, 472, 915, 1377.
WIGHT, *adj.* strong, active, 460.
WIGHT(E)LY, WYGHTELY, *adv.* with strength, might, 2822 ; quickly, 513, 3289.
WIS, *imperat.* 2 *s.* direct, 3414.
WISELICHE, *adv.* certainly, 1158.
WIST(E), WYSTE, *pret.* knew (how), 8, 119, 128, 189, 435, 529, 1537, 2499, 3539 ; *p.p.* 1148.
WITE, WYTE, *v.* blame, reproach with, 492, 1153, 2880 ; *pres.* 2 *s.* WITESTE, 2398.
WITHE, *prep.* by, 1778.
WLLE, *pres.* 1 *s.* will, 2592.
WODE, *adj.* mad, 384, 662, 1172, 1710, 1994, 2841.
WOKYS, *s. pl.* weeks, 2111.
WOLDE, *s.* subjection, control, 745, 3233.
WOLLE, *pres.* 1 *s.* will, 1495.
WONDYD, *p.p.* wounded, 3434.
WONE, *s.* abundance, 1083.
WONNE, *s.* dwelling, habitation, 3377.
WONNYNG, *s.* dwelling, 3561.
WO(U)NYD, *pret.* dwelt, 137, 332, 3636.

L

WOODELY, *adv.* madly, wildly, 3191.
WORCHE, *v.* work, 3683.
WORSHIP(PE), WORSHYP(PE), *s.* honour, reputation, 35, 1152, 2845, 2933.
WORSHIPPED, -ID, *p.p.* shown honour to, 1551, 1569.
WORSHIPPFFULLY, *adv.* with honour, 1117.
WORTHE, *v.* become, 1817 ; *pres.* 3 *s.* WORTHIS, gets, 782.
WORTHE, WORTHY, *adj.* worthy, strong, 2545, 2559.
WOUGHE, *s.* trouble, evil, wo, 1333, 1365, 1638.
WOUND, *v.* wend, go, 2863.
WOUNDE, *v.* hesitate, 1070, 3558.
WOUNT, *pret* 3 *s.* was wont, 26.
WRAKE, *s.* rack, ruin, 1695, 3567 ; trouble, suffering, 935, 948, 1092, 1181 ; vengeful spirit, 1451 ; mischief, 1675.
WYKKE, *adj.* severe, 3365.
WYLANLYCHE, *adj.* villainously, 1156.
WYNNE, *s.* joy, 3788.

WYNNE, *v.* to come, 1830.
WYTTERLY. See WETTERLYE.
WYTHSAYNE, *v.* gainsay, deny, 2406.

YA, *adv.* yea, 79, 1626.
YARE, *adj.* ready, 218, 349, 1420, 2702 ; *adv.* quickly, 983, 3536.
YAT, *s.* gate, 2864 ; *pl.* YATES, 2743.
YEDE, *pret.* went, 81, 346, 667, 986, 1331, 2280, 3952.
YEFF(E), YEUE, *v.* give, 2728, 3267, 3275 ; *pres. subj.* 3 *s.* YEFFE, YIFFE, 2643, 3671 ; *imperat.* 2 *s.* YIF, 3554 ; *pret.* YAFE, YAFF(E), 269, 2815, 2963 ; *p.p.* YEVE, 88.
YIF(E), YIFF(E), *conj.* if, 199, 1627, 1709, 2077.
YȝEN, *s. pl.* eyes, 1349.
YLKE, *adj.* same, 54, 366, 1934, 3639. See ILKE.
YO(O)DE, *pret.* went, 307, 1858, 2876, 3108, 3751 ; ran, 962, 3935.
YOLDE, *pret.* 1 *s.* yielded, surrendered, 2308 ; *p.p.* YOLDEN, 2797.
YVELLE, *adj.* difficult, 619.

INDEX OF PROPER NAMES.

N.B. All the variant forms of a name are given, but no attempt has been made to render the references for each form exhaustive.

Aggrawayne, 1718, 1764, 1910, 1916 ; Agravayne, 73 ; Agraveyne, 59 ; Agrawayne, 1676, 1692, 1728, 1832.
Arthur, 88, 337, 640, 955, 1048, 1681, 2388, 3082, 3964 ; Arthure, 1096, 1934, 2070, 2500 ; *gen.* Arthur, 5, 3346 ; Arthurs, 260, 2965 ; Arthuris, 3157, 3776.
Ascalot, 548, 747, 1054 ; Ascalote, 1011 ; Ascolot, 138, 297, 645, 1136 ; Ascolote, 1135.
Avelovne, 3516.
Avmysbery, 3569, 3954.

Barendowne, 3094, 3592.
Banndemagew, 2564.
Bedwere, 3386, 3400, 3519, 3758.
Benwike, 2305, 2474 ; Benwyk, 2707 ; Benwyke, 2534.
Boert, 230, 464 ; Boerte, 273, 432 ; Boerte de Gawnes, 788 ; Bors, 1344, 1443, 1888, 2214, 3607, 3808, 3921 ; Bors de Gawnes, 1326, 1772, 2084, 2548, 2746, 3802.
Bretayne, 3376, 3553 ; *gen.* Bretaynes, 2513.

Canterbery, 3002, 3119 ; Canturbery, 2982 ; Caunterbery, 3019.
Cornwale, 3267 ; Cornwayle, 3275, 3295.
Cryste, 3004.

Douer, 3589 ; Dover, 3042, 3794 ; Dower, 3055.

Ector, 299, 436, 789, 3807, 3946 ; Estor, 1327, 1394, 2492.
Engelond, 2435. See Yngland.
Evwayn, 129 ; Evwayne, 107, 230, 265, 408 ; Evway[n]e, 106.

Excaliber, 3448.

Fraunce, 2486.

Gaheriet, 1674, 1722, 1940, 1979 ; Gahereit, 1987 ; Gaheryet, 1931, 2020, 2025.
Gaheries, 1940 2020 ; Gaheryes, 1722, 1931 ; Gaherys, 1935.
Galehod, 43, 225 ; Galehud, 2587 ; Galyhud, 2572 ; *gen.* Galehodis, 261.
Gawayn, 824, 1041, 2751 ; Gawayne, 536, 600, 1115, 1720, 2218, 3593 ; Gaweyn, 570 ; Gaweyne, 576, 626 ; *gen.* Gawayne, 2899.
Gawle, 2487.
Gawnes, 2484 ; Gawnys, 1422.
Gaynor, 3566 ; Gaynore, 421 ; Gaynour, 3600, 3965 ; Genure, 515, 835, 901, 936.
Glassynbery, 3960.

Ihesu, 2642, 3562, 3894, 3968 ; Ihesu Criste, 534, 861 ; Ihesu Cryst, 2475 ; Ihesu Cryste, 1974, 2074, 3940 ; *gen.* Ihesu, 3929.
Ioyes Garde, 3845, 3901 ; Ioyus Gard, 2044, 2345, 2460 ; Ioyus Garde, 1669, 2079, 2110.

Kamelot, 420.
Karlyll, 2349 ; Karllyle, 2257, 2327.
Kelyon, 2466 ; Kerlyonne, 2529.
Kente, 2982, 3019, 3295.

Lancelot, 2916, 3590, 3884 ; Lancelot du lake, 1614, 3962 ; Launcelot, 53, 543, 1596, 2142, 3574, 3823 ; Launcelot de lake, 2589, 2640 ; Launcelot du lake, 629, 1410, 2779 ; Launcelote, 1682, 1945 ; Launcelote du lake, 1094 ;

Index of Proper Names.

Launcelott, 27, 81, 178, 1099; Launcelotte, 233, 706; *gen.* Launcelot, 2237; Launcelotis, 2046, 2329; Launcelottis, 594, 598.
London, 2992, 2996, 3800.
Lionelle, 1459; Lyonett, 3797; Lyonelle, 230, 432, 788, 1536, 2486.
Lucan, 2636, 3436; Lucan de boteler, 3232, 3416; Lucan de botelere, 3384; Lucan de bottelere, 2631; Lucane de botteler, 2695.

Mador, 883, 1449, 1644.
Mary, 3410; *gen.* Mary-is, 3863.
Mordred, 2518, 2998, 3228, 3560; Mordreit, 1862, 1904, 1908, 2522; Mordreite, 1675.

Northe Gales, 2580.

Rome, 2248.
Rowchester, 2255.

Salusbury, 3148; Salysbery, 3597.
Sangrayle, 10.
Scottis, 2099.

Walys, 2099, 3147.
Wynchester, 42, 340, 2984.

Yngland, 347, 2261, 2958, 3263; Ynglande, 2249, 2268; Ynglonde, 2098, 2273.
Yreland, 2098.

The manufacturer's authorised representative in the EU for product safety is
Oxford University Press España S.A. of el Parque Empresarial San Fernando de
Henares, Avenida de Castilla, 2 – 28830 Madrid (www.oup.es/en or product.
safety@oup.com). OUP España S.A. also acts as importer into Spain of products
made by the manufacturer.

www.ingramcontent.com/pod-product-compliance
Ingram Content Group UK Ltd.
Pitfield, Milton Keynes, MK11 3LW, UK
UKHW041902230426
12049UKWH00001B/3